Strategic Reassurance and Resolve

Strategic Reassurance and Resolve

U.S.-CHINA RELATIONS IN THE TWENTY-FIRST CENTURY

James Steinberg

Michael E. O'Hanlon

PRINCETON UNIVERSITY PRESS

PRINCETON AND OXFORD

Published by Princeton University Press, 41 William Street,
Princeton, New Jersey 08540
In the United Kingdom: Princeton University Press, 6 Oxford Street,
Woodstock, Oxfordshire OX20 1TW
press.princeton.edu

Library of Congress Cataloging-in-Publication Data

Steinberg, James.
Strategic reassurance and resolve : U.S - China relations in the twenty-first century /
James Steinberg, Michael E. O'Hanlon.
pages   cm

Summary: "After forty years of largely cooperative Sino-U.S. relations, policymakers, pol-
iticians, and pundits on both sides of the Pacific see growing tensions between the United
States and China. Some go so far as to predict a future of conflict, driven by the inevitable
rivalry between an established and a rising power, and urge their leaders to prepare now for
a future showdown. Others argue that the deep economic interdependence between the two
countries and the many areas of shared interests will lead to more collaborative relations in
the coming decades. In this book, James Steinberg and Michael O'Hanlon stake out a third,
less deterministic position. They argue that there are powerful domestic and international
factors, especially in the military and security realms, that could well push the bilateral relationship toward an arms race and confrontation, even though both sides will be far worse off
if such a future comes to pass. They contend that this pessimistic scenario can be confidently
avoided only if China and the United States adopt deliberate policies designed to address
the security dilemma that besets the relationship between a rising and an established power.
The authors propose a set of policy proposals to achieve a sustainable, relatively cooperative
relationship between the two nations, based on the concept of providing mutual strategic
reassurance in such key areas as nuclear weapons and missile defense, space and cyber operations, and military basing and deployments, while also demonstrating strategic resolve
to protect vital national interests, including, in the case of the United States, its commitments
to regional allies"— Provided by publisher.

Includes bibliographical references and index.
ISBN 978-0-691-15951-5 (hardback)
1. United States—Foreign relations—China—History—21st century. 2. China—Foreign
relations—United States—History—21st century.   I. O'Hanlon, Michael E.   II. Title.
E183.8.C5S84 2014
327.5107309'05—dc23
2013035849

British Library Cataloging-in-Publication Data is available

This book has been composed in Palatino LT Std

Printed on acid-free paper.

Printed in the United States of America

3 5 7 9 10 8 6 4

To our wives, Shere and Cathy,

and our daughters, Jenna and Emma and Grace and Lily

Contents

Acknowledgments

The authors are grateful to the Sasakawa Peace Foundation for support of this work; O'Hanlon and Brookings would additionally like to thank Herb Allen and Dan Lufkin, as well as Ian Livingston for outstanding research assistance. The authors are also grateful to Jeffrey Bader, Richard Bush, Erica Downs, Vanda Felbab-Brown, Martin Indyk, Kenneth Lieberthal, Suzanne Maloney, Theodore Piccone, Steven Pifer, Jonathan Pollack, Kenneth Pollack, Jeremy Shapiro, Peter Singer, Mireya Solis, several military fellows from the 2012–13 team at Brookings, and several anonymous reviewers for their invaluable input and ideas, as well as colleagues at Beijing University and elsewhere in China. Steinberg expresses appreciation to Andrea Baldwin and Kathleen Ciciarelli for their assistance and support, and to Kurt Campbell, a valued colleague, on understanding the challenges of the United States in East Asia, as well as to Presidents Clinton and Obama, and Secretaries Christopher and Clinton, for the opportunity to participate in shaping U.S. policy toward China over the past two decades. The opinions and characterizations in this book are those of the authors and do not necessarily represent official positions of the U.S. government.

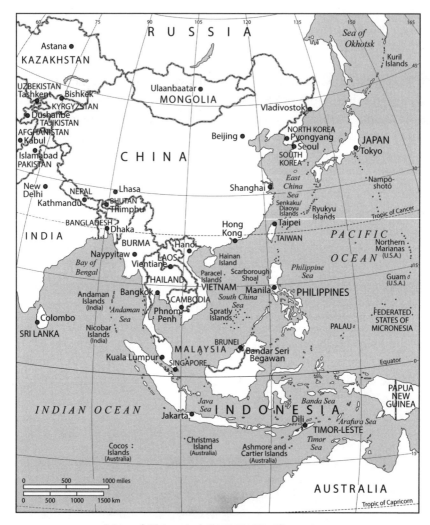

Map of China and the Asia-Pacific region

Source: Redrawn from University of Texas Libraries.

Strategic Reassurance and Resolve

1

Introduction

O n March 7, 2012, in a speech to mark the fortieth anniversary of President Nixon's historic trip to China, Secretary of State Hillary Clinton observed that "the U.S.-China project of 2012 . . . is unprecedented in the history of nations. The United States is attempting to work with a rising power to foster its rise as an active contributor to global security, stability and prosperity while also sustaining and securing American leadership in a changing world. And we are trying to do this without entering into unhealthy competition, rivalry, or conflict."[1]

With these sentences, she encapsulated what may be the most consequential foreign policy challenge of the twenty-first century. While there is a wide range of views in both the United States and China on how to manage bilateral relations, few dispute the assertion of leaders on both sides that the U.S.-China relationship is the most consequential bilateral relationship of our time, as China's spectacular economic growth, its military modernization, and its increasingly active role on the regional and global stages have focused attention on the prospects for cooperation or conflict between the United States and China in the coming decades.[2]

China's leaders have responded to the challenge with a formulation of their own: the call for a "new great power relationship,"[3] implicitly endorsing Secretary Clinton's argument that China and the United States must chart a novel approach in order to avoid the dangers of conflict that have characterized relations between established and emerging powers so often in the past.[4]

Both are responding to commonly held views among both policymakers and many academic international relations theorists that China, as a rising power, is bound to challenge America's regional and global hegemony and that America, the dominant power, is destined to resist.

Although the outcome of the contest is not foreordained, in this view the inevitability of it is. The immutable structure of the international system is based on states pursuing their national interest by seeking absolute or relative power dominance. For the proponents of this view, the coming contest is largely independent of the character and history of the two countries in question and of the choices made by their leaders.[5]

Their views find inspiration in Thucydides' explanation of the cause of the Peloponnesian War: "What made the war inevitable was the growth of Athenian power and the fear which this caused Sparta."[6] The United States may not be fearful of China, per se, but its leaders certainly recognize the tectonic implications of the rise of the People's Republic China (PRC) for international relations in the Asia-Pacific region and beyond. In any event, the tragic record of conflict over the centuries between rising and established powers has only reinforced Thucydides' argument since then.[7]

For those who embrace this view, the policy implications are clear. On the U.S. side, proponents argue that the core goal of U.S. foreign policy should be to sustain American dominance to ward off the inevitable challenge of emerging powers. It was embodied in the U.S. National Security Strategy of 2002: "Our forces will be strong enough to dissuade potential adversaries from pursuing a military build-up in hopes of surpassing or equaling the power of the United States."[8] The concept has been further underscored by leading academic strategists.[9]

Their views are mirrored on the China side by academics and former officials (primarily from the People's Liberation Army [PLA]) who share the view that conflict is inevitable and that China should not shirk from the challenge of taking on American interests.[10]

Others are less deterministic, but not much less pessimistic. Although conflict between China and the United States is not inevitable, they argue, it is highly likely. These analysts draw their pessimistic forecasts from a number of factors. Some point to the difficulty of achieving cooperation and avoiding conflict under uncertainty. Drawing on insights from game theory, they note that rational actors often compete even when they would be better off cooperating because they cannot "trust" the other side to keep any bargain between them rather than defect, as the game theory lexicon would phrase it.[11] Others point to the problems of misperception—what appears to one side as a legitimate strategy of self-defense may look to the other as preparations for offensive actions (the so-called security dilemma).[12] A third group focuses more on the specific traditions and cultures of the two countries themselves, each of which has a strong sense of unique mission and superior values. In the case of the United States and China, this can be depicted as the City on the Hill versus the Middle Kingdom. These self-images give each a legitimate claim, at least in its own eyes, to act as the dominant power—not only for its own narrow self-interest but for the greater good.

Of course, these are not the only views. Practitioners tend to reject deterministic accounts, not least because adopting such a view implies that the choices made by individual leaders are irrelevant to the future course of events. They are supported by historians who look at periods where power shifts have not been accompanied by war. They are further buttressed by theorists who argue that the so-called iron laws of state-to-state relations are really context dependent (with contemporary factors such as nuclear deterrence clearly being relevant) and finally by those who argue that in the globalized world of increasing interdependence, power shifts need not lead to zero-sum competition.[13]

This book proceeds from the premise that the future is not fully determined by factors beyond the control of policymakers in both countries; otherwise there would be little point in considering policy options at all. This is a modest assumption; our analysis does not depend on adherence to a particular school of international relations theory. As a number of academics have noted, even adherents of the so-called realist school have argued in favor of an optimistic view of the future of U.S.-China relations, while some liberal internationalists find a potential cause for pessimism from the application of their theory to the Sino-American case.[14]

Our core contention is that the outcome is contingent. It is contingent on a variety of both external developments and domestic factors in both countries—and in other places, particularly those in the Asia-Pacific region. To a large degree, the outcome of those interacting forces will be shaped by the conscious policy decisions of each country.[15]

This debate has enormous consequences for the United States, for China, for East Asia, and for world as a whole. If the pessimists are right, we are doomed to a rivalry that will at a minimum produce a costly and dangerous arms race and strategic competition that will imperil the prosperity and security of both nations and could even lead to war. If the optimists have the better argument, we have a chance to manage our relations to achieve important degrees of cooperation in common interests from promoting global economic prosperity to combating common challenges such as terrorism, international crime, climate change, and pandemic disease while mitigating the risks that come from areas of inevitable competition.

In our view, the pessimistic outcome is not inevitable. But there are powerful forces that make it quite possible, and perhaps even likely, in the absence of a comprehensive strategy by both countries to resist them. This book sets out an approach that seeks to bound the competition and reinforce the cooperative dimensions of our bilateral relationship.

Competition is inevitable in the U.S.-China relationship, just as it is in any relationship among states. The goal cannot realistically be a Kantian peace. The United States competes and occasionally has serious disagreements with even its closest allies—including those in Europe, as well as Japan and Canada. But few worry that these competitive dimensions of our relationship will lead to outright conflict. It may be too much to aspire to an equally cooperative relationship with China. Yet it is entirely plausible that the competition can be limited in ways to avoid the worst outcomes, particularly armed conflict, and to provide space for an important degree of cooperation on issues of common concern. Given the potential benefits of such cooperation and the costs of failing to work together on issues that no one country can solve by itself, there are powerful reasons to work toward this outcome.

To achieve this, China and the United States must directly address the most dangerous areas where competition can produce conflict: the military and strategic spheres. In this book we focus on core strategic areas—nuclear, conventional military, space, cyber, and maritime issues—that could trigger destabilizing arms races, foster crises, and eventually lead to conflict. This focus is not intended to shortchange the importance of other elements of competition and rivalry, particularly in the economic sphere as well as differences in values. These can both contribute to mistrust and provide their own sources of potential conflict, especially given the powerful political impact of economic concerns in both countries. Managing the strategic interaction is a necessary but not fully sufficient requirement for stable U.S.-China relations.

Much of the contemporary discussion concerning U.S.-China relations focuses on building mutual trust. Indeed, this is the formula adopted by

President Obama and former Chinese President Hu.[16] Trust of course is valuable. From Kissinger's extraordinary conversations with Zhou En Lai in 1971 and Nixon's subsequent dialogue with Mao to Scowcroft's secret visit to Beijing following Tiananmen in 1989 to President Clinton's unprecedented eight-day trip to China in 1998, candid high-level discussions and personal diplomacy have played a critical role in shaping Sino-American relations.[17] But trust building of this kind suffers from important limits—both horizontal (among diverse constituencies) and vertical (over time). Even if the two countries' leaders develop personal trust from repeated mutual interactions, as President Obama and President Xi have sought in their summit in Sunnylands, California, in June 2013 and elsewhere, it is far more challenging to extend that trust to all those who shape national policy. These various actors range from political critics of incumbents to the two nations' militaries to their publics at large. It is noteworthy that despite the personal relationship developed between Presidents Clinton and Jiang during their repeated interactions, the Chinese leadership as a whole (and especially the PLA) was reluctant to accept Clinton's personal assurances concerning the accidental bombing of the Chinese Embassy in Kosovo in 1999. In addition, active media in both countries tend to magnify disagreements—a factor especially important today, when public opinion in both countries exerts powerful constraints on the actions of policymakers. And even if there is contemporary trust, it is hard for today's leaders to bind the actions of their successors. The persistent anxiety in America over the true meaning of Deng Xiaoping's famous "hide and bide" exhortation of a generation ago—suggesting to some that China intended to conceal its strategic ambitions until powerful enough to pursue them effectively—is emblematic of this problem.[18] This concern is mirrored on the Chinese side by those who point to past presidential campaigns and contemporary congressional actions to question the long-term reliability of current assurances that the United States does not seek to contain China. Put more bluntly, achieving true trust is a high bar and may not be attainable in a comprehensive sense.

For this reason, there is deep insight behind President Reagan's admonition to "trust but verify." The core concept in this book, which we call strategic reassurance, is to identify concrete measures that each side can take to allay the other's concerns about its strategic intentions.

At its core, the goal of strategic reassurance is twofold: first, to give credibility to each side's profession of good intentions by reducing as much as possible the ambiguity and uncertainty associated with unilateral security policies; and second, to provide timely indicators and warnings of any less benign intentions to allow each side adequate time to adjust its own policies to reflect a new reality.

The concept has its root in theoretical work developed in the context of the Cold War, which led to concrete measures to achieve stability (both arms race stability and crisis stability) in the otherwise conflictual U.S.-Soviet relationship.[19] It took many forms, ranging from agreements on transparency and information exchange to limits on certain military modernization efforts and deployments. In each case the goal was both to provide credibility to claims of good intentions and to protect against "breakout" should those professed intentions prove false or change over time.

Some may argue that an approach that has its roots in the Cold War is both inapposite and inappropriate for a bilateral relationship that is less rooted in ideology. We disagree. If ideological adversaries like the United States and the USSR could find ways to stabilize their security competition, then surely the United States and China should be able to agree on steps to avoid the worst consequences of the security dilemma—and in doing so, to pave the way for a more constructive relationship beyond the "peaceful coexistence" of the Cold War era. At the same time, it is important to recognize the many ways in which the strategic interaction between China and the United States differs from the Cold War paradigm. Some of these (e.g., the absence of a global ideological competition, the degree of economic interdependence) facilitate strategic reassurance. Other factors (China's growing economic clout, the complex geopolitics of the Western Pacific, including the historic U.S. relationship with Taiwan) complicate the challenge.

There are a number of tools available to the United States and China that can contribute to strategic reassurance.

RESTRAINT

Neither the United States nor China can be expected to weaken its commitment to what each country sees as its fundamental national interests. Nor do we advocate that the United States exercise restraint by pulling back from a region of the world, the Asia-Pacific region, where it has important interests and allies.[20] But there is still much that can be done.

By forgoing potentially threatening security options each side can help re-inforce the credibility of its intentions. Restraint can take the form of agreed limitations or voluntary moves communicated either explicitly or implicitly to the counterpart. The credibility of restraint is greatest when it comes in response to explicit expressions of concern by the other side, though for po-litical reasons (the danger of appearing to provide "concessions") it is often based instead on an implicit understanding of the other's needs.

Restraint is a particularly powerful tool given that the U.S.-China re-lationship is a "multimove" strategic interaction. If voluntary restraint produces reciprocal response, trust is built; if instead the other side seeks to take advantage of restraint, its counterpart can adjust expectations ac-cordingly. Similarly, the failure to exercise restraint in the face of explicit or implicit requests can justify more pessimistic conclusions about in-tent.[21] Each side's reactions (or lack thereof) to the other's restraint can be seen as an opportunity for "learning," an important feature of managing U.S.-Soviet relations during the Cold War.[22]

In each of the sensitive areas discussed in this book, leaders on both sides should take into account the likely reaction of the other side before acting and weigh it against the anticipated benefits, keeping in mind that the relationship is a multimove strategic interaction rather than a one-move "game."

The history of the relationship shows both sides implicitly adopting ele-ments of restraint. For example, in considering both national and regional missile defense architectures, the United States has adopted a conscious, if implicit, approach that is neither designed to nor capable of seriously degrading China's nuclear capacity. It recognizes both the serious polit-ical consequences of any approach that would provide the United States with an effective first-strike nuclear option against China and the likely military consequences of such a move (Chinese expansion of its nuclear arsenal, greater focus on technologies that would evade interception, and asymmetric threats to the missile defense architecture such as antisatellite and anti–radar attack capabilities).

Another important example of restraint is Washington's approach con-cerning arms sales to Taiwan. Over the decades, the U.S. government, drawing on the 1979 Taiwan Relations Act, has carefully modulated arms sales, focusing on Taiwan's defensive needs (such as Patriot missile defense systems and mine-clearing ships) and seeking to avoid systems, such as surface-to-surface ballistic missiles, which, although arguably valuable to Taiwan's defense, could also represent an offensive threat to the mainland.

China, too, appears to have exercised some restraint in its own military modernization. Two notable examples are its limited deployment of strategic nuclear missiles and its apparent caution in developing comprehensive amphibious assault capabilities that would pose a threat of land occupation of Taiwan—perhaps in recognition that such a move might serve only to inflame anti-unification sentiment on the island and induce greater U.S. military sales to Taiwan.

Unlike the case with U.S.-Soviet relations, however, mutually agreed restraint has on balance played only a modest role in the U.S.-China context. There are a few other exceptions, such as the nuclear detargeting agreement announced in connection with President Clinton's visit to China in 1998 (a very modest step given the lack of verification measures associated with the verbal pledge). But such examples are few. The lack of formal agreements can be attributed in part to the lack of parity between the two sides in most areas, which makes a bargain more difficult to achieve,[23] and to both sides' desire to avoid Cold War parallels in building the bilateral relationship.

Instances of voluntary restraint remain relatively rare, and both sides have been disinclined to draw explicit attention to such moves out of fear that they will be criticized as unilateral concessions. But as we will see throughout this book, unilateral restraint offers a number of advantages over negotiated agreements: measures adopted unilaterally are more easily revised if circumstances warrant, are more easily established without complex and time-consuming negotiations (which sometimes exacerbate tensions rather than building confidence), and do not require intricate verification procedures.[24]

REINFORCEMENT

Closely related to restraint is the opportunity to provide the other reassurance through reinforcement by deliberately taking measures that are the logical outgrowth of benign intent and that give credibility to declaratory assurances.

This approach includes U.S. actions that are seen as consistent with the "one China" policy, particularly with respect to Taiwan and Tibet, such as votes that oppose Taiwanese membership in international organizations that require statehood as condition of membership.[25] On the Chinese side, the policy of not mating strategic missiles and nuclear warheads can be seen as reinforcing the credibility of its declaratory policy of no first use of nuclear weapons.

Of course the opposite effect can occur as well. In Chinese eyes, the failure of the United States to end arms sales to Taiwan and the continued interaction between American presidents and the Dalai Lama are seen as undercutting the credibility of U.S. assurances on "one China." For the United States, provocative actions by the PLA (such as the behavior of the pilot who collided with the U.S. EP-3 in 2001 and the shadowing of U.S. warships in China's exclusive economic zone more recently) raise questions as to whether China genuinely "welcomes" the U.S. military presence in the Western Pacific, as it officially claims.

TRANSPARENCY

Greater understanding of each other's capabilities is another tool that helps dispel misperception and limits the dangers of worst-case planning. Although transparency can never be complete (you don't know what you don't know, and each side will have compelling reasons to guard some vital secrets), experiences such as the open skies regimes during the Cold War and beyond illustrate how transparency can modulate strategic competition. Ship visits, officer exchanges, and the like, as well as publishing defense budgets and holding strategic dialogues, are examples of transparency.

RESILIENCE

Resilience is an important adjunct to strategic reassurance because it allows both sides greater leeway to exercise restraint without putting at risk vital national interests. In other words, it lowers the cost of being wrong about the other's intentions. It also increases the opportunity to make timely adjustments if reassurance is not forthcoming and therefore reduces the need for premature and potentially counterproductive "hedging." Given the inherently competitive nature of the relationship and the inevitability of uncertainty and misperception, efforts by each side to strengthen resilience to attack are generally stabilizing and desirable. They increase the opportunity to defuse crises while reducing the dangers of escalation, or preemption, or mistaken attribution of the source of an attack. Increasing the survivability of nuclear systems, including command and control, as well as the redundancy and defensive capabilities of cyber systems, particularly those connected to critical infrastructure, can help manage the tensions in each side's development of intelligence tools and offensive cyber capability.

Resilience also includes avoidance of dependence on the other's goodwill for critical needs. For example, in the case of the United States, this philosophy suggests developing alternative sources of supply for critical rare Earth metals, while for China it counsels diversifying sources of imported energy to reduce hypothetical vulnerability to disruption by the United States.

RESOLVE

The fifth element of the approach is, in some ways, the flip side of the previous four—each of which is designed to allay misplaced fears of hostile intent by signaling what each side does not intend to do. By resolve we mean making clear what interests each side believes are "worth fighting for" both figuratively and in some cases literally. Like the other elements of the strategy, resolve involves dispelling misperceptions, in this case by making clear what actions by the other are unacceptable and will elicit a firm response. Clarity about red lines is a key element of deterrence designed to reduce the danger of miscalculation.

While the basic concept is clear, putting strategic resolve into practice is complex. It is obviously impossible to specify ex ante each and every case in which a country will respond to actions by the other—the number of possible permutations is infinite and constantly changing. Moreover, there is a real danger that any specification of red lines will lead the other side to infer that there will be no response in the case of actions not covered by the red line (what lawyers call the presumption *expressio unius est exclusio alterius*)—a danger illustrated dramatically in U.S.-China relations by Acheson's speech defining the geographic scope of U.S. strategic interests in East Asia in 1950, which some argue contributed to the Korean War because it excluded the peninsula from the list of preeminent U.S. interests.[26] In addition, the need to sustain the credibility of assertions of resolve can lead to dangerous escalation—although, as we discuss at length in subsequent chapters, it is possible to design strategies that both reinforce credibility and allow for deescalation of crises. And there may be cases where a country wishes to establish a red line but where that may not require an actual threatened use of force. One example we discuss subsequently is Taiwan, where few can doubt that China sees the issue as fundamental to its interests, yet where Beijing has adequate nonmilitary means, working with other countries including the United States, to prevent any possible unilateral move by Taiwan toward independence.

For the United States, strategic resolve is itself a form of strategic reassurance—but in this case, reassurance toward its allies that the United States has the capability and will to maintain its security commitments. Done thoughtfully, this can also offer a measure of reassurance to China as well, since U.S. security commitments make a major contribution to regional stability by reducing the strategic competition between China and its neighbors.

Each of these elements—restraint, reinforcement, transparency, resilience, and resolve—addresses two of the most dangerous elements of competition that could undermine Sino-American political cooperation and ultimately lead to conflict: arms race instability and crisis instability. Arms race instability can be seen as a series of action-reaction moves as each side seeks to achieve a capabilities advantage over the other, igniting a sequence of steps that ultimately improves the security of neither. Examples of arms race competition in the U.S.-China relationship include the missile/missile-defense competition between the two in regard to China's recent buildup of short-range conventionally armed missiles near Taiwan, and the broader interaction between China's growing anti-access/area denial capabilities and America's Air-Sea Battle concept.[27]

Crisis instability is the danger that unanticipated events could trigger actions that inadvertently lead to conflict before each side can fully consider or adopt measures short of war to defuse the conflict. "Use it or lose it" capabilities—weapons that are vulnerable to attack if not used first in a preemptive mode—can lead to crisis instability, as can actions that provide little or no warning time (e.g., cyber attacks). The succeeding chapters discuss in detail steps that both sides should consider to help mitigate arms race competition and reduce crisis instability. These would be worthy aims in themselves, as the U.S.-Soviet relationship so clearly illustrated. But in the case of the United States and China, the potential benefit is far greater than just avoiding armed conflict. By managing the strategic relationship, the two sides will be much better positioned to pursue vital areas of common interest—from sustaining economic growth to combating common threats like nuclear proliferation, terrorism, organized crime, environmental degradation, and climate change.

Each of these strategies is based on the premise that the other side's long-term intentions are unknown and unknowable—and indeed changeable—but that it is possible to create a strategic interaction that increases confidence nonetheless. The two countries can do so by providing adequate warning to allow for adaptive actions to be taken in timely ways without jeopardizing national security or triggering security dilemma dynamics out of premature hedging behavior. By adopting these kind of measures, the United States and China can increase the prospects of avoiding a "lose-lose" rivalry as well as unintended conflict.

In the end, the long-term success of these approaches will depend on the extent to which China and the United States mutually believe that it is possible to accommodate what the other perceives as its vital national interest in ways that are consistent with its own. Put another way, it assumes that both sides can ultimately accept compromise as superior to outright competition—that the risks of competition outweigh the potential benefits. Neither side can be expected to give up its defense of vital interests, of course, or its central values—indeed the core function of resolve in this strategy is to make clear what can be compromised and what not. But one can be resolute at the same time that one reassures, if the two sides pursue this concept simultaneously. Reassurance is doomed if in fact each side believes that security really is a zero-sum game—as in the dynamic of the early days of the Cold War before each side came to accept peaceful coexistence and put it into practice.

This is the basic insight that animated the U.S.-China Joint Statement of 2009 in which both sides pledged to try to respect the other's "core national interest."[28] Of course, whether this approach can (or indeed should) succeed depends on how each defines which interests are core. If each defines its core or "vital" national interests in ways that are incompatible with the other's, confidence-building measures and crisis-avoidance steps of the kind suggested will ultimately fail to ameliorate the underlying conflict. For example, if China were to conclude that its security is incompatible with a U.S. military presence in the Western Pacific while the United States continued to believe that its alliance commitments and broader interests required such a presence, no amount of tactical reassurance or transparency could bridge the gap. Similarly, if the United States were convinced that its security was incompatible with continued Communist Party rule in mainland China or with truly voluntary unification between Taiwan and the PRC, the stage would be set for prolonged rivalry with growing risks of conflict.

There are many reasons to believe that U.S. and Chinese interests are not so fundamentally adverse as to preclude the approach we advocate here. The lack of intense ideological competition, as well as the absence of bilateral territorial disputes or imperial ambitions by either side, suggest grounds for hope. If nothing else, pursuing the approach we suggest here will help clarify whether the two sides' concepts of vital interests can be reconciled. As we discuss in the next chapter, there are also important forces that could lead to a more zero-sum calculus. Only by understanding the potential sources of conflict can we develop strategies to mitigate the dangers they pose.

Nothing in the history of U.S.-PRC relations illustrates the challenges— or the opportunities—of strategic reassurance more dramatically than the issue of Taiwan. Following the outbreak of the Korean War, the emphasis of U.S. policy was on resolve, embodied in the U.S.-Taiwan Mutual Defense Treaty of 1954 backed up by American military capabilities. But even in the early years, reassurance was a factor in shaping U.S. restraint on the KMT's ambitions to regain the mainland. Beginning with normalization in the 1970s, reassurance began to play a more prominent role: from the three communiques to President Clinton's public reaffirmation of the three "noes" in 1998 (no U.S. support for Taiwan independence, for "one China, one Taiwan" or for "two Chinas," or for Taiwan's membership in international organizations whose members are sovereign states) to President George W. Bush's criticism of Taiwan President Chen Shuibian's proposed referenda on constitutional reform in 2003. But throughout this period, reassurance was matched with resolve—from the Taiwan

Relations Act of 1979 and President Reagan's "six assurances" to Taiwan in 1982, through President Clinton's decision to send two aircraft carriers to Taiwan's vicinity following China's missile firings in 1996, to President Obama's authorizing continued U.S. arms sales to Taiwan in January 2010. Notwithstanding China's "core" interest in achieving unification with Taiwan, Washington's skillful blending of reassurance and resolve has not only avoided a military conflict between Beijing and Taipei but has managed to prevent the Taiwan issue from undermining U.S.-China relations and paved the way for more constructive Taiwan-PRC engagement.

Our concept of strategic reassurance leads us to more than twenty policy recommendations for both the United States and China in the chapters that follow. Some would be formal accords. Most would be more informal guides to action for each side or suggestions for unilateral but reciprocating steps of restraint, reinforcement, and transparency each might take. But as much as the specific recommendations themselves, it is the commitment by both sides to view strategic reassurance as a central organizing policy tool that counts. If this objective is prioritized just as much as each side's commitment to the traditional defense of key national interests, that bodes well for the future of the relationship. Indeed, our policy agenda is illustrative, limited by the opportunities and challenges facing the two sides in 2014. Adoption of a paradigm of strategic reassurance should impel policymakers and scholars in both countries to look continually for additional means of pursuing that goal. They must do so even as each country will naturally seek to remain resolute in defense of its fundamental interests. Strategic reassurance is a way of interacting, and of thinking, as much as it is any specific set of policies or accords.[29] But before developing these recommendations, it is important to focus squarely on the dynamics, and possible dangers, in the U.S.-China relationship today.

PART I

THE CAUSE FOR CONCERN

———◈———

The Sources of Conflict

The rationale for a doctrine of strategic reassurance begins with a clear-eyed assessment of the many tensions and sources of potential conflict in the U.S.-China relationship. They are significant and not automatically trumped by the two nations' mutual interdependencies and interests.

Much of the academic literature on interstate conflict focuses on the structural relations between states—that is, on their relative power. At times when one country has clear predominance over another, the weaker country is obliged to adapt itself to the dictates of the stronger.[1] But as the power relations become more equal—or as the challenger begins to surpass the former champion—the rising power has greater opportunity to pursue its own conceptions of national interest, independent of the wishes of the previously dominant country.

For some theorists, this "power transition" will inevitably lead to conflict because the dominant power will have an incentive to resist and thwart the challenger's rise, irrespective of the specific goals or interests of the challenger. For others, whether this power transition will lead to conflict depends on the degree to which the challenger is "dissatisfied" with the prevailing international order, because only if it believes that it is disadvantaged will it necessarily choose to use its newfound power to create a world more to its own liking in potentially disruptive ways.

Applying this analysis to the United States and China, the past four decades of relatively tranquil U.S.-China relations can be attributed to American dominance, to which China had no choice but to accommodate itself (excepting of course in part earlier conflicts in Korea and Vietnam, where it was less disadvantaged than in other geographic and military realms). Whether this can be sustained in the future will depend on the degree to which China will see its interests best served by accepting at least the core pillars of the international order established by the United States and its democratic, liberal market allies. If it does, then the relationship faces fair winds and calm seas.[2] If not, then we should expect China to seek to use its power to challenge the U.S.-led international system.

Of course, it is easier to pose than to answer this question. Undoubtedly China has benefited considerably from the international system presided over by the United States and its allies in many important ways. The international economic order has made possible China's extraordinary economic development, fostering opportunities for trade, investment, and technological innovation. (The United States has even tolerated Chinese infractions of the rules of this system fairly consistently, believing China's rise to be generally in its own interest.) This economic growth has been central to the Chinese Communist Party's continued hold on power and the relatively high degree of approval the party seems to achieve from the Chinese public. Major disruptions to the international security environment through increasing tensions or conflict with the United States could put this in jeopardy, even if China's growing economic and military power might make such a challenge possible.

America's security order has also helped assure the safety and security of the sea-lanes, so important to China's economic development for both exports and access to raw materials and energy. In effect, China has been a free rider on the U.S. Navy. The current international system also offers important benefits to China (not available to other rising powers)—for example, its veto-wielding membership on the Security Council and its privileged position as a nuclear power under the Nuclear Non-Proliferation Treaty.

Yet for all the reasons that China benefits from the U.S.-led status quo, there are also reasons why a Chinese leadership might wish to revise it in China's favor—beginning with certain territorial issues. First and foremost, of course, is Taiwan, which has over the past sixty years been the most contentious item on the U.S.-China agenda. Completion of the territorial recovery of China through the unification of Taiwan with the mainland has been a political imperative for the Chinese Communist Party. In recent years, there have been indications that China's willingness to accept the preferred U.S. approach—no alteration of the status quo by force or without the consent of both sides—may be fragile. This can arguably be seen by the adoption of the antisecession laws by the National

People's Congress in 2005 and the growing unwillingness in Beijing to countenance continuing U.S. arms sales to Taiwan. Chinese leaders continue to press with increasing insistence the need for Washington to live up to its commitment in the 1982 U.S.-China Communique to reduce the number and quality of arms sold to Taiwan.

In the military sphere, there are a number of other sources of dissatisfaction with the status quo. These include what Chinese leaders believe are unfettered and growing U.S. military operations in the air and waters near China, especially in China's claimed exclusive economic zones and the sensitive Yellow Sea. The American military's recently announced Air-Sea Battle concept, in the view of Chinese military leaders, is directly designed to sustain China's vulnerability to attack by assuring U.S. access to the Chinese mainland.

These dissatisfactions have their counterparts in the political sphere. Most notably, over the past two years China has expressed increasing dissatisfaction with the United States' direct political engagement on the issue of the South China Sea, where Washington's explicit advocacy of multilateral approaches is seen as an implicit siding with China's rival claimants in this set of territorial disputes. A similar Chinese concern stems from the U.S. assertion that the U.S.-Japan security treaty covers the disputed East China Sea and Senkaku Islands administered by Tokyo but claimed by both Japan and China (under the name Diaoyu in China). More broadly, Chinese leaders question the legitimacy and appropriateness of the United States' formal security "alliances" with Japan, South Korea, Australia, the Philippines, and Thailand, as discussed in the next section.

Other items on the grievance list abound. They range from American pressure on Europe to maintain the embargo on arms sales to China to the United States' willingness to use force outside UN auspices—from Kosovo, exacerbated by the accidental 1999 bombing of the Chinese Embassy in Belgrade, to Iraq to Libya (by some interpretations of the latter mission).

These strategic disagreements are of course matched by a comparable list of complaints about the U.S.-dominated economic order. They range from U.S. (and European) dominance in international economic organizations like the IMF and World Bank to the U.S. attempt to press a liberal trade agenda in regional and global trade fora. Taken together, this suggests a picture of China that has elements of both an embrace of the status quo and revisionism. Thus from a structural point of view, the outcome of China's rise would seem to be indeterminate—it is impossible to say with confidence based on these factors alone that China's rise will or will not lead to conflict with the United States and its allies. (And the degree of China's dissatisfaction with the status quo is closely tied to how the United States and others respond to China's complaints.)

THE AMERICAN ALLIANCE SYSTEM

Since the early days of the Cold War, U.S. strategy toward East Asia and the Pacific has been based on an alliance system of formal and informal security guarantees to regional partners. From the American point of view, this approach has not only benefited the allies themselves but offered considerable benefits to the other nations of the region, including China. America's alliance system, especially its defense pacts with Japan and South Korea, has allowed the two countries to develop in relative security without the need to seek military capacities analogous to those of the United States for their own defense capabilities, which could pose a threat to China. Perhaps most important, this situation has underpinned the willingness of the two to forgo the development of nuclear weapons, despite the emergence of China and more recently North Korea as nuclear powers. Given the histories of conflict between China and its two northeast Asian neighbors, this is a considerable security benefit.

The American presence has, for example, facilitated impressive improvement in the China-South Korea relationship over the years, which goes well beyond simple economic interdependence and the mutual pursuit of prosperity. Indeed, the formal treaty commitment has arguably allowed Seoul to build stronger political ties to Beijing without fear of dominance by its large neighbor.[3]

The U.S. security presence has also arguably helped China improve its ties with Southeast Asian neighbors, as the American counterweight makes it easier for Association of Southeast Asian Nations (ASEAN) states, Australia, and New Zealand to build close economic ties without worrying that these will lead to a dependency that would facilitate

Chinese coercion. Australia's recent Defence White Paper, with its conge-
nial language about both the United States and China, is a good illustra-
tion of this point.[4]

Similarly, from the American perspective, the ongoing security ties between the United States and Taiwan, following the abrogation of the U.S.-
Taiwan security treaty a generation ago, also benefit China. They have
provided Taiwan sufficient reassurance to engage China constructively
without the need to develop its own military forces (including potentially
nuclear weapons) to avoid coercion or conquest—and to avoid any pursuit of formal independence.

But China has never accepted the logic that it is the beneficiary of this
strategy, especially vis-à-vis Taiwan. Chinese leaders and analysts repeatedly criticize the U.S. alliance system as a relic of the Cold War era and
a source of conflict in the region, as well as a thinly disguised effort to
contain China. China has grown increasingly insistent in its opposition
to U.S. arms sales to Taiwan, moving from verbal criticism to concrete actions such as suspending military-to-military dialogues and threatening
retaliation against American firms that supply arms to Taiwan.

More recently, China has also alleged that U.S. alliances have helped
foment other conflicts in the region. China has made clear that it views
the U.S. formal alliances with Japan and the Philippines (as well as the
less formal U.S. ties to Vietnam) as factors contributing to conflicts in the
South and East China seas by emboldening regional actors to take more
aggressive stands against China. For this reason, China has resisted efforts
by the United States to participate through the ASEAN Regional Forum
in developing a Code of Conduct governing the South China Sea and has
challenged Washington's assertion that the Senkaku/Diaoyu Islands are
covered by the U.S.-Japan security treaty. While the United States repeatedly asserts neutrality on the underlying sovereignty disputes between
China and its neighbors, America's formal alliance ties could turn these
bilateral regional disputes into sources of tension or even conflict between
the United States and China.

More broadly, China has also increasingly asserted that the U.S.-Japan
alliance has contributed to unhealthy nationalism in Japan, including
momentum to revise Japan's "peace constitution" to allow more assertive military activities, which China views as a direct threat to its own
security.

STRATEGIC CULTURE

An important source of potential conflict stems from the strategic cultures of the two countries. Their contrasting national narratives tend to exacerbate the inherent tensions between rising and established powers. For the United States, two dominant strains, geographic isolationism and American exceptionalism, have combined to create a narrative that focuses on the country's purported ability to achieve security not through cooperation but through effective invulnerability, the ability to project power away from home shores, and the ability to dissuade others from "balancing" against U.S. power by having the United States provide global public goods. This has been due in the first instance to geography (notably, protection offered from two oceans) and later by technology (such as missile defense). The period of U.S.-Soviet coexistence based on mutual vulnerability might have satisfied strategic theorists. But it sat uncomfortably with the American public and helped inspire President Reagan's vision of closing the window of vulnerability and rejecting the logic of deterrence and mutual assured destruction in favor of strategic defense. American exceptionalism has fostered a belief that unlike past hegemonies based on power, which tended to be destabilizing because they invited competition and counterbalancing, American hegemony, because it is based on universal values and mutual interests, therefore will be sustainable.

By contrast contemporary Chinese strategic culture is deeply influenced by the experience of vulnerability in much of the nineteenth century and into the twentieth—the so-called century of humiliation—as well as the more distant (and somewhat mythologized) earlier times of Pax Sinica. Indeed, as many observers have noted, much of the Chinese Communist Party's legitimacy derives from its claim to have recovered China's sovereignty from foreign encroachment, first European and then Japanese. From Mao's assertion that "we have stood up"[5] to Xi Jingping's assertion that "realizing the great renewal of the Chinese nation is the Chinese nation's greatest dream in modern history,"[6] the restoration of China's glory has been a motivating force behind the party's claim to rule. This has led Chinese strategists to focus on trying to reduce the nation's vulnerability to outside aggression or coercion and to establish China as at least a co-equal with the United States in managing regional and global affairs. Combined with China's own sense of superior culture and traditions, this makes Chinese leaders especially disinclined to accept American hegemony as consistent with their country's own security and increasingly assertive in promoting China's right to set the terms of international affairs.

The broad challenges posed to China by dominant U.S. security thinking are further compounded by America's strong conventional wisdom in support of the rationality of "hedging" strategies—preparing for the worst, given the inherent inability to know for certain what path future China leaders will take.[7] In the minds of many Chinese strategists, however, this is tantamount to preparing to defeat China in a military conflict—thus stoking their own countermilitary strategy to deny the United States any ability to achieve such a victory.

It is difficult to reconcile these worldviews. Neither side is inclined to accept vulnerability; both reject the idea that their power should be viewed as threatening.[8] Yet each side's search for invulnerability and freedom of action increasingly leads it to take actions that are seen as inconsistent with the strategic aspirations of the other power—and inconsistent with the rhetorical commitment to constructive bilateral relations. For example, the Obama administration's "rebalancing" toward Asia, including its related military modernization and deployments and the new Pentagon concept of Air-Sea Battle, is collectively touted by Washington as a means of reinforcing freedom of navigation and the security of U.S. allies, but it is seen by China as thinly disguised containment. China's actions to reinforce its territorial claims in the South and East China seas, and the military activities to back up those claims (often described in America as part of an anti-access/area denial strategy), are explained by China as a legitimate response to provocations by others, but they are seen in the United States as signs of expansionist and revisionist aspirations.

REGIME TYPE

Another potential source of conflict between the United States and China derives from the two countries' political and economic regimes. There are several strands to this argument. First, stemming from variants of so-called democratic peace theory, is the view that the possibility of conflict between two states is enhanced when one of the countries is nondemocratic—that the absence of democratic checks on expansionist or aggressive actions, in this case within China, makes conflict more likely. (This argument is somewhat in tension with the view that growing democratization in China could itself contribute to conflict, which will be discussed shortly.) A second factor stems from the role of democracy and human rights promotion as core elements of U.S. foreign policy. In the United States, this policy is justified as a support for universal norms (embodied in the UN Charter and Declaration of Human Rights) rather than an attempt to undermine the Chinese Communist Party. Nonetheless, many Chinese argue that this strategy of "peaceful evolution" is a thinly disguised effort to undermine the regime.[9] These sources of conflict are exacerbated by divergence on the economic front, where China's statist model is seen to pose a direct threat to U.S. interests—whether through manipulation of the value of the RMB currency, favoritism to Chinese industries (through the doctrine of "indigenous innovation"), explicit and hidden subsidies to Chinese manufacturers, or even state complicity in intellectual property theft. Conversely China sees U.S. advocacy of liberal trade and investment policies as threatening to China's prosperity.

Another factor associated with regime type that contributes to the risk of conflict is the closed nature of Chinese government decision making. Secrecy and lack of transparency are the hallmarks of leadership deliberations, especially on matters related to national security. This fuels U.S. suspicion and mistrust and reinforces concerns that certain elements of the Chinese policy elite such as the PLA may have undue influence on some decision making.

From the Chinese perspective, the highly pluralist nature of the U.S. government, including the overlapping and sometimes conflicting roles of Congress, the executive branch, and courts, leads to questions about the sincerity and reliability of American commitments. For China, a case in point was the adoption of the Taiwan Relations Act immediately after the abrogation of the U.S.-Taiwan Security Treaty by the executive branch (following the agreement on normalizing U.S.-PRC relations).

DOMESTIC POLITICAL FACTORS

Like structural factors, domestic political considerations in each country also suggest a mix of forces potentially leading to either cooperation or conflict. On the optimistic side, there are many elements of the U.S.-China relationship that have positive-sum effects on domestic constituencies, such as the workers in China who benefit from exports to the United States and the consumers in the United States who benefit from China's low-cost production. China's large holdings of U.S. debt help keep interest rates low in the United States—a benefit to both the taxpayer and the homebuyer. U.S. farmers and aerospace workers benefit from exports to China, as do their Chinese customers.

But domestic political considerations also contribute to conflict. First, while in each country there are constituencies that benefit from the relationship, there are also those who feel victims—be they U.S. textile workers and tire manufacturers or Chinese workers in state-owned enterprises who are at the losing end of U.S.-brought World Trade Organization cases. Moreover, there are important asymmetries between those who gain and those who lose—with the pain of the losers often being concentrated and deep (e.g., loss of jobs) while the benefits are more broadly spread and shallower (as with lower prices to consumers).

In China, rising national pride and memories of past humiliations put increased pressure on leaders not to compromise with foreigners, including Americans. This nationalism is fueled by the emergence of a vibrant and often virulent community of microbloggers who challenge leaders at any sign of weakness. The Communist Party is especially susceptible to these pressures, given its dependence on nationalist credentials as an element of its legitimacy.

In the United States, too, nationalist perspectives tend to increase anxieties about China's rise, fueled by a narrative dating back to the Chinese Civil War about who "lost" China. Ideologically oriented cable news, radio, and Web sites play a role comparable to the microblogging site Weibo in the PRC. Although polling in the United States consistently shows no strong sentiment against China, only 37 percent of Americans expressed positive views of China in a 2013 Pew survey (while only 40 percent of Chinese indicated positive views of the United States).[10] Issues like Taiwan and trade tensions as well as cyber security provide ample grist for critics. Problems of history such as China's role in the Korean and Vietnam wars, and Tiananmen, lurk in the background as well. Overall, uncertainty about where the relationship is now headed in light of China's rise contributes to a certain tension in the public's overall mood about the PRC. Indeed, at most points over the last twenty years, 40 percent or more have worried about China as a future threat even as they have also tended to view U.S.-China relations in the present as reasonably good. Surveys indicate that the next generation of American leaders holds similarly mixed views about China.[11]

THE WAY FORWARD: MANAGING THE U.S.-CHINA STRATEGIC RELATIONSHIP

The foregoing discussion illustrates that there are profound forces at work that could undermine the goal of avoiding conflict and maximizing cooperation even though both countries have much to gain by a positive relationship. Without an explicit effort to address these sources of conflict through the tools of what we call strategic reassurance, the prospects for a poor outcome are great. Since neither side can guarantee the other what the goals and ambitions of future leaders might be, they need to craft a set of actions today that will reinforce the benefits of cooperation while undercutting the perceived necessity for hedging and confrontation, consistent with each's national interest.

We now turn to a more systematic discussion of the determinants of strategy in both China and the United States, in successive chapters. This discussion is central to our ensuing argument about how the two sides can mitigate their rivalry and advance their common interests in the security sphere—the subject of the remainder of the book. Only by understanding the forces shaping policy decisions in each country, as well as the historical backdrop to current debates, can each side appreciate the lens through which its own actions are perceived and the likely response those actions will evoke. Only with such perspective is it possible to develop a set of strategies that can reduce the danger of unwanted and unintended conflict, and increase the prospects of constructive cooperation.

Our objective is not to predict the future intentions of U.S. and Chinese leaders, an inherently problematic exercise for at least three reasons. First, prediction of this kind assumes a highly deterministic view of political behavior by states and/or leaders. Second, even if one subscribes to a deterministic view (which we do not), it is also necessary to specify in advance which variable(s) will determine future behavior. International relations

theory and political science are rife with competing hypotheses that prioritize particular variables to predict future outcomes. For example, political
transition theory, together with democratic peace theory and considerations of China's form of government, suggest more pessimistic outcomes,
while interdependence and nuclear peace theories suggest that leaders will
be constrained in their competition. Third, the actions of future leaders in
each of our two countries will depend to some degree on the choices the
other side makes, adding a further degree of indeterminacy to prediction.

At the same time, simply to conclude that future policies are inherently
unknowable is also problematic because it has led many theorists and
practitioners to fall back on a strategy of assuming the worst—or at least
preparing for the worst. In this view if you cannot know what is to come,
it would be foolhardy and reckless to count on benign outcomes—an un-
forgivable sin for officials charged with national security. Bureaucratic and
nationalistic politics can exacerbate the tendency. To be sure, preparing for
a range of outcomes, rather than depending on a single point forecast, is
a reasonable course under conditions of uncertainty. But when hedging
produces the very behavior in a potential adversary that was seen as necessitating hedging in the first place, it is clearly counterproductive.

Such a situation leads us to the need to examine the factors that might
influence future strategy. This effort is undertaken not with the goal of
making a prediction but to illuminate the core policy question: what actions each side can take, consistent with its own security and, in America's
case, that of its allies as well, that will reduce the chances that the other
side will pursue a strategy that leads to conflict. The goal is to focus on
the strategic interaction of the choices the two sides make to increase the
probability of better outcomes.

We believe that there are at least four elements that have been identified
by theorists and historians that could shape the choices of future U.S. and
Chinese leaders. The first is how each side understands its own national
security interests (the national security "narrative"); second, what strategies are seen by political leaders, the military, and other opinion shapers
as most likely to achieve those interests (related to "strategic culture");
third, how the choice of strategies is influenced by internal forces in each
country ("domestic politics"); and fourth, how each side understands the
other's likely strategy as well as the strategies of other key external actors
("strategic context").

It is important to recognize that none of these elements that go into shaping future behavior are fixed in stone. Each country's strategic narrative has evolved over time as internal and external circumstances evolve. Strategic culture also changes over time. Even within historical eras there are often lively debates about alternative strategies; consider, for example, the debate in the United States about what strategy to pursue vis-à-vis the Soviet Union after World War II. Domestic politics can be upended by inherently unpredictable exogenous shocks (such as natural disaster or pandemic disease) as well as long-term forces such as shifting technologies, global markets, and demographics. Nonetheless, these are the raw materials available to contemporary policymakers as they seek to ascertain the likely choices—or range of choices—of other states. It makes sense to learn as much as we can about the intellectual and political forces shaping the worldviews and influencing the future actions of Chinese and American leaders, before considering specific policies each side can pursue to advance the goal of strategic reassurance, and it is to that first task we now turn.

3

⬥

The Determinants of Chinese Strategy

Although U.S.-China relations have been largely stable over the past forty years, for policymakers the core question is whether the past will be prologue. If, as we suggest, structural factors alone are indeterminate in predicting the future of U.S.-China relations, it is important to consider what other factors might shape the policy each side will pursue. In this and the succeeding chapter on the United States, we begin with a summary of current declaratory policy and then examine four factors that may influence future choices: the definition of national interest, strategic culture, domestic politics, and perception of the other side's strategy.

CHINESE DECLARATORY SECURITY STRATEGY

Declaratory strategy has some value as a window into contemporary thinking and future choices. Its limitations are self-evident: it reflects the contemporary political environment (both domestic and external), it is geared to shaping public opinion and thus may not be an accurate reflection of true intentions, and in any event it cannot bind future leaders.[1] But it is still a useful starting point.

Chinese declaratory strategy has remained fairly constant since the end of the Cold War. Its dominant themes focus on the need to create a stable, peaceful international environment to facilitate China's economic development. As articulated in its 2013 defense white paper: "It is China's unshakable national commitment and strategic choice to take the road of peaceful development. China unswervingly pursues an independent foreign policy of peace and a national defense policy that is defensive in nature. China opposes any form of hegemonism or power politics, and does not interfere in the internal affairs of other countries. China will never seek hegemony or behave in a hegemonic manner, nor will it engage in military expansion. China advocates a new security concept featuring mutual trust, mutual benefit, equality and coordination, and pursues comprehensive security, common security and cooperative security."[2]

Originally articulated as a strategy of "peaceful rise,"[3] the term was amended to "peaceful development" out of concern that even a "peaceful" rise might seem threatening to the other countries in the region and beyond.[4] In recent years there has been an increasingly lively debate in China about the wisdom of this strategy, particularly from more nationalist voices that advocate a more assertive policy in line with China's growing power.[5] Under President Hu, these critics were strongly rebutted, as reflected in an authoritative article by State Counselor Dai Bingguo.[6] Although some have suggested that the early pronouncement of China's new leaders may herald a change of strategy under the rubric of "China Dream" and "China Revival," most Chinese officials continue to stress continuity with the core concept of peaceful development.[7] Chinese leaders have been at pains to justify all of the country's recent foreign policy actions within that framework—from its "defensive" military modernization to its territorial claims—as simply restoring China's historic lands.[8]

U.S.-China relations understandably play a central role in the declaratory strategy. Indeed, a prominent feature of every major bilateral encounter is China's desire to incorporate a formulaic characterization of the bilateral policy in official communiques, with an emphasis on cooperation and mutuality.[9]

Some scholars and analysts largely accept China's declaratory policy as a real expression of China's goals and objectives. They focus on the powerful domestic imperative of economic growth and the benefits of the current international order to China (including the opportunities for free riding) and suggest that the current approach is likely to prove durable.[10]

Others see possible change in the future. Avery Goldstein, for example, characterizes China's contemporary strategy as one of "transition . . . tailored to chart a course for its rise during an era of unipolarity; it is not designed to guide China once it has risen and circumstances are fundamentally different."[11]

Still others believe that the change has already begun and that the continued rhetoric of peaceful rise is a smokescreen for a China that has already decided to challenge the United States for regional, if not global, dominance.[12] They suggest that the weakening of U.S. economic power following the 2008 financial crisis and the ongoing budget challenges in the United States have led Chinese strategists to conclude that power relations have tilted decisively in China's favor, justifying a new, more assertive approach. They point to what they perceive as increased Chinese assertiveness across a range of foreign policy issues[13] and explicit calls by retired senior PLA officials for challenging U.S. hegemony.[14] Their skepticism about the value of declaratory statements is colored by the closed nature of the Chinese policymaking process. It is further fueled by the considerable attention accorded to Deng Xiaoping's exhortation that China should "hide our capacities and bide our time"[15]—an aphorism that has been seized upon by those who believe that China's declaratory acceptance of the international order has been a function of China's relative weakness and that its revisionist objectives will become increasingly clear as China's power grows and U.S. relative power declines. By this logic, China will hide its true ambitions and bide its time until in a position to do something about them. Advocates of this interpretation point to Chinese negotiating behavior over the years, which would seem to reinforce such a theory, given its typically disciplined and patient character.[16] Beyond official doctrine, and recent behavior, therefore, we must look deeper to understand the texture and complexity of Chinese national security thinking.

CHINESE DEFINITION OF NATIONAL INTEREST: THE NATIONAL SECURITY NARRATIVE

At the heart of the contemporary debate over China's future intentions is the question of how current and future Chinese leaders define their national security interests—a definition that is deeply shaped by Chinese leaders' and the public's perception of China's own history. Looming large over this question is China's experience in the century preceding the Communist Revolution of 1949, the so-called century of humiliation. Over this era, weak Chinese governments, both imperial and republican, suffered territorial incursions, economic exploitation, and vast human tragedy at the hands of foreign powers. This period began with the European incursions from 1839 during the Opium Wars and culminated in the expulsion of Chiang Kai Shek's KMT from the mainland by the Red Army and the CCP and the establishment of the PRC in 1949. But this sense of exploitation has deeper roots in Chinese history, for example, during the periods when China was subject to invasion by the Mongols.

At the highest level of generality, avoiding a repetition of these periods and reversing the losses that occurred during this time is a fundamental national imperative almost universally endorsed among Chinese. This objective is widely shared by both leaders and the public and has become the dominant form of political discourse to describe China's goals both to domestic and to foreign audiences.

There is disagreement over what it means to "reverse the losses" of these periods. Consensus does exist on the desire to avoid the vulnerability or weakness that made it possible for foreigners to exploit or coerce China. Symbolized by Mao's assertion that "we have stood up," during a period when China faced a challenging external environment and went to war with the United States as well as several immediate neighbors, this narrative has provided a compelling justification for investment in China's military modernization despite the continued high level of social and economic needs for China's own development.

However, the desire to avoid vulnerability admits of a range of solutions—from a highly defensive "fortress" China to a strategy that would be tantamount to restoring China as the dominant power in the region and beyond. The latter could include a return to the power and influence China exerted at the height of the Ming Dynasty half a millennium ago, when much of East Asia and Southeast Asia formed tributary relationships with China and the Chinese Navy held sway as far away as East Africa. For some Chinese strategists, this is a particularly compelling narrative because it couples China's interest in assuring its own security with a more benevolent public goods objective: spreading peace and prosperity throughout the globe, a narrative that bears a striking resemblance to the U.S. national security narrative discussed in chapter 4. The debate is closely linked to the one over Chinese strategic culture (discussed later in the chapter) concerning what strategy is most likely to provide China security.[17] As China increases its dependence on Middle East hydrocarbons and increases its global overseas investments in natural resources, protecting against "vulnerability" could be broadened beyond territorial threats to the need to protect vital sea-lanes of communication throughout Asia and much of Africa and beyond. The argument for broadening the zone of PLA activities and responsibilities could come to have additional resonance.

There is also a perceived imperative to restore lands "taken" from China during its period of weakness. During the sixty-plus years since the establishment of the PRC, many of the instances of Chinese use of force have been connected with territorial claims, ranging from India in 1962 and the Soviet Union in 1969 to the periodic uses of force in the Taiwan Strait from the 1950s to the missile firings of 1995–96. These areas are routinely identified as "core interests"—consistent with the leadership's oft-repeated definition of China's core interest as "sovereignty, unification and territorial integrity."[18] How extensive these claims may come to be remains uncertain. For example, some contemporary Chinese explanations focus on implementing what they believe to be the agreed World War II settlement, which was largely concerned with reversing Japanese territorial gains. But even this relatively modest framing includes important ambiguities about its scope, as we will see in the discussion about the dispute over the Senkaku/Diaoyu Islands.[19]

For most of the decades since 1949, this territorial imperative has focused on three highly emotive issues: Hong Kong, Tibet, and Taiwan. Indeed, many Chinese interlocutors explicitly identified these as constituting China's "core national interests."[20] The reversion of Hong Kong (along with Macau and the islands of Taipa and Coloane) was a singular achievement that culminated in the Jiang Zemin era, and that was celebrated with the same kind of pomp and national pride that typically accompany a major military victory. The ongoing effort to continually reconfirm Chinese sovereignty over Tibet against indigenous efforts at either self-determination or independence, and against what China perceives as external meddling designed to foster Tibet's separation from the motherland (even though the United States and other states do not contest China's sovereignty in Tibet), features prominently in China's foreign policy. This can be seen, for example, in the intense pressure on foreign governments to avoid contact with the Dalai Lama. In the case of China and India, the issue has contributed to direct military conflict. Similar motivations help explain China's heavy-handed efforts to stamp out the Uighur separatist movement in Xinjiang and China's hostile reaction to foreign support for Uighur activists.

Taiwan has been the most important focal point of China's effort to restore lost sovereignty. It has special resonance because the loss of Taiwan is tied to foreign actions—first by Japan and more recently by U.S. support to the Taipei government, which in the eyes of China's leaders and the public is the sole reason why unlike Hong Kong, Taiwan has not voluntarily returned to the motherland. Given the centrality of this national narrative, it is not surprising that Taiwan has been the most explosive flash point in U.S.-China relations, and the one place since the end of the Korean War that military conflict between the United States and China seemed most plausible. From the Quemoy and Matsu crises of the 1950s through the missile firings near the Taiwan Strait in 1995–96 and the threats surrounding the reelection of Taiwan's President Chen Shui-bian in 2000, China's leaders have played brinksmanship over the question of Taiwan and sovereignty.[21]

Yet despite the centrality of the Taiwan question, major conflict has been avoided. A variety of theories have been advanced to explain China's unwillingness to "force" the issue. They range from China's own military weaknesses, particularly in its inability to conduct a successful amphibious invasion, to concerns about vertical escalation if the United States came to Taiwan's defense, to concerns about the impact that the use of force would have on China's overriding economic development imperative, or, alternatively, to optimism that "time is on China's side" and that with China's growing economic and military clout, Taiwan would increasingly see a better future by voluntary reunification with the mainland.

Might China's restraint on Taiwan erode over time? Certainly China's increased military capacity expands some available military options, as we will examine in more detail in the discussion of China's military modernization and military strategy. The increased stridency of China's opposition to U.S. arms sales to Taiwan in 2010, including threats of economic retaliation against American firms associated with those arms sales, took many in the U.S. government by surprise. During the official visit of one of us (Steinberg) to China with Senior NSC Director Jeffrey Bader in March 2010, each of the meetings began with a detailed recitation of U.S. obligations under the third U.S.-China Communique to phase out all arms sales to Taiwan, as well as an insistence that the time had come, after nearly thirty years, to put that commitment into practice. Although tensions subsided shortly after the visit (due in part perhaps to China's desire to facilitate Hu Jintao's participation in the Washington Nuclear Security Summit in April 2010), this episode could be a harbinger that a stronger China will be less willing to acquiesce in this longstanding U.S. policy. And pressure for greater action could come from the Chinese public, which may grow less understanding of the leadership tolerating U.S. interference as China's power grows. But the economic risks and uncertainty remain high, and any use of force could have a powerful influence in shaping the attitudes and policies of China's neighbors—from Korea to the ASEAN countries. All of these act as a brake on more resolute Chinese actions.

In the end, China's approach likely will be shaped by its perceptions of the balance of political forces on Taiwan (particularly the strength of the independence movement) and, equally important, the impact of U.S. policy in either restraining or supporting those forces. U.S. policy does not support Taiwan independence but insists that any resolution of the dispute between Taipei and Beijing be peaceful and voluntary. American officials have argued that this diplomatic stance, plus some degree of U.S. military protection and "defensive" arms sales, serves to both reassure and restrain Taipei from pursuing a unilateral move toward independence. The relatively quick end to the Taiwan flap of 2010 and the willingness of President Hu to come to Washington for the Nuclear Security Summit in April 2010 suggest that at least in the near term China's leaders are reluctant to move to a more confrontational posture.

The South and East China Seas

Although the Taiwan issue has remained deeply contentious, the relatively stable and limited nature of China's territorial assertions during the early years of Sino-American rapprochement gave at least some reason to believe that China did not have far-ranging territorial ambitions and was not an inherently expansionist power. China's own leaders constructed a national narrative to suggest that recovery of Taiwan would put an end to China's own revisionist claims and would usher in an era of regional stability and peace.

Until recently, China had pursued a relatively cooperative approach to other territorial claims in the South and East China seas. This was the path taken with respect to the Senkaku/Diaoyu Islands dispute at the time of Sino-Japanese normalization[22] and continued through the 2008

Sino-Japanese agreement to jointly develop the Chunxiao gas deposits in the East China Sea.[23]

But growing tensions around China's territorial claims in the South and East China seas have raised questions about the elasticity of Chinese territorial ambitions and in particular whether China's growing economic and military power will lead not just to more forceful assertions of historical claims but to ever-expanding demands.[24] This concern is encapsulated in the debate about whether China is expanding its own definition of core national interests along with its expanding power. Contrary to some reporting, senior officials have eschewed the label "core interest" to describe China's South China Sea claims to date.[25] Still, the increasing forcefulness of China's rhetoric in support of the legitimacy of its claims, coupled with the dramatic increase in military and associated activity surrounding these claims, gives credence to the beliefs of those who worry that if unchecked China will become more hegemonic as its capability expands.[26] More recently, at least one Chinese official has suggested that the Senkaku/Diaoyu Islands are part of China's core national interests.[27]

With respect to the South China Sea, China has relied on a historical narrative buttressed by a reference to claims made by Nationalist China prior to the revolution.[28] Although the official territorial claim of the Chinese government appears to be limited to the islands themselves, some Chinese have suggested the sovereignty claim extends to waters within the "9 dash line" that covers most of the South China Sea. China's claim to the Diaoyu Islands is rooted in the assertion that the lands of the Ryukyu empire, of which the islands were a part, were in the past a tributary state that Japan illegally sought to annex in 1895 and were implicitly promised to China as part of the post–World War II settlement at Yalta and Tehran (these disputes are discussed in detail in chapter 6).[29] Some independent Chinese scholars writing in state-run papers have even raised the idea that Okinawa should be viewed as Chinese territory, although this has been rejected in official statements.[30]

Other Territorial Interests

At its extreme, this type of narrative might justify claims coextensive with the farthest expansion of the Qing/Ch'ing era (1644 through 1911, in its totality). That could in theory include what is now Mongolia and part of Russian Manchuria—although to date no Chinese leaders have suggested this as a legitimate objective. Indeed, China's recent history of resolving border disputes with Russia, Kazakhstan, and Vietnam suggests that China values amicable relations with its neighbors over preserving maximalist territorial gains.[31] However, the border dispute with India remains an inflammatory issue within a challenging relationship that China continues to face with one of its most consequential neighbors.[32]

Nonterritorial Interests

The Chinese national security narrative is not limited to the defense of the homeland and the recovery of lost territories. As China's economy has become increasingly dependent on global trade and access to natural resources, economic issues have come to play an increasingly important role in China's national security debate. More specifically, China's leaders and strategists have increasingly begun to focus on the need to assure, through military means if necessary, Chinese unimpeded access to vital sea-lanes and maritime resources.[33] As a corollary, some Chinese thinkers have also begun to focus on the need to reduce China's vulnerability to coercion by the United States by virtue of America's current domination of the open seas, as noted earlier.[34]

This economic dimension of China's national security narrative has broad-ranging implications—for the size and composition of China's naval forces, for overseas basing and access, for Beijing's diplomatic relations with key trading partners in the Gulf, Africa, and Latin America, and for its interest in both traditional and nontraditional threats to maritime security. We discuss this in greater detail in connection with maritime issues and basing in subsequent chapters.

To date, China's economic interests with other countries have generally not caused serious security friction with the United States. China has shown a willingness to curb at least some trade and investment with Iran in order to cooperate with the United States in addressing the Iranian nuclear program.[35] It has been tougher with North Korea in 2013 after Pyongyang's third nuclear test, with Beijing also imposing some sanctions there, for example on financial transactions. Finally, its nuclear nonproliferation record has improved over the years as well, with China tightening its controls over exports of sensitive technologies.[36]

China's defense white paper identifies a number of other interests that shape China's strategy, including "[t]he threats posed by 'three forces,' namely, terrorism, separatism and extremism." It also notes that "[s]erious natural disasters, security accidents and public health incidents keep occurring. Factors affecting social harmony and stability are growing in number, and the security risks to China's overseas interests are on the increase." Unlike the issues discussed earlier, however, many of these areas are avenues for possible cooperation, rather than competition, between the United States and China.[37]

STRATEGIC CULTURE

A second factor that could influence future Chinese national security policy is what scholars have come to call "strategic culture." The concept has been defined by Iain Johnston as "the way particular states (or state elites) think about the use of force for political ends . . . different states have different predominant sets of strategic preferences that are rooted in the 'early' or 'formative' military experiences of the state or its predecessor and are influenced to some degree by the philosophical, political, cultural, and cognitive characteristics of the state and state elites as these develop through time."[38] A number of scholars have sought to plumb Chinese history to determine whether there is a dominant perspective that shapes Chinese national security strategy, independent of structural factors (relative power or capability) prevailing during any given period. Like so many exercises of this type, however, scholars have drawn very different conclusions from the same historical record.

Two broad, but conflicting, schools of thought have dominated the debate. The first, which includes American historians as well as many Chinese scholars and practitioners, asserts that China has a distinctive strategic culture derived from Confucian-Mencian precepts and embodied in Sun Tzu's admonition to "win without fight or force"—a culture that eschews territorial expansion and "disesteems" the offensive use of force to achieve national security. Perhaps the most prominent American proponent of that view was Harvard historian John King Fairbank.[39]

More recently, Huiyun Feng reaches a similar conclusion from her analysis of Chinese strategic behavior, drawing on both historical case studies and analysis of Chinese rhetoric, which she terms "operational code."[40] Feng focuses on the dominant role of Confucianism in Chinese strategy:

"the Chinese way of expansion of the Chinese order was through cultural rather than military means and the final goal was not territorial or political rule over other states."[41] She contends, "my reading of China's history indicates that in over 2000 years of feudal rule the feudal empires of China seldom displayed aggressive intentions toward other countries nor made any attempts at expansion despite the capability to do so."[42] And "China does have a unique strategic culture, which is more peaceful and non-violent than the realpolitik Western one."[43]

This view has been echoed by both Chinese strategists and Chinese political leaders. This can be seen most vividly in the canonization of Ming era official Admiral Zheng He, whose far-ranging voyages at the height of Chinese power are cited as proof that China does not seek territorial conquest or forcible subjugation. At the government-sponsored commemoration of the six hundredth anniversary of Zheng He's travel, a senior Chinese official stated, "During the overall course of six voyages to the western Ocean, Zheng He did not occupy a single piece of land, establish any fortress or seize any wealth from other countries."[44] This view has been espoused by Chinese military leaders. For example, General Xu Xin, a former deputy chief of staff of the PLA, said that "the Chinese nation has a long tradition of honoring peace. As early as two thousand years ago, Confucius has emphasized that peace should be cherished."[45] Top PRC officials have made similar arguments frequently over the years.[46]

This view underpins the Chinese leadership's embrace of the "peaceful rise" or "peaceful development" theory of Chinese grand strategy. At its core it springs from a rational interest argument, that China's primary imperative is the peaceful international environment needed at least for now to facilitate China's economic development. But China's leaders seek to enhance the credibility of their assertions by reference to China's behavior during earlier eras of political dominance. Specifically, the contention is that China has historically used its power to produce global public goods.

An alternative view challenges the influence of the Confucian model in Chinese history, contending instead that the offensive use of force was widely accepted by Chinese leaders. In an influential study focusing on China's strategic behavior during the Ming era, Iain Johnston concludes that "Chinese strategic behavior exhibits a preference for offensive uses of force, mediated by a keen sensitivity to relative capabilities."[47] Johnston further argues, "Yet, in the Chinese case, at least, empires, especially at peak periods of power, often exhibited an offensive, coercive behavior rooted in a perception of adversaries as implacably hostile and threatening to the very survival of the system, and in a distrust of the long-term efficacy of accommodationist strategies."[48] Some go even further to question whether strategic culture was a factor at all, arguing that China's historic behavior conforms to realist assumptions about power: "Chinese grand strategy correlated with the rise and fall of its power. As China grew more powerful, it became more expansionist. Chinese strategic interests expanded as far as resources allowed, both on the Asian continent and across the ocean."[49]

It is not our objective to try to resolve the competing historical interpretive claims. Two important conclusions for our purpose, however, are that (1) different conclusions can be drawn from the historical record, but (2) contemporary Chinese leaders embrace the Confucian interpretation as a means of reassuring the international community of the pacific nature of China's intentions. So a key question is whether this paradigm in fact constrains Chinese international behavior—or whether it can be discarded or disregarded at will by future leaders.

There are many theories as to why this national narrative about Chinese history and strategic culture might constrain future action. Some suggest that embrace of the Confucian paradigm conveys legitimacy on the Communist Party's leadership, by rooting its claim to authority as a continuation of broadly accepted principles, independent of Communist ideology or raw power. Deviation from those principles would, therefore, weaken domestic support. Other arguments focus on the international level—that China has been successful in blunting balancing behavior by embracing this benign philosophy, and by doing so it has actually raised the bar on its own future behavior because it has in fact legitimated non-aggressiveness as an appropriate metric for others to apply to China.[50]

DOMESTIC DETERMINANTS OF CHINA'S EXTERNAL BEHAVIOR

As China's power has grown, there has been increasing attention paid to the question of how domestic factors will influence China's behavior in the current era. For all but the purest structuralist there is broad agreement that so-called unit-level factors influence how countries conduct foreign policy—but little agreement in China's case as to whether these internal factors are more likely to produce restrained or more aggressive behavior. Optimists point to the fundamental importance of sustained economic growth to the CCP's ability to sustain its monopoly of power, viewing it as a powerful constraint on actions that would increase the prospects of conflict. It provided the context to Deng Xiaoping's initial exhortation to modesty on the international stage as a necessary component to the success of his reform and opening-up strategy.[51] This is an argument frequently advanced by Chinese leaders as to why they can be trusted to be a responsible power with shared interests in sustaining a peaceful international environment.[52]

But other domestic factors point in the opposite direction. Another source of the CCP's legitimacy is rooted in nationalism, dating from Mao's early assertion that China has stood up and begun to reclaim China's historic legacy as a great power. That sentiment is reflected today in President Xi Jinping's call for China to be a great nation. To the extent that popular support for CCP rule depends on the party's vigilance in sustaining such an international role (much like the so-called mandate of heaven of earlier Chinese leaders, which could be forfeited by failure to protect the national interest), it could act as a constraint on conciliatory behavior by the Chinese leaders,[53] as well as a potentially important factor in intraparty and intragovernmental rivalry. The importance of this factor could become even more powerful if the other pole of the CCP's legitimacy, economic growth, begins to falter in the future.[54]

There is a rich and growing literature about domestic political influences on China's strategy, ranging from analysis of the impact of public opinion and social media to the impact of think tanks and interest groups to bureaucratic and institutional forces.[55] Each of these plays a role, but it is difficult to conclude which way these forces cut on balance and how important they are compared with other factors shaping China's policy.

Certainly China's policymakers regularly refer to the constraint of public opinion, referring in all apparent seriousness, for example, to occasional actions by the United States that "hurt the feelings of 1.3 billion Chinese" and to the impact of "netizens" on constraining the options available to China's leaders. There is at least anecdotal evidence to suggest that China's leaders actively seek out information on public opinion.[56] And it is certainly true that social media are increasingly active on the issue of U.S.-China relations—reflected in chat rooms such as the "Strong China forum" and more traditional media such as the highly nationalist *Global Times*. What is harder to say is the degree to which these sentiments are more broadly reflective of Chinese opinion and, perhaps more important, to what extent public opinion is an independent variable, or rather highly subject to manipulation by the leadership.[57] Given the extraordinarily active and intrusive role the central government plays in overseeing both traditional and new media, it is hard to fully credit the "what can we do in the face of public opinion?" attitude professed by Chinese policy interlocutors. But even if cynical in their initiation, nationalist and xenophobic sentiments may be easier for the party and government to unleash than to control.

This question of how the leadership reacts to and uses Chinese nationalism is particularly important because there are reasons to believe that nationalism per se is not inconsistent with constructive engagement with the United States or other international partners. Positive views about themselves do not necessarily imply hostile views about us.[58] And the deliberate "spin" put on U.S. policy would seem to be especially important given the relative fluidity of Chinese public attitudes toward the United States (in contrast, say, to the consistently very negative public attitudes vis-à-vis Japan).

Despite increased acceptance and availability of polling data in China on issues related to public opinion and national security, it is hard to know with great certainty what Chinese attitudes are and how variable or malleable they may be. One time series over the period 1998–2004, analyzed by Thomas Christensen, suggests that there are both short-term influences (e.g., the 1999 Belgrade bombing and the 2001 EP-3 incident) and long-term trends that affect Chinese attitudes toward the United States. There is at least the suggestion of a long-term cooling of views, more pronounced among the less educated and less well-to-do. Yet another poll by *China Daily* suggested that U.S. "likability" rose steadily from 2005 to 2009 but dropped sharply in 2010, which the analysts attributed to tensions that year including the Taiwan arms sales and the Dalai Lama's visit to the United States.[59]

There is certainly evidence to suggest a real change in Chinese attitudes toward the United States in recent years. According to a 2012 poll by the

Pew Research Centers Global Attitudes project, Chinese views toward the United States "have become significantly more negative in the last two years," with favorable ratings falling from 58 percent to 43 percent. The number who saw the relationship as one of cooperation fell from 68 percent to 39 percent, while those who considered it one of hostility grew from 8 percent to 26 percent.[60]

As noted earlier, the 2013 poll was similar, with U.S. favorability slightly lower, at 40 percent. Other polls are more optimistic but still show at least small declines in favorable opinion in China toward the United States among both the general public and elites[61] and increasing numbers who believe that relations are worsening.[62] Slight majorities of Chinese consider the United States "untrustworthy" (56.1% among the general public).[63] And over the past seven years, the U.S. military presence in Asia has emerged as a growing concern of the Chinese (especially among business and opinion leaders but to a degree among the public), on par with economic issues, though concerns about Taiwan have abated significantly. Pluralities of Chinese in all three groups think the U.S. military presence in the region will cause tensions rather than contribute to stability.[64]

The Chinese leadership has shown considerable dexterity in its domestic public messaging. It has rallied nationalist sentiment when it is seen to serve national and party interests, for example, in the aftermath of the embassy bombing in Belgrade in 1999 or following the announcement of the U.S. arms sale to Taiwan in 2010.[65] But it has then sought to turn it off when the leadership wished to create a more positive atmosphere, as before Hu Jintao's trip to the United States to participate in the Nuclear Security Summit in April 2010, just months after the arms sales announcement. It can also be seen in the decision of the leadership to put an authoritative end to the growing debate inside China by reaffirming the hide and bide approach during 2010 through the unusual publication of an article signed by China's top foreign affairs official, Dai Bingguo, in December 2010 in both Chinese and English.[66]

There is also considerable debate about the role of institutional interests and bureaucratic politics in shaping China's policy. Some of this is based on a priori assumptions about the strategies of institutional players—for example, the expectation that the PLA advocates for more forceful assertions of China's interest and is more likely to view American policy through a mistrustful lens, while the Foreign Ministry and at least some economic agencies are more likely to stress collaborative, positive-sum policies.[67] This view finds some support with reference to public remarks, especially by current and former PLA officials who often adopt a particularly strident tone,[68] as well as speculation about the significance of President Xi's ties to the PLA. But given the relative opaqueness of the Chinese policy process and the internal politics of the CCP, these conjectures are highly speculative.

China's Interpretation of U.S. Strategy

Of course, the PRC's policy is influenced not only by internal factors but by Chinese leaders' own assessments of U.S. intentions. This is of necessity a highly speculative inquiry, since the Chinese decision-making process is shrouded in secrecy and public pronouncements are as likely designed to shape public opinion as to reflect true attitudes, although pundits and experts have taken stabs at guessing what the real discussion might be behind the closed gates of Zhongnonghai.

In recent years there has been an increasingly public discussion involving think tanks, journalists, and former officials that at least offers a window into some of the competing theories about American goals—a discussion that almost certainly is familiar to the leadership. Broadly speaking, Chinese assessments fall along a spectrum with two poles. At one extreme they assert that the United States is determined to maintain its hegemonic position and resist China's rise (or even seek to undermine the regime). At the other, they accept the argument that the United States is prepared to "share power"—either of necessity, because of American decline, or by choice based on positive-sum views of the contemporary international system. It is not clear which "side" Chinese leadership tends to take in these internal debates.

Those harboring the more pessimistic assessment of U.S. intentions cite many factors in support of their view. These range from structural considerations (the inherent interest of the dominant power)[69] to strategic cultural factors (U.S. embrace of "offensive realism" as the core of its national security strategy)[70] to American domestic political forces. They cite a broad range of evidence in support of America's supposedly malign intentions, from the promulgation of the "China Threat" theory designed to delegitimize China internationally, to the refusal to honor the third U.S.-China Communique (to phase out arms sales to Taiwan), to support for human rights in China (as an effort to undermine the CCP through "peaceful evolution"), to the strengthening of U.S. security alliances and the "pivot" toward Asia to contain China militarily. The latter is also seen as sustaining the ability of the United States to hold hostage China's access to the global commons and to sustain a capacity to attack the Chinese homeland. This perspective is most often associated with commentators close to the PLA and security services (including former military officers), as noted previously, but can also be heard from academic "America" experts as well.[71]

On the other side of the debate are theorists who focus on U.S. interdependence as motivation for Washington to seek constructive relations with China.[72] This camp also includes those who argue that common interests outweigh differences (and thus will lead U.S. policymakers to pursue win-win approaches), as well as those who believe that declining American capacity will require the United States to accept a more co-equal role for China.

In public pronouncements, China's top civilian leaders most often side with the optimists—for example, in a speech by former vice foreign minister and now Chinese ambassador to the United States Cui Tiankai, where he laid out the case for why convergent U.S. and Chinese interests give confidence that the two sides will choose to pursue cooperation, and more recently by Cui in an interview with *Foreign Affairs* magazine, in which he stated the following:

> In the past, when one big country developed very fast and gained international influence, it was seen as being in a kind of a zero-sum game vis-à-vis the existing powers. This often led to conflict or even war. Now, there is a determination both in China and in the United States to not allow history to repeat itself. We'll have to find a new way for a developing power and an existing power to work with each other, not against each other. . . .
>
> . . . As for whether we are trying to change the rules of the game, if you look at recent history since China reformed and opened up, there has been a clear integration of China into the existing global

order. We are now members of many international institutions, not only the United Nations but also the World Bank and the International Monetary Fund. We have joined the World Trade Organization. We are taking part in many regional mechanisms.

So we are ready to integrate ourselves into the global system, and we are ready to follow the international rules. Of course, these rules were set without much participation by China, and the world is changing. You cannot say that the rules that were set up half a century ago can be applied without any change today. But what we want is not a revolution. We stand for necessary reform of the international system, but we have no intention of overthrowing it or setting up an entirely new one.[73]

But Chinese leaders are also careful to qualify their optimism with concerns about specific behavior that could be viewed as hostile, ranging from U.S. policy on Taiwan and Tibet, to interference in bilateral territorial disputes (as in the South and East China seas), to continued Tiananmen-era export controls, to American military activities around China's periphery.

These views frame the debate in China about the U.S. "pivot" or rebalance. It is not surprising that few if any Chinese welcome the Obama administration's decision to enhance its focus on the Asia-Pacific. But the extent of concern varies. Some see the rebalance as an ill-disguised plan to contain China. They point not just to the military front (increased deployments in the region, strengthened alliance ties, and a military modernization program focused on countering China's own growing military capacity) but also to economic strategies such as the Trans-Pacific Partnership trade negotiations that exclude China and, in this view, seek to weaken China's economic ties to key trading partners in the region. This perspective was evident at the 2013 Shangri-La Conference of Asia-Pacific Defense Ministers when a PLA general sharply rebutted U.S. Secretary of Defense Hagel's explanation of the goals of the U.S. rebalance.[74] Others, especially official commentaries, are more circumspect[75] but remain skeptical. The 2013 PLA defense white paper, for example, observes simply, "Some country has strengthened its Asia-Pacific military alliances, expanded its military presence in the region, and frequently makes the situation there tenser."[76]

CONCLUSION

This survey of the main "nonstructural" factors that could influence Chinese strategy going forward suggests that there is complex mix of forces that pull and tug Chinese decision makers toward more assertive or more accommodative policies.[77] What is important from our perspective is to consider how these factors might be used to improve the chances of more cooperative outcomes. For example, U.S. policymakers can reinforce the domestic political forces in China that are likely to support constructive Chinese strategies.[78] Similarly, the better U.S. policymakers understand China's own security narrative and the factors that influence Chinese assessments about U.S. strategy, the greater the possibility that Washington can craft its own policies in ways that will call forth reciprocal, positive Chinese actions. This view is similar to what two leading scholars, Kenneth Lieberthal from the United States and Wang Jisi from China, have argued in an important recent monograph.[79] For the practitioner, taking account of these competing explanations can at a minimum suggest a menu of policy strategies that can be used to address the underlying sources of tension in the relationship and a series of starting points to test which options to pursue. This approach lies at the core of our concept of strategic reassurance.

4

The Determinants of American Strategy

Just as historical traditions and experience provide the context for contemporary Chinese policy, whether the United States and China can constructively manage their relationship will be heavily influenced by the strategic traditions and concepts that dominate the American approach to national security policy. Powerful narratives rooted in interpretations of U.S. history influence the contemporary debate. They include the dangers of appeasing rising powers, the need for foreign policy to reflect American values, a belief in American exceptionalism, and the importance of overwhelming force and technological superiority for deterrence as well as war fighting. For many American strategists and political leaders, these precepts, together, have helped sustain a stable international order for decades—but they also combine to create enormous challenges to managing the U.S. relationship with a country such as China. This challenge stems both from inherent tensions between the American paradigm and China's conception of its own national interest, as well as deep doubts held by many in China that the reality of America's intentions is consistent with this benign narrative.

At the same time, other American security traditions, including fears of excessive international entanglement and military overstretch, can contribute toward policies that make it easier for America to avoid conflict with China. Such factors are currently on the rise in the aftermath of America's difficult experiences in Iraq and Afghanistan. The interplay between these competing traditions will strongly influence the way Sino--U.S. relations evolve in the coming years.

Strategy is not simply the province of executive branch officials and military leaders. Domestic politics in the United States also play a crucial role. Economic interests in particular help shape strategy, although their impact is complex—some economic issues tend to exacerbate the sense of strategic competition, while others highlight shared interests and interdependence. Key domestic constituencies also influence the debate—from groups concerned about human rights and religious freedom, to the defense industry, to the media.

Although there have been deep and substantial controversies throughout American history on the proper grand strategy for the United States, there has been a surprising degree of consensus on U.S. policy toward China in the four decades since President Nixon's first trip to the PRC. Despite continued challenges, from the suppression of dissent at Tiananmen Square, to the missile firings off Taiwan in the mid-1990s, to the frictions over maritime and cyber issues today, there has been a mainstream view that the United States should seek constructive relations with China. But for the most part, that view flourished at a time when China was too weak to present a serious security challenge to the United States (except of course in land conflicts in Asia).

In this chapter we examine U.S. strategic culture and traditions, as well as the domestic political factors that shape U.S. policy toward China, with an eye toward assessing how they could influence the course of the relationship in this new era. In the context of China's growing power and international role, will the United States act primarily a defensive power, avoiding conflict whenever possible and using force only when urgent and serious national security imperatives require it? Or will U.S. leaders be inclined to pursue a more activist strategy to preempt challenges to the country's current dominance, further expand the community of market-oriented democracies where possible, and be willing to use force under a wide range of circumstances to maintain the credibility of its regional security commitments? These broad parameters of the debate over which global strategy to pursue provide the context within which the specific challenges of managing U.S.-China relations will unfold.

STRATEGIC TRADITIONS AND THEIR INFLUENCE ON CONTEMPORARY AMERICAN SECURITY POLICY

Although the United States occasionally played an active role in international affairs in its early years (dating back to the conflict with the

Barbary Pirates, and again at the beginning of the twentieth century with the Spanish-American War and the "Open Door" policy toward China), it was not until the conclusion of World War II that U.S. strategic culture embraced the idea of a sustained and vigorous role on the world stage. A powerful narrative of "nonentanglement" dating from Washington's Farewell Address had pervaded U.S. political culture, despite the reality of an often more active role, from territorial expansion in North America to Commodore Perry's Black Ships in Japan and the occupation of the Philippines as well as the promotion of American economic interests in China.[1] America's self-image is reflected in George Kennan's metaphor that America—like democracies in general—is similar to a sluggish giant, slow to awaken to challenges abroad, though resolute and fierce once finally shaken from slumber.[2]

This view colored America's caution in entering the two world wars of the twentieth century. Indeed, even in the immediate aftermath of World War II, the United States made plans for a rapid demobilization. But the needs of occupation forces in Germany and Japan, impelled even further by Soviet assertiveness in the territories it occupied and ambitions along its periphery in Europe and East Asia, combined to check this proclivity toward disengagement.

The resulting post–World War II activist posture was not unanimous. It was challenged by Democrats like Henry Wallace and in the Republican Party by many, such as Robert Taft. President Truman struggled to build a domestic consensus in support of U.S. international engagement.[3] But over time the containment paradigm embodied in the Truman Doctrine and embraced by influential Republicans such as George Vandenberg came to dominate U.S. strategy.[4] Drawing on the perceived lessons of World War II, the need to avoid appeasement as well as the costs of military unpreparedness were seen as greater concerns than the danger of spiraling into war because of great-power competition.[5] This sentiment was reinforced by the Communist revolution in China and the North Korean invasion of South Korea.[6]

America's more activist strategy was reinforced because the competition between the United States and the "Communist bloc" was more than a great-power rivalry. It was also an ideological competition that was seen to threaten the American way of life, including individual freedom, democracy, and free markets as well U.S. security. As a result, the rivalry had a zero-sum quality; indeed, powerful voices advocated an even more aggressive policy of "roll back" rather than simple containment. The words of President Kennedy's inaugural address, to "pay any price, bear any burden in defense of liberty," captured the spirit of much of the times and framed U.S. strategy from Latin America to Southeast Asia.

Nonetheless, there were also elements of American strategy that tempered the competition, driven particularly by the danger of nuclear war. Thus even as Kennedy proclaimed the "twilight struggle" with communism, he proceeded to negotiate the first nuclear arms agreements with the Soviet Union. His successors went further through agreements such as the ABM Treaty of 1972 and the Helsinki accords of 1975. The idea of peaceful coexistence and negotiated limits on strategic competition came to characterize the U.S.-Soviet relationship.

Such a hedged strategy was not universally popular of course. These elements of détente and "rapprochement" drew criticism from elements in both political parties (from Democratic senator Henry Jackson to Republican presidential candidate Ronald Reagan) as well as influential strategists (such as Paul Nitze, Paul Wolfowitz, Jeanne Kirkpatrick, and the Committee on the Present Danger) on strategic grounds (as well as human rights grounds.) They led to the opposition to Carter's SALT II nuclear agreement with the Soviet Union in the Senate, as well as to the military buildup initiated under Carter and pursued vigorously under Reagan.

Thus, while conventional accounts focus on the continuity and dominance of "containment" as the core of U.S. Cold War strategy, there were ongoing debates over a variety of specific approaches carried out in the name of containment. The latter ranged from Eisenhower's nuclear-heavy New Look, to Kennedy's bear any burden, to Reagan's military buildup and missile defense ambitions.[7] There was considerable fluctuation in conventional military thinking, as well as in nuclear strategies and doctrines.

The end of the Cold War presented the United States with a kind of strategic tabula rasa. Should the United States protect its national security by returning to its traditional narrative of a power largely content to stay at home and remain disengaged from the world's quarrels except in rare circumstances of direct threat to the United States? Or should the United States assume a more sustained global role to buttress a Pax Americana designed to preserve national security, promote American values, and advance U.S. economic interests?

The debate between these two broad paradigms and the myriad intermediate positions between them[8] provide the context for the choices facing U.S. policy toward China and for the prospects for peacefully managing the relationship between the two. We now turn to four key components of the broader strategic debate: primacy versus sufficiency; the use of force and military strategy; the influence of values; and role of economic interests.

Primacy versus Sufficiency

One of the most important debates in American grand strategy, particularly since the end of World War II, has been the question of the need for the United States to achieve and maintain overwhelming military dominance to assure its security. There has been no simple consensus on this point.

American military power reinforced by the atomic bomb and rooted in U.S. economic might proved decisive in World War II, and for many American political leaders as well as "realist" strategic thinkers, peace through strength was the resulting watchword. The idea was that unparalleled American military and economic strength could provide security for the United States and stability for the rest of the world.

This view was challenged, however, by those who believed that the United States could not afford to shoulder that burden, and that in any event would be better served by collective security arrangements such as the UN and NATO rather than by unilateral American hegemony. Their view was reinforced by strategists who argued that the atomic bomb changed the calculus of power and rendered meaningless the pursuit of hegemony, since even a weaker, poorer adversary armed with nuclear weapons could wreak untold harm. This school of thought recognized the need to develop a modus vivendi with the Soviet Union to limit the dangers of inadvertent conflict or the escalation of peripheral conflicts to a direct confrontation between the two nuclear powers themselves. Especially as time went on and Soviet nuclear capabilities grew, this school was largely content for the United States to sustain strategic nuclear parity and act as a status quo power, willing to tolerate, at least in the short term, Soviet spheres of influence in Central and Eastern Europe, and Communist control in China, North Korea, and North Vietnam. But following Kennan, it insisted that Britain, Japan, the Soviet Union, and Germany as well as contiguous Western European industrial zones could not all be allowed to fall under the sway of a single hostile power.[9]

This latter approach was of course itself challenged by members of the first school, who characterized it as appeasement, rejected the 1975 Helsinki accords as a codification of an unacceptable status quo, and opposed arms control agreements as damaging constraints on U.S. power. The ambitious nature of their approach was later embodied in President Reagan's 1982 Westminster address and his famous demand that Gorbachev "tear down that wall."

The end of the Cold War brought renewal of the debate over the question of whether the United States should adopt primacy as the organizing principle for U.S. strategy. For some Americans, the U.S. "triumph" in the Cold War was brought about because the United States under President Reagan abandoned a status quo approach to the Soviet Union. Through a more muscular confrontation, it brought the Soviet Union to its knees and liberated Central and Eastern Europe. The moral was clear: the United States needed to sustain its primacy and build on the unipolar moment. This view surfaced early in the post–Cold War era, reflected in views publicly reported to have been advanced in draft Defense Department planning documents during the first Bush administration,[10] in the advocacy documents of the influential Project for a New American Century, and finally officially embodied in the first George W. Bush national security strategy report in 2002.[11]

Nor was the view limited to so-called neoconservatives. Many identified as liberal or progressive argued that American primacy brought with it vital global public goods. From President Clinton's and Secretary Albright's characterization of the United States as an indispensable nation,[12] to the expansion of NATO in the early post–Cold War years, to the more explicitly hegemonic calls for an American Empire,[13] political leaders and strategists charted a liberal model for the United States as a non–status quo power.

These perspectives coalesced in their most muscular form in the early years of the second Bush administration, specifically after the 9/11 attacks. In this period, security concerns about the possible nexus of weapons of mass destruction and terrorism, combined with a broader agenda to restore American power after what was perceived as a period of weakness under President Clinton, led President Bush to adopt a strategy that included the preventive use of military force and regime change as embodied in the intervention in Iraq.

Others advocated a more restrained approach, seizing on the end of the U.S.-Soviet competition as an opportunity to return to America's historical (pre–World War II) role as an "offshore balancer"—intervening abroad only when there seemed little choice in the face of the rise of a major hostile power. Perhaps best captured in certain policies of the first Bush administration, this approach led to caution about expanding NATO or involvement in the early political struggles in post-Soviet Russia and Ukraine, opposed involvement in the Balkans in the 1990s, and questioned the U.S. interest in places like Rwanda, Somalia, Haiti, and Libya.[14] Other theorists saw an opportunity for constructing a system of great-power cooperation in major security matters and favored American restraint for that reason.[15]

The election of President Obama reflected a swing toward this latter pole, though far from a full embrace of offshore balancing. Obama's campaign got its impetus from his early opposition to the Iraq war.[16] While Obama has continued the historic focus on the U.S. global leadership role (he explicitly repeated Clinton's characterization of the United States as an "indispensable nation" and has rejected the notion of American decline), there has been greater focus on building cooperative relationships with allies, neutrals, and emerging powers and about avoiding any tendency by the United States to act as the world's policeman.[17]

This trend seems to mirror U.S. public opinion. While Governor Romney's national security platform in 2012 focused on restoring a stronger international role for the United States, public opinion surveys suggested little appetite for U.S. hegemony after a decade of conflict. The Chicago Council on Foreign relations observed, on the basis of its 2010 poll:

> for some years . . . the Chicago Council surveys . . . have shown Americans uncomfortable with America's hegemonic role. In the current survey a large majority (79%) agree that the United States is playing the role of world policeman more than it should be. This finding is unchanged from 2008, and large majorities have taken this position since the question was first asked in 2002. On the question . . . about the U.S. role in solving international problems, asked repeatedly since 2002, only small minorities (8% in 2010), have thought that "as the sole remaining superpower, the United

States should continue to be the preeminent world leader in solving international problems."[18]

THE USE OF FORCE AND MILITARY DOCTRINE

A second and related debate has been over when and how the United States should use force to promote U.S. interests. This debate pitted those (beginning with Kennan himself) who believed that the competition between the United States and the Soviet Union should be waged primarily on the economic and political front, and those who advocated more "kinetic" measures. From controversies over the U.S. response to the Soviet interventions in East Germany and Hungary to the Eisenhower Doctrine in the Middle East pledging military support to regional states that might need it to resist Soviet encroachment, support for authoritarian but anticommunist governments in the Caribbean and Latin America in the 1950s and 1960s, to Vietnam, Angola, the Horn of Africa, Afghanistan, and Nicaragua, the United States oscillated between more or less political and military responses to perceived Communist expansionism. Its policies ranged along a spectrum from simple financial support, as in Greece and Turkey in the 1940s, to arming of proxies and covert action, as in Cuba, Angola, Somalia, Afghanistan, and Nicaragua, to direct intervention with main U.S. combat forces as in Lebanon and Vietnam as well as various smaller wars such as the 1965 invasion of the Dominican Republic[19] and the 1983 intervention in Grenada.

The debate turned over two related issues: when to intervene and what kind of military interventions to undertake. One perspective, often associated with Reagan-era Secretary of Defense Caspar Weinberger and Chairman of the Joint Chiefs of Staff Colin Powell, argued that the United States should only use force when clear national interests were at stake (in the case of Weinberger, vital interests) and that when force was used, it should be "overwhelming."[20] Arrayed against this view (sometimes associated with Secretary of State George Shultz and later Secretary Albright)[21] was the argument that the United States needed to be prepared to use force in a broader range of circumstances, with more limited objectives and more tailored military tools.

This debate began in the Cold War era but took on particular salience after the collapse of the Soviet Union, focusing on issues like the U.S. interventions in Haiti, Bosnia, and Kosovo (supported by those who believed that U.S. military capacity should be used for humanitarian and political objectives)[22] but opposed by those, including advisors to the first President Bush, who believed that these interventions squandered American power.[23] During the Obama years, the debate over the intervention in Libya again brought forth the two perspectives, as has the debate over Syria.[24]

The "how" to use force question was influenced by competing views about U.S. military strategy. Debates about how to employ force, although primarily confined to the military academies and security think tanks, occasionally have engaged the broader public.

During the Cold War, America's initial military posture in Europe and beyond was largely static. Following the Soviet acquisition of the bomb, U.S. policy was dominated by defensive concepts: early U.S./NATO planning was built around primarily defensive measures—preventing breakthroughs along the inter-German border and defense in depth across the German plains. This conventional strategy was backed up by nuclear "massive retaliation," which was driven not by war-fighting plans but a kind of "doomsday machine" deterrent concept. Even after the United States began to move toward a more nuanced nuclear posture, the emphasis remained on assured response and deterrence rather than prevailing in a nuclear conflict—a perspective that found its expression in the ABM Treaty of 1972.

Still, some military planners argued that this approach not only ceded the initiative to the potential adversary and relied on a nuclear threat of dubious credibility but also failed to take advantage of NATO's technological edge. Their views were reinforced by strategists who doubted the efficacy of the defensive/retaliatory paradigm. This rethinking culminated in more offensive approaches, such as NATO's Airland Battle doctrine, to deter war in Europe by developing the capacity to interdict Soviet reinforcements headed toward the central German front and the proposal to develop the neutron bomb, a more "usable" nuclear weapon. It fueled the move to abrogate the ABM Treaty and build missile defenses (the Strategic Defense Initiative), to abandon offensive nuclear arms control, and to develop powerful, accurate ballistic missiles (the MX and Trident II, in large numbers potentially), which some saw as a way to decapitate the

Soviet leadership and/or destroy Soviet nuclear forces, along with a naval capacity to threaten the Soviet submarine fleet carrying sea-launched ballistic missiles in its bastions.

In the post–Cold War context, this perspective led to a focus on how the United States could exploit its technological advantage over potential adversaries—from information technology to control of space—to deliver a powerful offensive capability, one that was very much on display in operations in Kosovo (1999) and Afghanistan (2001) and Iraq (2003). It also led some to question the value of multilateral operations, because they constrained American freedom of action and America's ability to exploit its technological advantages.[25]

American confidence in the ability to achieve its political goals through the use of military power was tempered by a national aversion to casualties. In the decades after Vietnam and before 9/11, American decisions on both when and how to use force were shaped by a reluctance to risk military casualties. The loss of 241 Marines in a suicide bombing led to the end of the U.S. military operation in Lebanon in 1983 under President Reagan. The death of 18 American servicemen in Mogadishu brought about the end of the U.S. operation in Somalia in 1993 under President Clinton. The Balkans wars were fought with minimal risk to Western soldiers. Any inclination to halt the Rwandan genocide of 1994 was constrained by concerns about U.S. military casualties.[26] Together these limited interventions and noninterventions earned the United States the nickname of "the reluctant sheriff" in Richard Haass's memorable phrase.[27] Casualty aversion shaped the U.S. role in Libya in 2011, as well.

Similar debates have shaped the U.S. approach to maritime strategy. For its first century of existence, the United States was most focused on defending its seagoing merchant marine from attacks by the dominant naval powers (primarily Britain) and pirates. In these early decades, the United States did not have the wherewithal to aspire to maritime hegemony in any event. But as U.S. capacity began to expand and its economic interests grew, strategists such as Alfred Thayer Mahan began to consider a more expansive role for the U.S. Navy—including the capacity to project naval power globally to advance U.S. economic interests and to provide basing and support arrangements for the fleet.[28]

Nonetheless, through the early twentieth century, the United States continued to accept (and "free ride" on) Britain's preeminent naval power. It stayed out of wars involving Japan and Russia, and initially sought neutrality when Germany and Britain went to war at sea in 1914. It agreed to the Washington Naval Treaty, which attempted, unsuccessfully, to stabilize military competition among several major powers, including the United States, by allocating generally equitable fleet sizes to various states.

World War II changed all that. America wound up with the only serviceable global Navy in the conflict's immediate aftermath. The Soviet Union and China were both relatively weak and focused on internal or nearby challenges. The European colonial powers liberated their former colonies and headed home, focusing more military energies on facing off against the Warsaw Pact than on ruling the seas or overseas territories. Over time, Britain abandoned its global maritime role and ultimately decided not to sustain its earlier commitments to the Persian Gulf region, leaving a vacuum that the Eisenhower administration and other subsequent presidents chose to fill by expanding U.S. military commitments there. Similarly in East Asia, the demilitarization of Japan left the U.S. Navy as the only maritime force capable of checking the Soviet Union.

The early years of the Cold War saw the apex of this American dominance. The United States came right up to China's shores during the Taiwan crises of the 1950s. It sought a comprehensive preemptive capability against early generations of Soviet ballistic-missile submarines. It built much of its plan for the conventional military defense of Europe around the assumption of assured access to Atlantic shipping lanes.

Even with the arrival of a much better Soviet Navy in the latter half of the Cold War, the United States retained ambitious goals for operating in oceanic domains. The Reagan administration's maritime strategy envisioned attacking the Soviet Union with amphibious and other naval assets that would sail around Scandinavia to the Kola Peninsula. Once the Cold War ended, the United States regained a measure of the predominance it had enjoyed in the late 1940s and 1950s, employing it to conduct "carrier diplomacy" in the Taiwan Strait in the mid-1990s and to project power into the Middle East to fight Iraq and pressure Iran. Naval doctrine focused on assuring unfettered access to the maritime commons, not simply to protect shipping and transit but as a platform for the United States to project power against potential adversaries. The Air-Sea Battle concept (discussed in more detail in chapter 5) follows this tradition in some ways, albeit with a less confrontational motivation than much of

Cold War military policy. It seeks to respond to the rise of China and the more general spread of advanced antiship and other precision-strike technologies with better defensive and offensive capabilities on the part of the U.S. Navy and U.S. Air Force in particular so that American forces can continue to defend allies and interests abroad.

But even at the height of U.S. maritime dominance, there were constraints on U.S. hegemony. As the Cold War went on, Soviet naval forces were increasingly capable of jeopardizing America's access to Atlantic shipping lanes; they could also have complicated U.S. operations in the Western Pacific. American naval predominance never extended to the distant reaches of Africa or even South America in most meaningful ways. The six-hundred-ship Navy advocated under Reagan by Secretary of the Navy John Lehman ultimately was judged unaffordable. Large-scale carrier formations came under increasing scrutiny because of their cost and potential vulnerability.

Over the last dozen years or so, an alternative to the "Lehman" model has begun to take shape, one that focuses more on cooperative strategies to secure the maritime domain and protect sea-lanes for commerce. Rather than relying on unilateral U.S. hegemony, this approach, embodied in the U.S. maritime strategy of 2007, suggested that collective efforts were both necessary and more desirable as the most stable approach to maritime security. As the official Navy/Marine Corps/Coast Guard report on the strategy put it, "We believe that preventing wars is as important as winning wars. . . . Maritime forces will be employed to build confidence and trust among nations through collective security efforts that focus on common threats and mutual interests in an open, multi-polar world. . . . Although our forces can surge when necessary to respond to crises, trust and cooperation cannot be surged."[29]

Values

Closely linked to the debate about primacy versus coexistence has been the debate over values in U.S. strategy. For some in the "primacy" camp, the need for American dominance was driven not simply by a realist view of international politics but from the specific nature of the Soviet Union as an ideologically motivated state seeking to impose its way of life on others. Following Reagan, this meant the problem was not that the Soviet Union was an empire but that it was an "evil" empire and inherently expansionist. Coexistence with such a state was impossible; one side or the other had to prevail. This view was reinforced by those who believed that the United States had a moral responsibility to vindicate its views on democracy and human rights through its global strategy.

This values-based view of American strategy has deep roots in American history, dating back at least to Thomas Paine's and others' advocacy of U.S. support for the French Revolution and by many who argued that the United States should actively support the Bolivarian revolutions in Central America in the early 1800s.[30] It achieved its early high point in U.S. strategy with Wilson's Fourteen Points. These were often counterbalanced by more "realist" views, embodied most succinctly in John Quincy Adams's counsel that the United States should be "the well-wisher to freedom and independence of all [but] the champion and vindicator only of her own."[31]

During the Cold War this debate was front and center. It extended from the Truman Doctrine to Kennedy's "bear any burden" exhortation, to Carter's human rights policy to Reagan's challenge to the "evil empire" and his support of freedom fighters from Nicaragua to Angola as well as the military intervention in Grenada. For those focused on human rights and democracy, it was not sufficient for the Soviet Union to leave others alone; the United States had a responsibility to press for self-determination and human rights in Russia itself. For them, Article III of the Helsinki agreement was more than an affirmation of the UN charter. It was also an argument for embedding human rights in U.S. policy, expressed, for example, by the Jackson-Vanik amendment and the broader idea of linking political and economic relations to a country's human rights performance.

Others offered more realist views. The perspective was perhaps best encapsulated in Article I of the Helsinki agreement's commitment to respect the sovereignty of all signatories—which, for the United States, meant acceptance of the communist regime in the Soviet Union, so long as Moscow accepted the sovereignty of others.

With the end of the Cold War, there was renewed focus on the role of values in American strategy. With the dark cloud of possible superpower nuclear conflict removed, some argued that the United States should feel more free to take an active role in supporting democracy movements and challenging nondemocratic regimes—in effect, to adopt a more explicitly non–status quo strategy, implied at least in both the Clinton and Bush administrations' national security strategies.[32] The values dimension took on an increasingly important role in the Bush administration's justification for toppling Saddam Hussein,[33] an argument that helped win support from human rights groups and some Democrats. Although some criticized the Bush democracy strategy for imposing Western values at the point of a gun, there remained a strong values-based strain under Obama, contributing to the decision to intervene in Libya.

ECONOMICS AND STRATEGY

A fourth important strand in U.S. strategic debates has been the matter of the proper role for economics in shaping foreign policy. From the earliest days of the republic, much of the debate about U.S. engagement abroad concerned the importance of economic interests and their interaction with security policy. In Asia, economic interests were a primary driver of U.S. policy through the nineteenth century.[34] During the Cold War, the tensions between these goals were muted. In part this was because they were aligned—the Marshall Plan served both security and economic goals, since economic recovery was seen as essential to keep more countries from falling prey to Soviet designs and influence as well as to rebuild valuable markets for U.S. goods.[35] Even where there were real trade-offs, the stakes were low—U.S. trade with the Soviet Union was minimal and unpromising, so there were few costs associated with security-related sanctions against the USSR. But the issue did arise from time to time, in contexts as diverse as the Cuba trade embargo and the disputes over the Soviet gas pipeline to Europe in the 1970s and 1980s, as did longstanding debates about the desirability of continuing support for monarchies and nondemocratic governments in the resource-rich Middle East. This led to debates about how far the United States should subordinate economic goals to concerns about both security as well as human rights and democracy.

Two competing perspectives have dominated the American debate from a security perspective. One has focused on the costs of economic engagement for U.S. security, since interdependence limits U.S. leverage and freedom of action. It can be seen, for example, in the thinking of strategists who have prioritized U.S. energy independence as a way of avoiding costly entanglements in the Middle East with fragile governments that do not all share American values and interests.[36] The other perspective, rooted in liberal international relations theory, sees economic engagement and interdependence as powerful forces in muting security competition and rivalry. This view took expression in the ideas of Cordell Hull and the liberal trade and investment era ushered in by Bretton Woods after World War II, which focused on the security benefits of a more integrated economic world.

PUBLIC ATTITUDES TOWARD U.S. GRAND STRATEGY

Beyond the debates among strategists and policymakers, what has the American public typically felt about the country's broad role in the world? Presumably much can be deduced by observing the behavior of those whom the voters have elected to office. But it is also worth examining public opinion directly as measured in surveys.

During much of the Cold War, especially during periods of heightened national security anxiety, American views were often rather hawkish. But that has not always been entirely true—and in any event, it has changed considerably over the last quarter century.

Throughout the post–Cold War era, Americans have told pollsters that they favor a more cooperative approach to global security and a greater sharing of the burden with other countries. For example, one 1996 poll showed that 74 percent favored multilateralism while only 12 percent favored isolationism and 13 percent favored American preeminence.[37]

The country's reluctance to use force in major ways, with or without a coalition, can also be seen in recent history. Consider the 1991 Gulf War, now often remembered as a convincing display of American power. Yet at the time, the Senate voted only 55–45 to authorize the use of force, hardly an overwhelming expression of national consensus to evict Saddam Hussein from Kuwait.[38] Those Americans listing international affairs as their top issue of concern typically numbered less than 10 percent in the 1990s.[39] That is similar to the current situation.[40]

Americans have also tended to say by large majorities—65 to 75 percent in recent years—that the country should focus more on its internal challenges and less on foreign affairs.[41] In the words of Derek Chollet and James Goldgeier, who chronicled U.S. strategy between 1989 and

2001, "[Americans] are not eager to hear a call for new global missions—especially military ones. Yet at the same time, American voters do prefer a strong military and often do vote for candidates—Reagan, both Bushes—who promise just that." As Chollet and Goldgeier continue, in writing about their fellow citizens, "they know that without American leadership, it will be impossible to solve global problems."[42]

Americans do tend to prefer to "maintain superior military power," according to Chicago Council on Global Affairs polling over the years. But the majority in favor has been modest—typically 50 to 55 percent over the last two decades—and the concept is somewhat vague in any event.[43] In 2012, two-thirds of Republicans favored that the country retain such superiority, but slightly less than 50 percent of either Democrats or independents did so.

Regardless of their preferences, Americans increasingly question whether their country will remain the strongest in the world. In a 2013 Pew poll, 47 percent said they expect China to become the world's leading superpower (if it is not already), up substantially from the 36 percent who felt that way in 2008.[44]

Americans tend to be pragmatists about the use of force. They are relatively casualty averse but are willing to tolerate difficult and costly military operations if they feel the country's core security is at stake and have some degree of confidence that operations can be effective. Recent polling on the Afghanistan war illustrates these tendencies. With the war now more than a dozen years old and with casualties and frustrations mounting, two-thirds of all Americans recently indicated that they no longer considered the effort to have been worth it. Yet perhaps recognizing the continued relevance of the area to U.S. national security, in the same mid-2013 poll they also favored (by a modest majority) keeping a residual American force in Afghanistan after 2014 when the current International Security Assistance Force mission ends. Of course, it helps that any such enduring mission would presumably be modest in scale and associated risk.[45]

Strategic Traditions and China Policy

These broad perspectives on U.S. grand strategy and the use of force provide the general context for the development of American strategy toward China, from the Open Door until today. Differing views over the roles of security, values, and economics in foreign policy have influenced both high policy and public opinion toward China.

During the first decades of U.S. engagement in China, economic interests predominated as the United States focused on maintaining access to China's markets against the mercantile aspiration of European powers. Economic interests also drove security policy and proved to be an important element of the argument for the development of U.S. sea power. Debates about the wisdom of territorial acquisition in the Western Pacific were often based on the perceived need to assure access to markets and control of the sea-lanes. And value issues also played a role, fueled by the presence of U.S. missionaries who saw in engagement with China an opportunity to spread Christian values. The values dimension was reinforced with the establishment of the democratic Republic of China and the ascendancy of Sun Yat-sen. Both security and values helped undergird the bonds that led to the Sino-American alliance in World War II.

The Chinese civil war and the ensuing Communist victory put debates over each of these dimensions in sharp relief and have continued to shape U.S. policy debates up to the present. We discuss each element in turn.

Security: Containment, Cooperation, and Competition

Competing perspectives on security heavily influenced the U.S. approach toward China in the post–World War II era.[46] A key issue was whether and how to view a Communist victory in China—as a zero-sum loss to the United States in its competition with the USSR, or a development that (by virtue of China's weakness or its lack of affinity for the USSR) could offer opportunities to promote U.S. interests through engagement.[47] With the advent of China's entry into the Korean War, the former view came to dominate American policy and contributed in part to the slow U.S. adaptation to China's increasingly hostile relations with Moscow. It formed a backdrop to key decisions during the Cold War, including what response if any the United States should make to China's development of nuclear weapons.[48] As discussed later in the chapter, it was also an important element in shaping U.S. policy toward Taiwan.

But even at the height of this confrontational posture, there were constraints on how far the United States would go in challenging China, and even more so in actively pursuing regime change in Beijing. Washington settled for an in-place armistice in Korea that left the China-backed

Communist government in power in North Korea. The United States declined to provide active support to Taiwanese plans to retake the mainland. Equally significant, the Johnson administration considered, but ultimately decided against, taking preemptive action against China's nascent nuclear program—in effect accepting that China would have at least some capacity to deter U.S. action through nuclear retaliation.[49] American policy reflected a view that U.S. security interests were compatible with a Communist government in Beijing—long before China had adopted the path of reform and opening up.

The initial rapprochement with China was heavily influenced by Nixon's and Kissinger's concerns about the global power balance. Drawing China closer to the United States—and away from the USSR—enhanced Washington's position vis-à-vis Russia at a time when Soviet military modernization (especially nuclear modernization) was seen to be eroding U.S. dominance. China was seen as too weak to be a threat to the United States but strong enough to provide additional counterweight to America's rival, partly by virtue of its large land armies that had frustrated America in Korea but that posed little ongoing threat to core U.S. interests in the region. It was no accident that some of the most important early elements of Sino-American collaboration involved security, including intelligence cooperation and discussions of arms sales.[50]

More recently, however, with the remarkable growth of China's economy as well as the dramatic increases in PRC military spending and operational capability, China has become the focus of the debate over the role of primacy in America's strategy. Since the initial steps toward normalization in the 1970s, canonical U.S. policy, pursued by presidents of both parties, has asserted that the United States welcomes a strong and prosperous China, that the Sino-American relationship is not zero sum, and that there are substantial prospects for great-power cooperation between the United States and the PRC to promote peace and stability in East Asia and beyond. But that view is challenged both by political leaders and by scholars who argue that for the first time since the collapse of the Soviet Union, it is possible to imagine in concrete terms a challenge to U.S. primacy. As China's power has grown, there has emerged a more explicit school of thought that China's rise poses a direct threat to American primacy and thus to American security and that therefore the United States needs to check China's capabilities.[51] From this perspective, strengthening U.S. security alliances with partners around China's periphery and encouraging cooperation among them are central to sustaining a favorable power balance in the region. Continued arms sales to Taiwan, and for some, affirmative opposition to Taiwan's unification, form a part of this overall strategy. Advocates of this approach in particular strongly support significant restrictions on technology exports—including dual-use capabilities—for fear that they will enhance China's military capabilities.

For those who believe that U.S. primacy is the core means of achieving American national security and maintaining regional peace, the only acceptable outcome is Chinese acquiescence in a U.S.-led security order. This could happen either by Beijing's voluntary acceptance of that order or because superior American capacity and unquestioned resolve block any effort by China to overturn it. Proponents of this view argue that irrespective of China's current intentions, the only way to be sure that China will behave as a status quo power in the future is to maintain such overwhelming U.S. superiority that China will have no other choice.[52]

For those who believe global interdependence makes the concept of "primacy" (especially in the military/security sense) less relevant or even counterproductive—or in any case unsustainable in the future in the same way it has existed in the recent past—the question is not how to thwart China's relative rise. The challenge, rather, is to shape it so that China makes a positive contribution to peace and security—or at least does not threaten the vital interests of the United States and its allies. From this perspective, China's economic and political evolution over time open the possibility, if not the certainty, that even a more powerful China will have a substantial stake in the status quo and perceive its dominant interest as achieving a modus vivendi with the United States. Seen from this perspective, efforts to sustain U.S. primacy will not only prove futile at some level but will undercut the opportunities for gain from cooperation and turn a positive-sum outcome into a lose-lose proposition.[53]

Military Strategy and the Use of Force

These competing perspectives also inform the debate over what military strategy the United States should pursue in East Asia and how it should structure its overseas military presence and employ its armed forces. Those who favor primacy advocate a robust approach to basing and military operations, as well as active efforts to counter what they perceive as Chinese challenges to that presence such as China's so-called anti-access/area denial strategy and its perceived attempt to intimidate rival territorial claimants. From this perspective, the United States needs to sustain unquestioned superiority across all war-fighting domains—especially space, maritime, and cyber—as well as the ability to project power against China, both from a strengthened presence in East Asia, through new bases and other cooperative agreements with allies and partners as proposed by the "pivot," as well as long-range capacity from the United States. Although few to date have advocated a China-centric approach to missile defense, proponents of this general approach see value in the overall enhancement of U.S. theater and strategic missile defense for possible application against China.[54] They question the value of military-to-military exchanges as potentially providing China knowledge about U.S. capabilities that could be used by China to counter those capabilities.

Those who accept a growing role for China focus more on confidence-building measures and the elaboration of rules of the road for military activities—such as the proposed Code of Conduct in the South China Sea—as well as multilateral frameworks for buttressing regional stability like the East Asian Summit and the ASEAN Regional Forum. They promote collaborative military efforts including joint exercises and non-traditional missions like antipiracy and disaster response, and focus on enhancing military-to-military dialogue and transparency. They caution about the dangers of offensive-minded doctrine (notably aspects of Air-Sea Battle) and elements of U.S. and allied military modernization (such as high-end strike aircraft based near China, long-range conventional ballistic missiles, and other advanced or exotic long-range systems) that can fuel an arms race, as well as operations like certain types of maritime surveillance that can lead to inadvertent crises.[55]

Values

The values debate has also played a prominent role in American China policy from the end of World War II to the present, as the strategic arguments for opposing the Communist takeover, and thereafter for refusing to recognize China, became entwined with "principled" opposition to the

Communist regime. Nixon's strategically motivated normalization was opposed on both the left and the right as a betrayal of U.S. values. The crackdown during and following Tiananmen forced even the first Bush administration, with its strongly pro-engagement instincts, to accept sanctions and an interruption in the steadily warming U.S.-China relationship. Concerns about a range of human rights issues and what measures should be taken to promote human rights in China continue to form an important dimension of U.S. policy, pitting those who believe that Washington should take active steps against those who advocate a more hands-off approach (either because they believe that internal Chinese developments will best achieve the desired objective or that the focus on human rights impedes the pursuit of other interests).

The values debate is not wholly independent from security concerns. For some who accept that power relations between rising and established powers are not inherently zero sum (citing the example of the United States and Britain during the twentieth century), they nonetheless believe that in this case, the autocratic nature of the Communist Party means that China's policy will necessarily be hostile to the United States.[56] They further point to the important role that the military plays in Chinese decision making and harbor concerns about whether there is full civilian control of the military. From this perspective, actively supporting democratic change and human rights not only is consistent with U.S. values but also can help bring about "peaceful evolution" of the Chinese political system that would make China's rise less threatening. They therefore champion direct support for activists in China, including measures to undermine China's information control system, as well as a forceful role in challenging China's human rights policy in international fora. They support continuation of the so-called Tiananmen sanctions for human rights as well as security reasons.

Most Americans believe that human rights and democracy should play some role in U.S. foreign policy. But many argue for a nonconfrontational approach with a country like China and particularly avoiding punitive measures like sanctions, which they believe are either ineffective or counterproductive, preferring dialogues on human rights and the rule of law to make progress. There is virtually no support in any camp for an active regime-change strategy, given China's growing power and its economic importance to the United States.

Economics

The economic dimension of strategy has come to play an increasingly important role in shaping the debate over U.S.-China relations, beginning with the era of reform and opening and accelerating with China's remarkable economic growth over the past two decades. But even those who prioritize economic interests in developing American policy toward China are divided about how best to advance those interests: there are those who see the growing interdependence of the two economies as both an economic boon and an emollient in security relations, and those who believe that the economic relationship is disadvantageous to the United States because of China's mercantile and predatory policies.[57] Members of the latter school further tend to believe that U.S. dependence on China for trade, investment, and finances makes the country too reliant on a potentially hostile power and thus constrains the United States' ability to assert forcefully its strategic interests.

These economic debates are particularly significant because unlike the security and to some extent the values debates, they involve distinctive political constituencies in the United States, which in turn have an impact on electoral politics and policymaking. They range from business and workers in industries and sectors that benefit from Chinese trade and investment (such as agriculture and aviation, as well as state and local officials seeking to attract foreign direct investment) to those who feel most harmed (e.g., certain manufacturing firms and workers believe they are victims of Chinese intellectual property theft).

Many of the economic debates have at least implicit security overtones. For example, during the debate over China's entry into the WTO (and the associated requirement that the United States grant permanent normal trading relations status to China) some proponents argued that WTO membership would contribute to a more constructive Chinese approach on international relations. Debates over how "tough" the United States should be with respect to Chinese trade law violations often turn on the potential impact, or lack thereof, on cooperation on security issues. Even trade agreements, like the U.S.-Korea Free Trade Agreement and the proposed Trans-Pacific Partnership (TPP), are sometimes promoted in terms of their broader impact on U.S.-China relations (in these two specific cases, as means of countering growing Chinese influence on its neighbors by virtue of the latters' economic dependence on trade with China).

High-tech trade has been another area where the debate has crystallized. Those focused on security concerns continue to oppose loosening export restrictions on China and resist Chinese inward investment in the United States that might have adverse security consequences for the United States (CNOOC-Conoco, Huawei), while others argue that these are areas of comparative advantage for the United States and offer win-win opportunities for economic benefit and closer political relations between the two countries.[58]

Cyber, too, is an arena where security and economic concerns have merged. The growing alarm in the United States over perceived Chinese cyber intrusions is seen as both a security threat (espionage and the potential for offensive actions that could interfere with military operations and critical infrastructure) and an economic threat (vast theft of U.S. intellectual property). These concerns have led some to advocate imposing economic and political sanctions on China, while others have focused on dialogue and cooperative strategies.[59]

Taiwan and U.S. Strategy

In many ways, the debate about U.S. policy toward Taiwan brings together (as it has done since the late 1940s) all these strands of competing strategic paradigms. Although virtually all U.S. policymakers have accepted the "one China" framework developed in connection with the process of normalization of U.S.-China relations in the 1970s, there have been important differences about what that means in practice. Those focused on the strategic competition between the United States and China advocate vigorous political and military support for Taiwan. They argue that maintaining Taiwanese de facto (if not de jure) independence is a major barrier to China's military expansion beyond the so-called first island chain (and therefore key to continued U.S. maritime primacy).[60] It also represents a strong values statement in support of Taiwan's vigorous democracy and advances U.S. economic interests by keeping Taiwan's technology and economic capacity beyond the control of the PRC.

Although few (if any) today advocate outright abandonment of Taiwan (including an end to arms sales), some are prepared to accept the peaceful unification of Taiwan, so long as it is not the product of coercion. They argue that Taiwan's integration with the mainland can foster a more open and competitive economic system in the PRC while promoting the diffusion of democratic values and that improved Taiwan-mainland relations would lessen the danger of direct conflict between the United States and China.[61]

Domestic Politics, U.S. Public Opinion, and Sino-American Relations

Domestic political factors have played and continue to play a significant role in the evolution of America's China policy, particularly since the Communist Revolution in 1949. In the early years, there was a heavy Cold War overlay, vividly seen in the Senate contest between Richard Nixon and Helen Geohagan Douglas and in the purge of the State Department China hands during the Red Scare of the McCarthy era. Even after Nixon's opening to China undercut the Cold War rationale for a tough policy toward the PRC, China continued to play a prominent role in U.S. presidential elections. From candidate Reagan's opposition to Carter's normalization, through candidate Clinton's critique of George H. W. Bush's response to the Tiananmen protests, to candidate Romney's critique of Obama's alleged softness on China's currency policy, presidential challengers have routinely attacked what they claim to be too accomodating U.S. policy toward China—and in many cases forced the incumbent to adjust, most notably in President Bush's decision to sell F16 aircraft to Taiwan in 1992.[62] Even when China policy played a less prominent role (e.g, in 2000 and 2008), few candidates (incumbent or challenger) have highlighted U.S.-China cooperation as an affirmative plank of their candidacy.

Congress, too, has been a contentious arena for U.S.-China relations, and not just on economic or human rights issues. Both President Carter and President Reagan were forced to backtrack on commitments to China with respect to Taiwan arms sales because of congressional opposition (culminating in the Taiwan Relations Act in 1979 and the so-called six assurances that accompanied the signing of the third U.S.-China Communique in 1982). During the Clinton years, for example, congressional concern about Chinese behavior, from alleged stealing of nuclear secrets to theft of missile technology, put the administration's China policy on the defensive. In 2000, Congress established the U.S.-China Economic and Security Review Commission "with the legislative mandate to monitor, investigate, and submit to Congress an annual report on the national security implications of the bilateral trade and economic relationship between the United States and the People's Republic of China."[63] Congress also mandated that the Department of Defense issue an annual report on "The Military Power of the People's Republic of China," mirroring a Cold War report on Soviet military power.[64]

U.S. public opinion toward China on security issues often has been less alarmist than what is reflected in actions and rhetoric by Congress. Indeed, according to one influential poll, "The development of China as a world power is viewed by a minority (40%) as a critical threat. The 2012 results are striking when contrasted with attitudes in the 1990s and early 2000s, when nearly six in ten considered the development of China as a world power a critical threat."[65] By more than 2 to 1, in that 2012 poll, Americans favored "undertak[ing] friendly cooperation and engagement" (69%) rather than "actively work[ing] to limit the growth of China's power" (28%).[66]

Still, the situation is hardly simple. Other surveys suggest that security issues still trail economic and human rights issues as sources of American's concerns toward China.[67] But there also are polls suggesting that a broad cross section of Americans view China's rising power as a military threat.[68] And China's favorability ratings among Americans, according to Pew, dropped from around 50 percent in the 2009–11 period to 40 percent in 2012 and 37 percent in 2013.[69]

CONCLUSION: THE FUTURE OF AMERICAN STRATEGY

While U.S. policy has been characterized more by continuity than change over the past four decades, there are reasons to think that the core consensus is under stress. The way in which American policy will evolve depends to some degree on events internal to the United States. For example, a vigorous economic recovery may increase U.S. self-confidence and reduce worries about being overtaken by China. In addition, security developments outside East Asia—for instance, renewed terrorist attacks on the homeland or renewed conflict in the Middle East—could also influence grand strategy, and with it the U.S. approach to East Asia.

But the discussion suggests that there are powerful forces in the United States, rooted in strategic traditions and domestic politics, that will tend to favor U.S. policies that could accentuate, rather than mitigate, the sense of rivalry between the United States and China and lead to rising tensions and an arms race between the two. The same is true in key allied capitals, perhaps most notably in Tokyo. At the same time, this chapter also shows there are significant forces working in the opposite direction and that such a pessimistic outcome, while highly possible, is far from certain.

Given these competing tendencies, America's future strategy will be heavily influenced not only by factors internal to the United States but also by the choices Beijing will make—in its own domestic politics, in its economic policies, and, most important in our view, in its security policies. A China that takes concrete measures to demonstrate its peaceful intentions and willingness to contribute to global public goods is likely to strengthen the arguments of those in the United States (and throughout the Western Pacific region, including among key American allies) who see U.S.-China relations in largely positive-sum terms. Alternatively, a China that appears to validate the skeptics' narrative through increased efforts to leverage its enhanced power at the expense of others will call forth a more confrontational approach by the United States.

This is, of course, the mirror image of the dynamic in China. As the previous chapter showed, although there are proponents of both futures for U.S.-China relations, the choices made by the United States and its allies will have an important role in determining the choices that China will make.

This dynamic on both sides of the bilateral relationship underscores why the idea of mutual strategic reassurance is so critical to managing the relationship going forward. Put simply, this discussion should help show that the course of the relationship is not predestined but that a positive outcome will depend on affirmative efforts by China and by the United States to address each other's concerns and thereby generate an affirmative momentum to combat the tendency to rivalry.

PART II

Strategic Reassurance in Practice

5

---❈---

Military Spending and Military Modernization

After a period during which a half-dozen military powers had comparably sized defense budgets and the United States spent tenfold as much as any other country, the global distribution of military budgets is changing. China has moved into a category all by itself as the world's number two military spending power. Meanwhile, although U.S. defense budgets are coming down, they remain very high by comparison with the military budgets of other countries and will still modestly exceed America's own Cold War average, in inflation-adjusted or real-dollar terms, even once planned reductions are complete. The growth of Chinese defense spending has been an important factor in fueling concerns in the United States about Chinese strategic intentions, while in China the continued high levels of U.S. military spending are seen primarily as reflection of a determination to maintain dominance over the PRC. At the direction of Congress, the U.S. Department of Defense now issues an annual report on military and security developments involving the People's Republic of China—a report that inevitably evokes comparison with the Soviet military power reports of an earlier era of superpower competition. How each side manages the mutual suspicions associated with defense spending can play an important role in either fueling mistrust or building mutual confidence.

Though the precise future course of Chinese military spending cannot be forecast, and is undoubtedly unknown even in Beijing, China's ever-expanding economy virtually ensures some substantial level of defense budget growth in coming years. To expect otherwise out of China is not realistic; as Robert Kagan writes, wondering about whether a growing China will increase its military might is like wondering if a tiger will grow teeth.[1]

Americans have sometimes raised concerns about the purpose of China's defense spending growth, questioning whether it reflects legitimate security needs or less benign objectives. For example, on a trip to Asia in 2005, Secretary of Defense Donald Rumsfeld stated, "It is estimated that China is the third largest military budget in the world, and clearly the largest in Asia. . . . Since no nation threatens China, one must wonder: Why this growing investment? Why these continuing large and expanding arms purchases? Why these continuing robust deployments?"[2] And that was before China became clearly the world's number two military power, when its military spending was half or less what it is now.

This continued growth in Chinese military spending will occur even as America's deficits and the end of its wars in Iraq and Afghanistan usher in an era of U.S. spending cuts. Over the next decade, for the first time in modern history, American and Chinese military budgets will probably begin to converge, even if net U.S. superiority is likely to endure for at least two to three more decades.[3]

The key question is whether this change in relative defense spending, and with it, relative capability, is inherently threatening to the United States. And conversely, does China need to match U.S. spending and capabilities in order to meet its security needs? If the answer to both of these questions is "no" and both sides can find a dynamic equilibrium that accepts a long-term relative, but declining advantage for the United States, the possibility of a costly and destabilizing competition in military spending can be reduced even as general international stability is preserved.

To understand whether such an equilibrium is possible, we need to examine current capabilities and future trends for U.S. and Chinese military spending and their implications for each nation's own national security objectives. We begin with a look at the broad economic resource base available for defense spending, then at overall levels of military spending, and finally to the modernization strategy pursued by both sides.

In 2010, according to purchasing power parity methods, China's economy was just over $10 trillion in size while the U.S. economy was just under $15 trillion.[4] For reference, Japan's and India's were each between $4 trillion and $4.5 trillion, Germany's was somewhat more than $3 trillion, and Russia's GDP was slightly below $3 trillion. Britain and France each had slightly more than $2 trillion in economic output and Italy slightly less than $2 trillion.

It is not unreasonable to think that China's economy might grow at 8 to 9 percent a year for the next decade and perhaps at 7 percent a year thereafter for a stretch. If, accordingly, China's economy doubles in size again over the next decade, the resource bases from which China and the United States fund their respective military establishments could converge quite a bit. And while it is increasingly hypothetical to project out that far, by 2030 current trends could place China ahead of the United States in overall economic output and income, meaning that by then, the two countries' annual defense budgets could become comparable if China continues to devote at least 2 percent of GDP to its armed forces and if the United States reduces resources for its own to 3 percent or less as now projected.

Some more specific statistics on industrial capacity underscore how much of a seismic shift has already occurred:

- China has recently edged ahead of the United States as the world's top manufacturing power, as indicated by the "value added" metric.[5]
- China now produces roughly one-third of the world's ships (with Japan and South Korea the other two big producers).[6]
- China is the world's largest producer of motor vehicles, making more than the United States and Japan (numbers two and three, respectively) combined in 2011.[7]
- China makes almost half the world's steel.[8]
- China mines almost all of the world's rare Earth metals at present and holds half the world's total reserves of these key inputs to modern industry.[9]

Chinese public statements reflect this new level of capacity. The defense white paper from 2011 talks about how China's "comprehensive national strength has stepped up to a new stage" (while the same paper warns elsewhere that "international military competition remains fierce").[10]

The situation may not be changing quite as rapidly as the above statistics would suggest, however. Discarding the purchasing-power parity method and returning to the classic method of sizing international economies through use of simple exchange-rate conversions, China's current position is still impressive, but less spectacular. Its current gross national income ([GNI], similar to GDP), while indeed more than Japan's and ranking second in the world, was $5.7 trillion in 2010. And this method of assessing economic strength is arguably more appropriate for gauging power internationally. This is especially so in areas such as high-technology weaponry where China's relatively underdeveloped economy offers it no inherent advantages, as argued by George Gilboy and Eric Heginbotham.[11] If China grows at 8 to 9 percent a year, its income will indeed again double, but to about $12 trillion by 2020 or so (expressed in constant 2014 dollars), when America's might be $20 trillion. Lower growth rates of, say, 6 to 7 percent, eminently plausible as well, would delay the doubling until roughly the mid-2020s. Either way, in 2030 and perhaps beyond, the United States might still maintain a modest lead in GNI/GDP.[12]

Even using purchasing-power parity methods, China's capacity to generate military capability may be less formidable if several other perspectives are kept in mind. First, consider per capita income. In 2050, when China will likely have 1.4 billion people with an average income of $30,000, the combination of the United States, EU, and Japan will have a billion—and they will have an average income more than twice that of China.[13] Second, the United States remains far and away the most innovative and scientifically strong nation on Earth, with the best institutions of higher learning and strongest attractiveness to entrepreneurs and investors from around the world (even if its public school performance metrics lag).[14] It is still a "melting pot" in a way that China is not, and is not likely to become, allowing it to draw on global talent. Third, even energy trends are now favoring America, in light of the revolutions in natural gas and unconventional oil as well as other developments on the North American continent.[15]

Fourth, in judging the relative economic capacity to support military investment, it is important to keep in mind that the United States has capable allies while China does not. America and its formal allies together continue to account for at least two-thirds of global GDP and military spending; a looser coalition can be said to account for perhaps three-fourths of each.[16]

Moreover, any straight-line projection of China's economic capacity does not take into account the many challenges China faces in sustaining high levels of growth, including demographic trends, severe pollution problems that threaten the environment and public health and seriously erode the Chinese quality of life, resource constraints, and inefficient state-run industries and banks among other things.[17]

To take one example, ensuring adequate usable water will be a huge task. Two-thirds of China's cities already have water shortages, more than 40 percent of its rivers are severely polluted, and 80 percent of its lakes suffer from eutrophication. China will have to rebuild much of its water infrastructure and revamp many of its water usage patterns, including in industry, to keep its factories humming and its populations alive in the years and decades ahead.[18] This and other large infrastructure require-ments will represent both a challenge to continued growth and a drain on public resources that might otherwise be devoted to military spending.

In addition, China continues to lag badly in innovation, high-quality education, and research vis-à-vis the United States and the West in gen-eral.[19] And because of China's complex and often opaque political and legal systems and other constraints, it ranks only twenty-ninth in the world in the annual competitiveness index according to the World Eco-nomic Forum.[20]

In short, China's future growth makes it virtually certain that mili-tary spending will rise and with it military capability. But the extent of resources available for spending on the armed forces is less certain than straight-line projections of China's trajectory might suggest. And perhaps even more important, there are reasons why China's leaders might wish to avoid devoting ever larger shares of the country's national income to defense spending.

MILITARY SPENDING

Not only are the United States and China now the world's top two eco-nomic powers, they are also clearly the world's top two military big spenders. Over the last decade, U.S. defense spending has actually in-creased quite a bit more than China's in absolute terms. But that will likely not be true in the current decade. With the United States now scaling back, even as China continues on the same trajectory as before, fundamental questions must be asked about where the two countries are headed. Their respective military budgets appear on a trajectory to converge in the years ahead.

U.S. Military Spending

U.S. defense spending is remarkably high compared to similar expenditures by other countries. According to the most commonly accepted comparative measurement by the International Institute for Strategic Studies in London, U.S. military expenditures have recently represented more than 40 percent of the world's total. Officially, they include nuclear weapons costs in the Department of Energy budget, war costs and normal retirement benefits for former military personnel, but not Veterans' Administration budgets for those incapacitated by their military service. This level of spending reflects the unique, global role played by the U.S. military. But it is also quite high compared to the spending in other periods when U.S. responsibilities were considerable; for example, during the Cold War the U.S. share was often in the range of 30 percent of the global total.[21]

But this situation is unlikely to be sustained, as U.S. spending is almost surely headed significantly downward in real terms in the coming years. By 2012, U.S. defense spending as a fraction of the nation's GDP had begun a gentle decline, back to 4.1 percent. It had been as high as 4.8 percent of GDP in 2010. With the initial spending cuts from the Budget Control Act (nearly $500 billion over ten years relative to earlier plans, even without counting the effects of sequestration or related additional budget cuts) and reductions in war spending, that figure is expected to reach 3.1 percent of GDP by 2015 and decline further thereafter.[22] It could be lower still if some variant of sequestration continues in effect or if a budget plan with similar implications is enacted (of course it could also be higher at least temporarily if, for example, war against Iran occurs).

That figure of roughly 4 percent of GDP is high relative to the levels of other countries. But it is just half of typical U.S. levels of the early Cold War decades and about three-fourths the average figure during the Reagan years. U.S. defense spending is also now just under 19 percent of federal government outlays, headed to 14 percent or less by 2015 according to current plans, in contrast to being nearly half of federal spending in the 1960s.[23] It could easily decline further as a result of likely future deficit reduction efforts (perhaps by another 10 percent were the Congress to adopt something along the lines of the Simpson-Bowles proposal).[24]

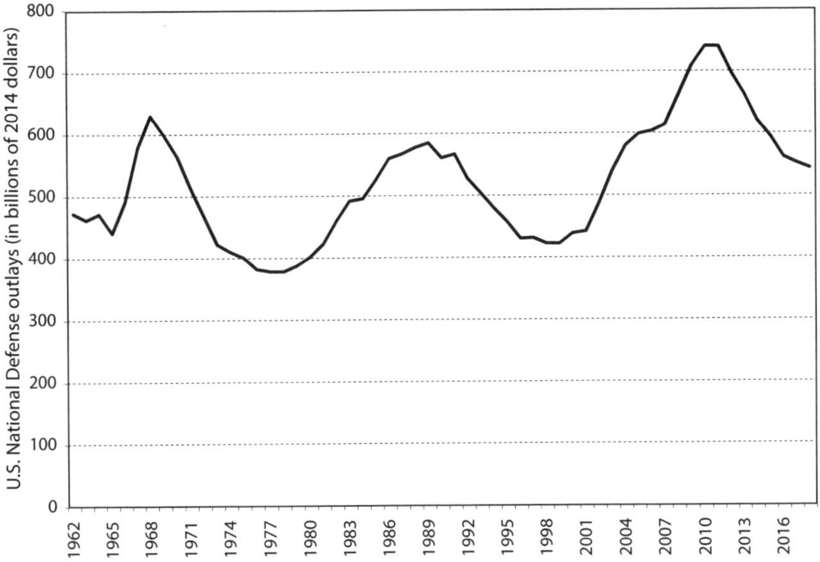

FIGURE 5.1. U.S. National Defense annual outlays, FY 1962–2018

Source: White House Office of Management and Budget, *Historical Tables: Budget of the U.S. Government, FY2014* (Washington, DC, April 2013), 151–52.

Note: Figures are based on the president's budget request for 2014. Totals include all war and enacted supplemental funding and include Department of Energy national security spending.

Even with these likely reductions, American defense spending will remain impressive. National defense spending in 2012 was roughly $645 billion. In constant 2014 dollars, it will remain $550 billion by 2017, including expected residual war costs.[25] (Full sequestration or the Simpson-Bowles plan would shave about another $50 billion or so off the 2017 figure.) In 2012 and 2013 it still exceeded the Vietnam and Reagan-era peaks in real-dollar terms. For comparison, the Cold War average for national defense was about $475 billion as expressed in 2014 dollars.[26]

The military resources available to the United States are even more impressive when one takes into account the spending of U.S. allies and security partners. Even though there has been concern about the downward trajectory of allies' and partners' spending, the totals remain significant: Britain and Japan each spent roughly $60–65 billion in 2012, Saudi Arabia just over $50 billion, France nearly $50 billion, and Germany around $40 billion.

Others near the top of the global rankings include South Korea, Australia, and Italy at $29 billion, $25 billion, and $24 billion, respectively. Next on the list were more U.S. allies or close security partners—Israel ($19 billion), Canada ($20 billion), the UAE (nearly as much, it would appear, though exact figures for that year are unavailable), Turkey ($17 billion), Spain ($12 billion), the Netherlands ($10 billion), and Taiwan ($10 billion). An important neutral country, but certainly not an unfriendly one toward America, India, spent about $39 billion. Although it is not a formal American ally, it is modernizing its forces impressively in a way that Beijing cannot ignore.

Among American contemporary adversaries, the leading spenders are Iran ($24 billion), North Korea (about $2–5 billion, though estimates are imprecise), Venezuela ($6 billion), Cuba (less than $1 billion), and Syria (perhaps $2 billion based on previous year estimates).[27] All these latter allocations are comparatively modest. So are, of course, the resources available to groups such as al Qaeda and the Taliban, which measure in the tens or hundreds of millions of dollars a year at most.[28]

When NATO and East Asian allies are figured in, the Western alliance system accounts for 70 percent of global military spending. When countries having security partnerships with the United States such as Israel and the Persian Gulf sheikdoms are tallied too, the broader U.S.-led global alliance system's military spending exceeds 75 percent of the world's aggregate, while its military manpower represents about half the world's total.

But simple comparative metrics are hardly adequate to determine proper force sizing or budget levels. An important reason for America's high defense spending is its large number of overseas interests and allies. Allies add to the strength of the Western alliance. But their power projection capabilities are very modest, tens of thousands of troops in aggregate at most, meaning that their ability to help in missions distant from home territory is severely circumscribed. They also add burdens on the United States because of formal and informal security commitments. With several dozen formal security partners and large military deployments in three main regions of the world (East Asia, Europe, and the broader Middle East), as well as smaller commitments in numerous other places, the United States has many actual and potential military obligations. Moreover, these distant theaters are all hard to reach for American forces,

TABLE 5.1. Global distribution of military spending, 2012
(millions of current dollars)

Country	Defense expenditure	Percentage of global total	Cumulative percentage
United States	645,700	38.9%	39%
Formal U.S. allies			
NATO			
Canada	20,240	1.2%	40%
France	48,121	2.9%	43%
Germany	40,356	2.4%	45%
Italy	23,631	1.4%	47%
Spain	11,782	0.7%	48%
Turkey	16,954	1.0%	49%
United Kingdom	64,080	3.9%	52%
Rest of NATO[a]	55,232	3.3%	56%
Total NATO (excluding U.S.)	280,396		
Total NATO	926,096		
RIO PACT[b]	57,260	3.4%	59%
KEY ASIA-PACIFIC ALLIES			
Japan	59,443	3.6%	63%
South Korea	28,978	1.7%	65%
Australia	25,093	1.5%	66%
New Zealand	2,321	0.1%	66%
Thailand	5,503	0.3%	67%
Philippines	2,609	0.2%	67%
Total key Asia-Pacific allies	123,947		
Informal U.S. allies			
Israel	19,366	1.2%	68%
Egypt	5,510	0.3%	68%
Iraq	14,727	0.9%	69%
Pakistan	5,878	0.4%	69%
Gulf Cooperation Council[c*]	77,662	4.7%	74%
Jordan	1,750	0.1%	74%
Morocco	3,374	0.2%	74%
Mexico	5,119	0.3%	75%
Taiwan	10,316	0.6%	75%
Total informal allies	143,702		
Other nations			
Non-NATO Europe	19,985	1.2%	77%
Other Middle East and North Africa[d*]	16,546	1.0%	78%
Other Central and South Asia[e*]	9,453	0.6%	78%

(continued)

TABLE 5.1. (continued)

Country	Defense expenditure	Percentage of global total	Cumulative percentage
Other nations (continued)			
Other East Asia and Pacific[f]	20,793	1.3%	79%
Other Caribbean and Latin America[g*]	275	0.0%	79%
Sub-Saharan Africa	19,162	1.2%	81%
Total other nations	86,214		
Major neutral nations			
China[h]	180,000	10.8%	91%
Russia	59,851	3.6%	95%
India	38,538	2.3%	97%
Indonesia	7,741	0.5%	98%
Total major neutral nations	286,130		
Nemeses and adversaries			
Iran	23,932	1.4%	99%
North Korea[i]	5,000	0.3%	100%
Syria*	2,296	0.1%	100%
Venezuela	6,089	0.4%	100%
Cuba	99	0.0%	100%
Total nemeses and adversaries	37,416		
Total	1,660,765	100%	100%

Source: International Institute for Strategic Studies, The Military Balance, 2013 (New York: Routledge, 2013), 548–54.

*At least part of the numbers here are from prior years as 2012 is not available.

[a] Albania, Belgium, Bulgaria, Croatia, Czech Republic, Denmark, Estonia, Greece, Hungary, Iceland, Latvia, Lithuania, Luxembourg, Netherlands, Norway, Poland, Portugal, Romania, Slovakia, and Slovenia.

[b] Argentina, Bahamas, Bolivia, Brazil, Chile, Colombia, Costa Rica, Dominican Republic, Ecuador, El Salvador, Guatemala, Haiti, Honduras, Nicaragua, Panama, Paraguay, Peru, Trinidad and Tobago, and Uruguay.

[c] Bahrain, Kuwait, Oman, Qatar, Saudi Arabia, and United Arab Emirates.

[d] Algeria, Lebanon, Libya, Mauritania, Tunisia, and Yemen.

[e] Afghanistan, Bangladesh, Kazakhstan, Kyrgyzstan, Nepal, Sri Lanka, Tajikistan, Turkmenistan, and Uzbekistan.

[f] Brunei, Cambodia, Fiji, Laos, Malaysia, Mongolia, Myanmar, Papua New Guinea, Singapore, Timor Leste, and Vietnam.

[g] Antigua and Barbuda, Barbados, Belize, Guyana, Jamaica, and Suriname.

[h] IISS values equal 102,436. We feel U.S. Department of Defense estimates are more accurate and have used them.

[i] North Korea value is an author estimate.

adding to the difficulty of the potential missions—and limiting the utility of comparative defense budget analysis, since potential enemies would generally be fighting on or near their home turf.

Nor is it likely that all or even most major U.S. allies would participate in any given major military contingency. The Iraq war experience certainly highlighted this fact, as has the 2013 Syria debate in reaction to President Bashar al-Assad's use of chemical weapons on August 21 of that year. And in the Asia-Pacific specifically, the defense spending levels of most American allies reflect an ambivalence about keeping pace with China. In recent years Japan's defense spending as a percent of GDP has not increased above the historical norm of 1 percent, although Prime Minister Abe is talking about modestly exceeding that figure now. Japan's 2013 defense white paper also talks about new capabilities for maneuvering troops in disputed maritime areas and for denying to an adversary missile-strike options.[29] But it will be difficult for Japan to go very far in such directions in light of its economic and budgetary pressures. Taiwan's spending is about 2.2 percent of GDP and Australia's has dipped well below that 2 percent figure, inadequate to sustain the plan put forth in Australia's 2009 defense white paper. South Korea is the stalwart—at 2.5 percent. But that is a modest level, especially given that it faces an immediate and formidable foe immediately to its north.[30] To date, whatever concerns China's neighbors may have about China's military buildup, they have not been reflected in strong pressure for increased defense spending.

Chinese officials and scholars are less reassured by another, equally important explanation for the disproportionately large U.S. defense budget: the United States seeks a major qualitative advantage in military capability. It is not interested in a "fair fight," that is, an even competition. Rather, it seeks a major military edge. Such superiority, so the logic goes, should enhance deterrence by reducing the likelihood that other countries will choose to challenge the U.S. military. While high spending cannot totally overcome the distinct possibility that the underdog will win in war, it can certainly make the underdog's job much harder.

The premium that the United States places on operating globally, and with a high-tech advantage, leads among other things to large budgets for the Navy and Air Force. Each of these has a budget comparable in size to that of the U.S. Army. It is unusual for a country's air and naval capabilities each to cost as much as its ground forces.

Some of this defense spending also arguably benefits China as well. China, like most trading nations, is a "free rider" on the protection provided by the U.S. military for global sea-lanes. The PRC contributes modestly outside of its own neighborhood today—in counterpiracy operations around the Gulf of Aden (where it had sent eighteen ships over a total of seven deployment cycles as of late 2010, and more since),[31] as well as certain UN peacekeeping missions (in which it now has nearly two thousand troops in aggregate).[32] But it has neither the capabilities nor the will to keep the global commons secure today. Of course, the benefit of this global public good also conceals a cost to China: a dependence on the United States that could be turned against China if relations became more confrontational.

Altogether, the U.S. military possesses an enormous inventory of expensive and modern equipment. In this regard, it is not only its current high level of defense spending that is relevant but the aggregate total of what it has invested over the years and decades. Military equipment typically lasts up to thirty years, sometimes even longer, if suitably maintained and when necessary refurbished. Most everything the United States has purchased over that time is at least as advanced as what China buys today, moreover. As one rough metric for the effects of American military modernization over the years, therefore, consider that the sum total of U.S. Department of Defense procurement spending from 1981 through 2013 has been about $3.3 trillion. Even if one discounts some of that for wear and tear, it gives a sense of the magnitude of the investment (and that figure does not even include research, development, testing, and evaluation accounts—or the considerable maintenance funds spent to refurbish equipment after it has been used for a time).[33]

Qualitative dominance also helps compensate for the modest size of the U.S. armed forces, which have been severely strained in the process of trying to stabilize two midsize nations of about 25 million people each in recent years. The active-duty American military, at about 1.5 million uniformed personnel including activated reservists, is certainly not large in historical or current international perspective. Not only is it down from the range of 2.0 to 2.25 million that characterized the post-Vietnam Cold War U.S. military (and much higher levels during Vietnam and Korea), it represents less than 10 percent of the world's current total of 22 million individuals under arms. China leads the way at 2.3 million active-duty personnel. India at 1.3 million and North Korea at 1.2 million are not too far behind the United States by this measure. (Russia is next at about 850,000 active-duty personnel; South Korea, Pakistan, Iran, and Turkey occupy the following tier in terms of size, with armed forces ranging from 500,000 to 650,000 active-duty personnel each.)[34]

Of course, America's stock of advanced weaponry should not lead to complacency. Should new technologies render some or much of it obsolescent in the future, it will hardly provide any guarantee of future preeminence. But since most of it has been modernized, linked in with increasingly advanced command and control networks, equipped with better munitions, and otherwise improved over the years, it can on balance be viewed as providing the United States a substantial edge today.

Chinese Military Spending

The People's Republic of China's official military budget, converted into dollars at market exchange rates, was $78 billion in 2010. That reflected average increases of about 11 percent a year in real terms over most of the last two decades, slightly more than China's average GDP growth rate.[35] As of 2013, China's official budget had grown roughly 45 percent further in nominal terms, to some $114 billion.[36] But these figures, which do not include spending for large internal security forces of roughly comparable financial magnitude,[37] represent just the starting point for gauging China's military resource allocations.

There are two main reasons why the PRC official number substantially understates actual military resources. First, because of limited transparency in its official papers and budgets, it fails to include many defense activities commonly recognized as intrinsic to a military budget by standard NATO definitions (or common sense). These feature some types of military compensation, military-related research and development, nuclear weapons and intelligence activities, and paramilitary forces. Altogether, the absence of these categories of expenditure creates a significant error in the official budget, though the accuracy of official budgets has improved with time.[38] Correcting accordingly, the International Institute for Strategic Studies estimated China's overall defense budget in 2010 to be $111 billion.[39] The corresponding 2013 number would exceed $150 billion.[40]

Second, as a developing economy, China (like many other countries) has a number of military-related costs that are quite modest by Western

TABLE 5.2. Defense expenditure estimates of the People's Republic of China (converted to constant 2014 U.S. dollars)

	Estimate
China, 2013 reported[*]	120
China, 2012 reported[*]	112
Department of Defense[a]	127–190
Stockholm International Peace Research Institute[b]	152
RAND Corporation[c]	~190
International Institute for Strategic Studies	118
Central Intelligence Agency, 2006 est.[d]	4.3% of GDP

Sources: Stockholm International Peace Research Institute, "Background Paper on SIPRI Military Expenditure Data, 2011," April 17, 2012, http://www.sipri.org/research/armaments/milex; James Dobbins, David Gompert, David Shlapak, and Andrew Scobell, "Conflict with China: Prospects, Consequences, and Strategies for Deterrence," RAND Corporation, 2011, p. 1, http://www.rand.org/pubs/occasional_papers/OP344.html; U.S. Department of Defense, "Military and Security Developments Involving the People's Republic of China, 2012," May 2012, p. 6, http://www.defense.gov/pubs/pdfs/2012_CMPR_Final.pdf; International Institute for Strategic Studies, *The Military Balance, 2012* (New York: Routledge, 2011), 233; Central Intelligence Agency, "The World Factbook: China," October 4, 2012, https://www.cia.gov/library/publications/the-world-factbook/geos/ch.html; International Monetary Fund, 2011 World Economic Outlook, http://www.imf.org/external/index.htm; Bradley Perrett, "Changing Pace," *Aviation Week*, March 18, 2013.

[*] The official defense budget does not include all spending on military and security.

[a] 2011 prices and exchange rates.

[b] 2011 prices and exchange rates.

[c] 2011 prices and exchange rates.

[d] In 2006, China's GDP was $2,712 billion under normal measures and $6,240 billion under PPP measures (2011 U.S. dollars).

standards. When China's defense budget is expressed in dollars, therefore, and a comparative sense of its military resource allocation is sought, it is valuable to consider purchasing-power parity as well.[41] Using purchasing-power parity (PPP) methods, the International Institute for Strategic Studies estimated China's overall defense spending for 2010 at $178 billion.[42] The U.S. Department of Defense is in general accord, offering an estimate of $120–180 billion for China's effective spending level in 2011.[43] The upper end of that range might be about $200 billion for 2013. This methodology can be challenged for areas such as research, development, and production of weaponry, where China's relatively lower

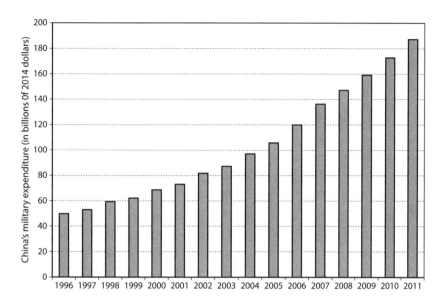

FIGURE 5.2. China's military expenditure estimates from the U.S. Department of Defense

Source: Office of the Secretary of Defense, "Military and Security Developments Involving the People's Republic of China 2010" (Washington, DC, August 2010), 42; Office of the Secretary of Defense, "Military and Security Developments Involving the People's Republic of China 2011" (Washington, DC, August 2011), 41, http://www.defense.gov/pubs/pdfs /2011_CMPR_Final.pdf; Office of the Secretary of Defense, "Military and Security Developments Involving the People's Republic of China 2011," (Washington, DC, August 2012), p. 6, http://www.defense.gov/pubs/pdfs/.

Note: Range for 2011 was $120–180 billion (in current dollars). Given previous estimates, we have used the higher number. Estimates by the International Institute for Strategic Studies, as reported in its annual publication *The Military Balance*, are about one-third lower, per year, than those reported by the Department of Defense. In 2011, its estimate for China's military expenditure was $111 billion. By 2030, based on GDP projections, China's military budget could reach $500 billion if it remains steady as a fraction of GDP.

domestic costs reflect a lower quality of scientific and engineering expertise in at least some domains of industry. As such, there is an argument that even though PPP measures are informative, the higher estimates commonly offered with this methodology tend to overstate China's actual military resource levels.[44] CIA estimates may have been particularly prone to this tendency at times.[45] For the sake of accuracy, we generally employ PPP measures in this book but try to use the most realistic (and therefore not the highest) figures available.

In addition, Chinese military spending, while reasonably large in absolute terms, represents less than 2 percent of GDP at present, around half the U.S. total by the same metric. That is largely because for all its spectacular progress, China remains a developing country with many other demands on its resources.

What about the breakdown of Chinese spending across different types of activities and accounts? Over the last decade, for example, the defense budget has been split relatively evenly among personnel, operations, and acquisition. Given that some areas of research and development, and foreign arms acquisitions, are off budget, that probably means that China spends a comparable percentage of its total military resources on acquisition as does the United States.

The People's Liberation Army has progressed quickly in modern times. As Admiral Robert Willard, former Combatant Commander of Pacific Command, put it in 2009: "In the past decade or so, China has exceeded most of our intelligence estimates of their military capability and capacity, every year."[46] This is a natural result in many ways of China's extraordinary economic growth, its corresponding growth in military spending, as well as the improvement of its scientific and manufacturing base and higher standards for its military personnel and training.

And even though China's defense spending as a percent of GDP has been modest, there are Chinese military leaders who try to use this fact to strengthen their internal case for more resources now and in the future. In the Deng Xiaoping era, China's defense budget stagnated as state policy directed the lion's share of available resources toward economic development rather than military investment. Chinese military leaders have reminded civilians of this fact ever since. In terms of bureaucratic politics, their case for greater military spending over the last two decades has been buttressed by common knowledge of the "lost decade" for the military that preceded the more recent and headier days.[47]

And while China's military remains large, as noted, China has also streamlined its force structure substantially over the last generation, while also making many changes to modernize its forces and improve the rigor and sophistication of their training and doctrine.[48] Its Navy and Air Force now have greater roles and resources than in the past. The quality of their technology has begun to reflect this reorientation of defense priorities.[49] At the same time, China has had to spend more money per person on salaries and training in order to attract and properly prepare its person-nel for advanced military operations, especially as the Chinese economy's growth makes it hard to attract the best and brightest into the armed forces. (China still has about 800,000 conscripts in its armed forces, but a much higher percent than before is now professional.)[50]

Future Defense Spending: Toward a Partial, Dynamic Equilibrium

As we have seen, U.S. defense spending is likely to steady somewhere in the $550 billion range for much of the rest of the decade. Chinese spend-ing is currently around $150–200 billion and seems likely to approach $300 billion by decade's end. Such a ratio of spending by the two coun-tries' military forces as projected for roughly 2020 should be seen as rea-sonable and acceptable to both—a case we attempt to outline here. It is not a call for a formal arms accord locking in any such spending ratio; nor is it a suggestion that these levels could be frozen into place indefinitely. But neither side should find such relative spending levels unsettling and nei-ther should feel any acute need to improve the ratio to its own advantage.

Both countries seem to invest between one-third and two-fifths of their military resources on new technology and acquisition more generally. But of course they begin from much different starting points. America's cumulative stock of modern military equipment exceeds $3 trillion in value. China's total procurement of military weaponry over the past three decades has accelerated quickly, but it has probably not exceeded $500 billion in aggregate. That number is in fact generous; it is based on the assumption that most investment spending has gone into procurement (rather than R&D) and that investment has represented a relatively steady one-third of overall Chinese military spending throughout the period. Of that total, only a fraction—probably less than half—has been for mod-ern equipment. By this measure, of total modern equipment stocks, the United States retains at least a 10:1 advantage over China without even counting U.S. allies.

If trends continue, what are their implications for the overall Sino-U.S. strategic relationship, and what steps can the United States and China take—individually or together—to reduce the risk that defense expendi-ture increases will increase strategic instability? Former U.S. national se-curity advisor Zbigniew Brzezinski has argued that "a systematic effort by the two states . . . to reach some sort of agreement regarding longer-range

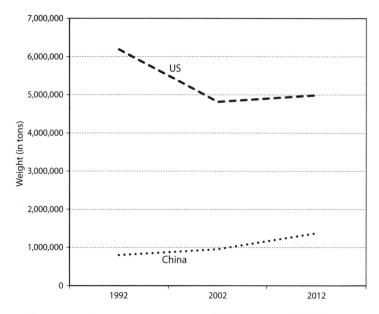

FIGURE 5.3. Tonnage comparison of Chinese and U.S. Navies

Source: International Institute for Strategic Studies, *The Military Balance, 2012* (New York: Routledge, 2011), 54–58, 233–36; International Institute for Strategic Studies, *The Military Balance, 2001–2002* (New York: Routledge, 2001), 19–23, 189–90; International Institute for Strategic Studies, *The Military Balance, 1991–1992* (New York: Routledge, 1991), 19–22, 152–54; NAVSEA Shipbuilding Support Office, "Ship Battle Forces," Naval Vessel Register, http://www.nvr.navy.mil/nvrships/sbf/fleet.htm; United States Navy, "U.S. Navy Active Ship Force Levels, 1886–present," http://www.history.navy.mil/branches/org9–4.htm; United States Navy, "Vessels: Navy Equipment," http://www.navy.com/about/equipment/vessels .html; Federation of American Scientists, "United States Munitions and Weapons Systems," http://www.fas.org/programs/ssp/man/uswpns/index.html; *sinodefense.com*, "Chinese Naval Forces," http://www.sinodefence.com/navy/default.asp; Federation of American Scientists, "People's Liberation Army Navy," http://www.fas.org/man/dod-101/sys/ship /row/plan/index.html.

Note: For China, we have included Patrol and Coastal Combatants. Though these ships are not included in the current 287-ship U.S. Navy, or in the U.S. tonnage here, a large conflict between nations would likely be near territorial waters of China. The weight (in tons) of Patrol and Coastal Combatants for China by period is as follows: 66,613 (2012); 80,691 (2002); 127,431 (1992). Some additional estimates are also included in the tallies for China, as not all specifics of the PLA Navy are known. The 1992 tonnage for the United States may be low or high in our tabulation because of the rapid decrease in U.S. ships during the post–Cold War period. Any error in weights is less than 10 percent.

military plans and measures of reciprocal reassurance is certainly a necessary component of any longer-term U.S.-Chinese partnership."[51] But what might the broad thrust of such an agreement be, and is it really possible to codify it?

There is certainly no "right answer" on what the relative sizes of American and Chinese defense budgets should be. Even measuring their respective spending levels is hard for reasons noted earlier. More fundamentally, each side's natural desire to protect its own national security will lead it to prefer an outcome that is suboptimal from the other's point of view. The two sides are unlikely to agree on a simple ratio of respective military spending levels that would satisfy them both.[52] In addition, the pace at which China modernizes (and America scales back spending) will matter too. Gradual change is probably less risky and destabilizing than rapid change, especially since the current international order would appear fairly stable.

One way to approach the question of a sustainable equilibrium in defense budgets is to examine the respective defense obligations and needs of China and the United States. The latter operates globally, of course, while China remains a regional power. But they both have significant numbers of missions that generate the need for military spending.

This task is challenging analytically, largely because it is not possible to divide the U.S. military into neat and tidy regional pieces. It is in fact rare to have a combat formation that could be usable in only one part of the world. Most American forces are based in the United States and are deployable to whatever region national command authorities might choose to send them. The Army drew down large numbers of European-focused forces to fight in Vietnam as well as Desert Storm in 1991 and the wars of the last decade. One of two brigades previously based in Korea was sent to Central Command's operations in the Iraq/Afghanistan theater in recent years (after which it returned to the United States, not Korea). Looking to hypothetical scenarios in the future, there are no dedicated American forces for addressing instability in South Asia, peacekeeping operations, humanitarian relief in Africa or South or Southeast Asia, or a range of other possibilities. That is not how the force structure is built, organized, or tasked.

Still, rough breakdowns have been attempted. One approach to how the United States allocates its forces around the world was done by the

TABLE 5.3: Kaufmann estimates of Department of Defense's
spending by geographic region under the "base force"
of first Bush administration (in percent)

Strategic nuclear deterrence	15
Tactical nuclear deterrence	1
National intelligence and communications	6
Northern Norway/Europe	5
Central Europe	29
Mediterranean	2
Atlantic sea-lanes	7
Pacific sea-lanes	5
Middle East and Persian Gulf	20
South Korea	6
Panama and Caribbean	1
United States	3

Source: William W. Kaufmann, *Assessing the Base Force: How Much Is Too Much?* (Washington, DC: Brookings, 1992), 3.

late William Kaufmann shortly after the Cold War ended. Kaufmann's geographic approach subdivided America's military missions by overseas theater: Europe, the Atlantic sea-lanes, the Far East, the Persian Gulf, Latin America, and Africa. Most combat formations were assigned accordingly, though some were attributed to American territorial defense or to missions such as nuclear deterrence and intelligence. The allocations were constructed such that their sum total equaled the aggregate defense budget.

Kaufmann's last breakdown was done in 1992, when the Pentagon still worried about a possible Russian resurgence. He estimated that a large fraction of the overall defense budget then was still for the defense of Europe.

More recent estimates would give a different answer. Notably, Europe certainly is the location of far less American military attention today than twenty years ago. The Obama administration's January 2012 defense strategic guidance white paper stated that "Most European countries are now producers of security rather than consumers of it."[53] In other words, America's forces in Europe, and broader commitments to Europe, focus more on preparing for allied operations beyond the continent than on defending Europe itself.

The Western Pacific region is now seen as just as important as the broader Persian Gulf region. Indeed, some might argue that it has become even more important. The frequent use of the term "pivoting to Asia" in and out of government since 2010 has made some think that the United States is leaving other regions behind to focus on East Asia. In fact, the Obama administration's formal statements and documents have also employed the term "rebalancing" to describe the reorientation toward Asia, while underscoring that the broader Gulf region remains a commensurate priority as well. For example, the Department of Defense budget request in February 2012, reflecting the new strategic guidance from the month before, succinctly explained the first major tenet of American defense policy as follows: "Rebalance force structure and investments toward the Asia-Pacific and Middle East regions while sustaining key alliances and partnerships in other regions."[54] This latter term, rebalance, is both more accurate and more consistent with the future policy approach we counsel.

Former Secretary of Defense Leon Panetta's June 2012 speech at the Shangri-La Security Dialogue in Singapore suggested that in coming years, the Pacific would receive the focus of 60 percent of American maritime assets and the broader Atlantic region only 40 percent. As he put it, "And by 2020 the Navy will repleposture its forces from today's roughly 50/50 percent split between the Pacific and the Atlantic to about a 60/40 split between those oceans. That will include six aircraft carriers in this region, a majority of our cruisers, destroyers, Littoral Combat Ships, and submarines."[55] Four Littoral Combat Ships will operate from Singapore, in fact. The Marine Corps will rotate up to 2,500 Marines at a time in Darwin, Australia. More modest but notable shifts are also occurring in Air Force assets in the region. Secretary of Defense Chuck Hagel stated at the 2013 Shangri-La conference that 60 percent of many Air Force assets will also focus on the Asia-Pacific region.[56] Missile defenses are being buttressed somewhat, too, with North Korea's threat providing the main impetus.

One needs to be careful in interpreting these changes. In fact, the Pacific Fleet can provide assets to the Persian Gulf itself, so the 60–40 split does not necessarily mean that 60 percent of U.S. naval assets will deploy exclusively to the Pacific in the years ahead. Air Force assets are even more easily and quickly redeployed than are ships. And in fact, some aspects of the 60–40 Navy apportionment preceded Panetta's speech by several years, dating back to the George W. Bush administration.[57] But this set of announcements does nonetheless reflect a partial shift.

In any event, taking the above into account, and recognizing that the 2012 defense strategic guidance white paper emphasizes the Persian Gulf/broader Middle East region as well as the Western Pacific region, an updated version of the Kaufmann methodology might very roughly go as follows:

- Some 35 percent of total U.S. defense spending efforts could be attributed to the Asia-Pacific, primarily East Asia and the Western Pacific (and this has likely increased by no more than a few percent as a result of the rebalancing policy).[58]
- Perhaps 30 percent of spending is principally envisioned for the Middle East.
- Ten percent might be for Europe, and 5 percent for the Americas, with a small percent to Africa.
- Some 20 percent could be viewed as supporting central activities (such as command, control, communications, intelligence, central supply, and central administration, according to the Department of Defense's breakdown of the budget by program).[59]

On these grounds, American strategists could make a good case that U.S. defense spending at a level at least twice that of China should not be viewed as an effort to achieve dominance over China but as a way to address the global tasks concerning the U.S. armed forces. Americans might further add that no major allies are presently engaged in sustained and significant military buildups in the region, and Americans as well as Japanese should not oversell Japan's very modest current steps to increase defense spending.

That conclusion could be justified not only by how the American defense budget might be notionally divvied up regionally but also because China's armed forces no longer have major threats to face along their land borders as a result of Beijing resolving most of its territorial disputes and improving relations with most neighbors (India remains an important exception).

The PLA budget might be loosely estimated to devote perhaps 70 percent of its total resources to the east of the country, 10 percent to other borders and global activities, and 20 percent to central activities. This is a notional and imprecise allocation. But it is plausible in light of the fact that five of seven Chinese military districts and a proportionate share of major military bases (and of course all of the country's Navy) are contiguous to the country's eastern borders and the sea.[60] This reflects the fact that, notwithstanding recent flare-ups with India over disputed borders, China does not currently appear to perceive itself as facing major land threats from neighbors and deploys the majority of its military power and concentrates the majority of its military modernization on regions toward the country's littorals in the east. Its 2013 defense white paper also focuses primary attention on security challenges in its maritime areas.[61] The situation could change if China decides to develop military capabilities and patterns of behavior to defend its economic interests in the broader Middle East or Africa, for example, or if those economic interests evolve substantially with time.[62] But any such changes are still a good ways off at present.

Of course, predominance in spending does not necessarily translate into victory on the battlefield. For example, during the Korean War, the United States fought China at a time when it enjoyed military superiority over the PRC but found itself in a type of campaign that minimized its ability to employ its strengths to good use. Similar challenges were faced by the United States against Vietnam, aided as it was by limited numbers of Chinese military personnel on the ground. The very difficult experiences in Iraq and Afghanistan underscore the point further, in more recent years.

Still, the U.S. war-fighting experience in modern times from Desert Storm to Iraq and Afghanistan, to Bosnia and Kosovo and Libya, makes it battle-hardened and extremely competent in actual operations. Its ground forces and special forces as well as close-air support capabilities are now particularly experienced. By contrast China's military, which last fought in a border war against Vietnam in 1979, is much less experienced. China has shown appreciation for the remarkable capabilities of the U.S. military in areas such as information technology, precision strike, and advanced command and control and communications. It coined the term "local war under high technology conditions" to reflect the lessons it learned by watching America's military in action. In so doing, it began to appreciate, for wars like Operation Desert Storm and Iraqi Freedom, how much the nature of modern combat has changed.[63] It has sought to develop new doctrines employing cyber attacks, accurate missile strikes, more proficient modern air forces and air defenses, and the like as a result.[64] But it must harbor doubts about its ability to employ such capabilities effectively against a military with so much practical experience, should it ever wind up in battle against the United States. Indeed, it is right to harbor such doubts, given the inherent challenges of modern military operations.[65]

China's planners can take note of the current U.S. intentions to slow down somewhat from the global military pace of activity of the last decade. The events of September 11, 2001, changed American strategic culture for a time. But that time may be coming to an end. U.S. politics seem likely to return toward the strategic posture of the period before the tragedy. Americans were quite comfortable fifteen to twenty years ago with a level of defense spending only two-thirds the present figure. In the last presidential race before 9/11, the difference in proposed annual defense spending between Vice President Al Gore and former governor George W. Bush was only $5 billion—out of a budget at that time around $400 billion in 2014 dollars, or less than 3 percent of GDP.[66] These relatively restrained budgets, and minor differences between the two candidates, were notable as well because they came at a time when national debt was less than half its current level relative to GDP (meaning the country could have afforded a larger defense budget if it had wanted to).[67]

Building on the previous discussion about U.S. global defense obligations, China might consider that the United States has two major and challenging parts of the world where it seeks to operate effectively, whereas China at this point really has only one. The United States' large number of overseas interests and allies also requires, among other things, continued balance in its defense investments, even if some strategists wish to emphasize maritime, air, and space domains so as to better challenge China.[68] As for China, earlier periods when it had to worry about the Soviet threat along its northern border or Vietnam to its south now appear over.[69] Moreover, America's areas of greatest interest and concern are far from its shores, raising the difficulty and expense associated with defending them, while China can use military facilities and other assets on its home territory to support forces operating in the area of greatest concern to its own policymakers and public.

Looking at the world in these terms, China should not "need" a defense budget more than half as big as that of the United States. This is not to argue that the United States and China should seek to reach a formal agreement codifying a 2:1 military spending ratio. In addition to generating irresolvable and counterproductive disputes about what counts as military spending, such an accord could introduce perverse incentives. For example, if "allowed" to spend half as much as the United States by a bilateral agreement, China might then feel obliged to spend at that level, as a Chinese academic pointed out in an informal discussion in Beijing in August 2012 to one of us. But it does suggest a rough benchmark that can help inform each side's interpretation of the other's intentions. Put crudely, China should understand that the U.S. superiority in overall defense spending is not necessarily a sign of hostility toward China but rather a reflection of its global interests and roles. Conversely, the United States should understand that up to a point the growth in Chinese defense spending reflects real security concerns associated with the overwhelming advantages now held by the United States and its allies—and with demonstrable weaknesses in the current PLA.

Of course, such a 2:1 ratio could not be permanent. As the two countries grow at disparate rates in future years and face different internal arguments about resource allocations in their respective national budgets, this ratio would prove at most a temporary zone of convergence in a longer historical trajectory. We do not presume to foresee, or constrain, the nature of the U.S.-China military relationship indefinitely. Indeed, perhaps someday the two nations can become security partners, collaborating on protection of global resources and sea-lanes to some extent at least, for example. We only suggest that as a 2:1 ratio is likely approached in the years ahead, both sides see it as not unnatural and not fundamentally threatening to their own interests. China might, as it approached that level, choose to slow its rate of military spending growth as a result. The United States might accept such a Chinese level rather than see it as a fundamental threat that required direct response—especially if, as noted, the Chinese slowed their rate of military spending increases once they reached this general spending zone.

The distribution of Chinese defense assets and obligations—and therefore the case for increased military spending relative to the United States—could change if China began to play a more global role, as noted. This might happen, for example, if the PLA became more engaged over the years in helping stabilize the Persian Gulf. It is still fairly early to think about it, but any such eventual development would be transformational in its implications for global security and the U.S.-China security relationship. It could offer the United States significant benefits, in terms of burden sharing. It would also carry risks, including reduced Chinese vulnerability to U.S. coercion as an asymmetric response to possible Chinese assertiveness in the Western Pacific, and greater Chinese ability to threaten American interests.

Such a tectonic change in China's global military role would require major rethinking about what would constitute a working equilibrium in the two countries' respective military spending levels. For this reason both sides need to be open to the possibility that things could change in the future. That is not only because of China's growing capabilities, together with possible improvement in U.S.-China security cooperation down the road. It is also because North America's expected movement toward energy self-sufficiency may weaken or otherwise change the political and strategic inclination of the United States to guarantee the stability of the Persian Gulf region in the years ahead, among other possible changes in global politics.

Of course, both sides could find reasons to complain about such a 2:1 ratio. China could raise issues about U.S. allies' capabilities and note that stabilizing spending ratios with a U.S. edge would lock in place the advantages of the accumulated assets of an American military that had been modernizing for decades. The United States could argue that it was upholding an international order that benefited all peaceful nations including China, a costly endeavor that requires a large defense budget. But there is a potential utility to the 2:1 framework in the years ahead anyway. It might help provide at least some bounding to a looming military competition that could otherwise take on an unregulated and unanchored character, stoking anxieties and exacerbating competitive dynamics in both countries. And perhaps even more important, it can help form a point of reference for a more robust and transparent dialogue on the goals of each side's military modernization. A significant change in the ratio could be seen as destabilizing and should trigger a need for a more intensive dialogue about the justifications for departing from that framework.

Beijing and Washington have made a start in dialogue and transparency about overall military spending, but they still have a long way to go.

China currently publishes white papers on its own military, going back to the 1990s, and the United States publishes annual documents on its own military as well as China's. Senior military leaders visit each other's country fairly regularly, and often each other's bases (the Congressional Research Service lists fifteen times that Americans have been the first foreign nationals to visit various Chinese bases or units in the last twenty years). Former Secretary of Defense Leon Panetta, on a trip to China in September 2012, gave a speech at the PLA Engineering Academy of Armored Forces and visited the headquarters of the North Sea Fleet, as well as a frigate and a diesel submarine there. (However, because of Chinese objections the two countries have made only limited headway in discussing delicate subjects such as nuclear forces, Korea contingency plans, and Taiwan during such visits, a subject to which we return in the next chapter.) Military officials have met annually for thirteen years as part of the Defense Consultative Talks. In 2012, they were held in Washington between Under Secretary of Defense for Policy James Miller and Lt. Gen. Qi Jianguo, deputy chief of the People's Liberation Army general staff. Related discussions have also taken place under the rubric of Defense Policy Coordination Talks. Starting in 2011, senior military officials on both sides joined senior civilian officials in the ongoing U.S.-China Strategic and Economic Dialogue. It will soon be time for these dialogues to move beyond immediate issues and focus on longer-term matters of strategic planning and defense budgeting as well.

A key topic of future discussion should be how to share the financial burden of securing the global sea-lanes in the years and decades ahead. Gradual increases in Chinese spending associated with a more active and collaborative role can help assuage concerns that its increased spending and associated global reach were destabilizing. Change that was either too slow or too fast could be problematic. If too slow, Washington could view Beijing's military modernization as doing nothing to share the burdens of global responsibility to help uphold the international order, but if too fast, a Chinese buildup in power projection capacities and activities could incite fear not only in the United States but in many other parts of the world. The United States and its allies will need to work hard to overcome their fears and accept a greater Chinese international security role provided that the latter is pursued incrementally and responsibly.

Innovation, Modernization, A2AD, and Air-Sea Battle

Of course, stability in bilateral relations depends not just on how much China and the United States spend on their militaries but on how they spend. The two countries have ambitious military procurement programs that have triggered concerns about the strategic objectives behind their military modernization.

Current Modernization Efforts

On the Chinese side, it seems clear that key elements of its ambitious modernization program are specifically tailored to counter U.S. capabilities. Some of the relevant technologies include advanced submarines, more and increasingly accurate ballistic and cruise missiles, homing munitions on antiship ballistic missiles,[70] antisatellite weapons, and modern stealthy combat aircraft.

The Chinese are developing a DF-41 long-range intercontinental ballistic missile that may be able to carry multiple nuclear warheads. China is also building Jin-class submarines and developing long-range nuclear-tipped ballistic missiles known as the JL-2 to deploy on them.[71]

China is acquiring the conventionally armed DF-21D antiship ballistic missile with a range of perhaps 1,500 kilometers and the intended capability, if suitably queued to the vicinity of a target, to attack ships at sea including aircraft carriers.[72] It is developing a J-20 stealthy aircraft and there are reports of a J-31 in the works as well. It is also now building, among other things, 25 or more J-11B ground attack jets a year. Perhaps 400 of its overall combat aircraft inventory or some 25 percent are now relatively modern (and about that number are capable of midair refueling).[73] Some questions have been raised about the quality of the J-20, however, and it may not be as capable as Western stealth aircraft.[74]

China has bought a dozen Kilo-class diesel-electric submarines from Russia. It is also building much better submarines of its own than before, at the pace of two to three a year, including the nuclear-powered Shang class of vessels as well as the conventionally powered Song and Yuan classes. These submarines carry the advanced H-6K/M cruise missile among other armaments. It is reported to be developing new classes of submarines as well.[75]

China has also purchased four Sovremenny-class destroyers from Russia and is building its own destroyers such the Type 052B Luyang I and the Type 051C Luzhou; the former are equipped among other things with the SS-N-22 Sunburn antiship missile. It acquired a non-nuclear-powered aircraft carrier from Russia, the *Varyag* (later renamed the *Liaoning*), which can carry up to 50 planes, and has announced plans to build a second carrier.[76] It is developing the WJ-600 long-range unmanned aerial vehicle and seeking a hypersonic "space plane" known as the Shadow Dragon. It is building Type 071 and 081 amphibious assault ships as well.[77]

On the U.S. side modernization efforts include some of these same types of systems but generally more advanced models. As noted, Chinese technology often lags that of the United States by fifteen years or so. American procurement plans have become somewhat uncertain in recent years as a result of the lack of proper annual appropriations, necessitating so-called continuing resolutions, and sequestration. But the plans at least have been calling for building some 10 ships a year, including one or two Virginia-class attack submarines and a similar number of DDG-51 Aegis-class destroyers (and in some years a new CVN-21 class aircraft carrier or large amphibious vessel). The country has also been purchasing about two dozen semi-stealthy F/A18E/F Super Hornet naval aircraft and two to three dozen F-35 stealthy attack aircraft a year. It has been continuing purchase of the V-22 tilt-rotor Osprey aircraft and of 180 advanced missile-defense interceptors for the THAAD program, as well as other missile defense systems.[78] The Department of Defense is also planning to develop a new stealthy long-range bomber. (Some propose that the United States also extricate itself from the 1987 Intermediate-Range Nuclear Forces [INF] Treaty with Russia on the grounds that it may need conventionally armed medium-range ballistic missiles to counter China's capabilities in this area of technology, though there is no such program at present.)[79]

American strategists view Chinese programs as part of a comprehensive anti-access/area denial (A2AD) approach that the PLA might employ against U.S. forces in its vicinity. By this logic, the PLA would seek to push U.S. forces back from areas near China, both for defensive reasons and to have a greater ability to dominate waters near Taiwan and in the South and East China seas. Chinese writers tend to talk less of A2AD and more of controlling seas out to the "first island chain" including Taiwan and

Okinawa and the western Philippine islands, and eventually out to the "second island chain" including central Japan and Guam; they characterize these aspirations as exclusively defensive.[80]

On the American side, the new Air-Sea Battle concept advocated by the U.S. Navy and Air Force seeks to use new technologies to counter these perceived Chinese initiatives (as well as similar ones by other countries) and preserve American access and freedom of movement.[81] It emphasizes improved command and control, precision strike, advanced defenses, robotics, submarine operations, and the use of air and space domains. As such, it has defensive as well as offensive elements. It is not a formal Pentagon strategy, but it has now been codified in a formal Department of Defense document, part of which reads as follows:

> The ASB Concept is a limited but critical component in a spectrum of initiatives aimed at shaping the security environment. Similar to other concepts, ASB makes important contributions in both peace and war. The improved combat capabilities advocated by the concept may help shape the decision calculus of potential aggressors. Additionally, continued U.S. investments in the capabilities identified in the concept reassure our allies and partners, and demonstrate the U.S. will not retreat from, or submit to, potential aggressors who would otherwise try and deny the international community the right to international waters and airspace. When combined with security assistance programs and other whole-of-government efforts, the ASB Concept reflects the U.S. commitment to maintaining escalation advantage during conflict and sustaining security and prosperity in the global commons.[82]

The blend of offensive and defensive instincts reflected in Air-Sea Battle, as well as in China's "informatization" and precision-strike endeavors, underscores the nature of the dilemma posed by the strategies pursued by the two countries. Each side tends to see the other's efforts in these respective areas as not just natural defensive strategies but threatening and even provocative.[83] Each side of course stresses the benign and legitimate goal of its modernization. For example, as Bernard Cole recounts, Chinese strategists are acutely aware of how often their country has been attacked by sea over the years and decades, by many foreign powers, and use this perspective to make the case that their plans are strategically defensive.[84]

On the U.S. side, the former Air Force chief of staff and the chief of naval operations recently argued that the emerging Pentagon concept is about preserving U.S. military access around the world—and denied it was focused against any specific country.[85] Since access is a necessary prerequisite to presence as well as various nonthreatening activities, that would seem an uncontroversial goal for the United States.[86] But since, for China and the United States, each country is the other's major strategic and military planning challenge, based on their respective sizes and technological capacities, each tends to plan around the least benign interpretation of the other's capabilities, irrespective of the denials offered by the other.[87]

Because military equipment takes such a long time to design, develop, and deploy (often stretching into decades), military planners are obliged to try to anticipate military requirements far into the future—in effect, to anticipate future threats and potential adversaries before they emerge and develop the tools to meet those uncertain contingencies.[88] And in the interest of preparedness there is a strong temptation to focus on the most stressing future scenarios and most capable prospective adversaries, even though the probability of the threat is remote or uncertain—a strategy termed "hedging." Given their capacities, the United States forces therefore become an obvious benchmark against which Chinese strategists are inclined to plan, and vice versa. Chinese experts regularly remark on the impressive dominance and high-tech capabilities of the modern American military as evidenced in missions like Operation Desert Storm in 1991 and the precision bombing during the Kosovo war, and argue the PLA needs to change its ways to compete.[89] In an era of improving precision strike in military affairs, the world's two best-resourced military establishments will almost inevitably continue to push in these directions.

The challenge then becomes to find a way to work toward mutually acceptable strategies that each country can employ for its own legitimate security needs without threatening the fundamental interests of the other. In an age of precision strike and sophisticated C4I, the time-honored maxim that "the best defense is a good offense" is especially compelling to military planners. But there should be ways for each to elaborate a military strategy that does not seem at its core to threaten the security of the other. Neither country seeks the demise of the other; neither has any territorial claims against the other; the two sides' political differences while significant are hardly existential.

Indeed, it is clear from actual behavior that both sides practice elements of restraint in their military planning and force posture. Despite its ambitions in some areas of military capability, China to date has not pursued a nuclear modernization program design to achieve parity with the nuclear superpowers in its strategic forces—much less in achieving a "first strike" capability. Indeed, it does not even seem that interested in establishing itself as clearly the third-ranking nuclear power, though it surely could do so by doubling or tripling its forces if it wished. While it has built new amphibious units involving several thousand troops over the past decade, it has not created a large amphibious assault fleet that would credibly threaten Taiwan with invasion.[90] (It has, however, improved training for such missions, perhaps for purposes of intimidation.)[91] And while it is creating capabilities like aircraft carriers in fits and starts, the scale and pace of its program differ little from what India is attempting to do, and at present China's capabilities are extremely limited in this domain. (Although it may not be a deliberate policy choice by Beijing, on balance, in areas of defense technology like advanced aircraft, China often remains fifteen years or more behind Western states and Russia, with all these states also displaying some reluctance to share their best technology with China.)[92]

The United States has shown elements of restraint in its modernization programs, particularly but not exclusively in the strategic dimension. The U.S. ballistic-missile defense program, for example, is not designed to be effective against the Chinese strategic missile forces. Offensive nuclear forces are coming way down in size and scale. (We discuss this more in chapter 7.) U.S. arms sales to Taiwan are limited to "defensive systems," and though the Chinese regularly challenge sales of dual-mission systems like F-16 aircraft, the United States has scrupulously avoided the sale of some capabilities (e.g., surface-to-surface missiles) that could pose a more serious threat to the mainland.

Future Restraint

Given that both sides in principle abjure a strategy of directly threatening the survival of the other, what options are available in defense planning and force posture to give credibility to these assurances and reduce the dangers associated with a bilateral arms race? Two interrelated approaches have been proposed, one focused on limiting weapon systems, the other focused more on doctrine and operations.

The difficulties associated with either approach are myriad. Defense analytical tools do not allow for a precise definition of a stable balance of power. Measuring military power, and predicting combat outcomes, is inherently difficult, with methodological uncertainties typically in the range of at least 50 percent of most relevant quantifiable variables. Predicting the winner and loser in a given scenario is itself difficult. Indeed, equally armed militaries do not typically fight to a draw in war in any event. The possibilities that innovative tactics, strong leadership, effective surprise, and other factors will help one side defeat another even when they appear evenly matched before battle make it generally unrealistic to define a correlation of forces that would provide mutual defensive advantage to two sides. It is for that reason analysts have identified the problem of the "security dilemma" as an inherent difficulty of coaxing two competing powers to restrain military competition; steps one country views as defensive another will often see as offensive, or potentially so, and they may also disagree on the likely military implications of any given series of steps (often they will underrate the potential of their own initiatives and exaggerate the likely value of those of the possible adversary). A final consideration is that since the roles of the two countries in the Asia-Pacific region have been asymmetric (including, especially, U.S. security commitments to allies), parity would not be a goal that the United States could accept anytime soon even if Beijing was willing.

History has shown the difficulty of approaches based on banning or capping the deployment of specific weapons or military technologies. It is implausible and unrealistic to ask Beijing to deny itself technologies that might challenge existing American power projection capabilities (even if it would be highly desirable from an American perspective that Beijing decided no longer to hold the threat of forceful reunification over Taiwanese heads, a point to which we return in a later chapter). It is also difficult, moreover, to imagine the United States failing to respond to such Chinese measures—unilaterally giving up the capability to operate its forces forward near Chinese territory.

A subsequent chapter on strategic competition—in areas of nuclear weapons, space, and cyber capabilities—does include some suggestions for restraint and for arms control. These represent either relatively new or extremely dangerous areas of military competition where at least codes of conduct and targeted forms of regulation make sense.

But in classic conventional weaponry, it is harder to see the case for formal arms limitation. Conundrums abound in attempting to elaborate possible arms control regimes. Consider, for example, China's ability to mount an amphibious assault against Taiwan. It would be desirable in principle to see China codify what has been its effective policy—not to build up a big amphibious fleet. But an amphibious attack is probably not the most promising way for China to use force against Taiwan anyway. Therefore, seeking formal commitments to limit China's potential here, perhaps at the cost of some commensurate American concessions on its own forces, could be worse than an opportunity cost; it could have perverse and counterproductive effects, driving China to use its military resources to acquire capabilities that might actually be even more threatening to Taiwan.

Or consider China's aircraft carrier ambitions. Persuading China not to build up aircraft carriers at the cost of negotiated restriction on U.S. carriers would not necessarily advance U.S. interests, given America's global responsibilities and its need to be able to come to the forward defense of overseas allies in the Western Pacific and elsewhere.[93]

Despite these difficulties, there are promising avenues that can help reduce tendencies toward a looming arms race. Informal arms control may make sense where formal negotiations do not. For example, a unilateral decision by China to restrain its capabilities in areas like those discussed earlier could have important benefits, by reducing the requirements on the U.S. side to meet its regional responsibilities, and it could therefore lead the United States in turn to unilateral decisions to slow aspects of its modernization or force buildups. Through dialogue, rather than formal negotiation, each could understand the direction of the other's plans and make adjustments accordingly. Given the long time frames associated with developing and fielding major new systems, the risks of surprise or breakout are relatively low—and the potential benefits are considerable in reducing strategic mistrust due to excessive worst-case planning.

Even if most categories of weapons systems seem unpromising for formal limits, are there exceptions? Perhaps specific classes of weapons that are especially destabilizing might warrant special efforts. Ballistic missiles in particular come to mind—in the past they have been subject to specific control regimes, including the INF agreement between the United States and the Soviet Union and the Missile Technology Control Regime (which focuses on exports of missile technology rather than deployments). Indeed, this is an area that has attracted particular attention. Thus, for example, China might accede to the INF Treaty. (Under that treaty it could retain short-range missiles that if suitably deployed in southeastern coastal China could still hold targets on Taiwan at risk—though as we argue later, it would be optimal that China simply stop threatening the use of force against Taiwan.) A downside of the complete elimination of medium-range missiles by China, however, is that the PRC might then increase its intercontinental ballistic missile (ICBM) arsenal to hold targets in Russia and India at risk with long-range missiles instead, since China undoubtedly views its medium-range missile force partly as a deterrent against those countries. But any increase in ICBM stockpiles would also increase Chinese capacities against the United States.

Michael Swaine has suggested limiting American arms sales to Taiwan in return for limits on Chinese weapons such as ballistic missiles that are built and deployed with a specific focus on Taiwan.[94] The United States might resist entering into a formal agreement that affects the interests of Taiwan, especially in light of the "six assurances" offered Taiwan following the adoption of the third U.S.-China Communique in 1982.[95] Still, a policy of reciprocal restraint (e.g., U.S. restraint in arms sales if China cuts its missile force unilaterally)[96] would be consistent with U.S. commitments, since Taiwan's defensive needs would be reduced by virtue of Chinese actions. In other words, in consultation with Taipei, the United States could ratchet back its intentions to sell Taiwan advanced missile-defense systems if China scales back the missile threat it poses to Taiwan. Since Beijing has dramatically increased the missile threat to Taiwan in recent years to well over a thousand surface-to-surface missiles (arrayed against roughly one to two hundred advanced surface-to-air missile defense interceptors on the Taiwan side), a move to reduce the Chinese missile forces—as well as a freeze on the modernization of any remaining missile force—would be an appropriate first step to trigger a virtuous cycle. Of course, even in this case problems of verifiability and the possibility of rapid breakout pose serious complications. For this reason, proposals simply to redeploy China's medium-range missiles to other parts of the country would provide little or no reassurance since such a redeployment could be quickly reversed.

Establishing the counterfactual is difficult, too—it is hard to know what arms Washington would have offered Taipei absent Chinese restraint, so it would be potentially hard to persuade Beijing that restraint has been exercised in future arms sales simply because they were less (in quality or quantity) than they might have been.[97] Still, by limiting sales to Taiwan of its most advanced weapons systems, the United States can make a good-faith attempt in this domain, using strategic dialogues to explain how it had determined its recent arms sales and then watching carefully the Chinese response as it determines appropriate next steps. (We discuss contingencies involving Taiwan more in the next chapter.)

Other potentially destabilizing systems might warrant attention. The United States is increasingly concerned about Chinese long-range precision-strike capabilities (especially cruise and ballistic missiles that could threaten the U.S. fleet in the Pacific). China could show restraint in production of missiles such as the DF-21, as well as its other new advanced antiship cruise and ballistic missiles with capacity to attack U.S. ships operating in the Western Pacific. But this of course would have important implications for China's core strategy of area denial—and so might require reciprocal steps limiting U.S. maritime operations in and around China—which could have significant implications for U.S. relations with its allies and partners in the Western Pacific unless cleverly designed. We return to this subject in our chapter on basing and deployments.

If China were prepared to cap the buildup of certain classes of such weaponry while perhaps scaling back short-range missile threats to Taiwan, the United States could also go slow on two aspects of its force modernization. First, it could clarify that any development of a new long-range bomber would be gradual and only intended to replace existing bomber fleets, not to expand them. This suggestion would run at direct cross-purposes with the advocates of Air-Sea Battle who favor a larger American bomber force. But bombers are more able to threaten inland Chinese targets than are short-range jets and the United States could make a meaningful show of restraint by agreeing not to overemphasize such weapons in its future inventory. Second, the United States should exercise caution in developing other new categories of weapons designed to create more long-range strike opportunities, such as arsenal ships with long-range cruise missiles or mobile offshore bases that could be deployed relatively near Chinese coasts or conventionally armed ICBMs. This type of restraint would also apply to futuristic weapons with inland-attack potential such as orbiting kinetic energy weapons and intercontinental hypersonic weapons of various types.

As for other systems, even though no formal deal on numbers of amphibious ships or aircraft carriers makes sense, for the reasons noted earlier, it is also important that neither side seek rapid buildups and that both share information with the other about the rationale behind even modest changes. For example, the U.S. decision to base 60 percent of its naval forces in the Pacific as part of its "rebalancing" toward that region, while an important signal of resolve to support U.S. security commitments, should also be explained as a relatively modest step. It is intended in part to compensate for America's smaller Navy in current times relative to recent decades; it also does not reflect a radical change, as forces based in the Pacific often go to the Persian Gulf rather than the East Asian littoral, so the strategic magnitude of the shift is in fact modest. This rationale should figure more prominently in U.S. explanations of the goals of the rebalance.[98] Similarly, while some degree of Chinese naval expansion is understandable, China can contribute to strategic reassurance by moderating the growth of its amphibious and aircraft carrier capacities.

If negotiated limits on weapons system production offer modest prospects for restraining military competition, are there operational constraints that might also help promote stability? Here, too, the Cold War experience suggests some options. The Treaty on Conventional Armed Forces in Europe (CFE) between NATO and the Warsaw Pact limited deployments in and around the line of confrontation between the two blocs, with the goal of reducing the risk of surprise attack and constraining a conventional forces arms race. Might understandings on doctrine and deployments contribute to building strategic trust? As noted earlier, a significant source of growing mistrust and security competition has arisen out of the competing military strategies of the two sides. Many U.S. strategists see China's focus on anti-access/area denial capabilities as an effort to drive the United States out of the Western Pacific and undermine the confidence of U.S. allies, ultimately leading to Chinese hegemonic domination of the region. Many Chinese planners in turn see the Air-Sea Battle concept along with U.S. domination of space and cyber realms as an effort to place the very survival of China, or at least its territorial cohesion, at risk. Can these doctrines be modified in ways that enhance stability without undermining critical interests?

With respect to deployments, there are many obvious difficulties in adapting the CFE model to the Western Pacific. CFE focused heavily on land forces and forward-deployed forces. Land forces are largely irrelevant to the U.S.-China context, and the mobility combined with long-range strike capability of air and naval forces makes geographic force limitations less effective for them. China has no deployed forces on foreign soil, so limits would have to be applied to its territorial forces. For the United States, CONUS-based forces are inherently multitheater in capability and responsibility, so Washington would have difficulty accepting limitations based on East Asia considerations alone. Thus the CFE model of limits on force deployment is not a productive model for U.S.-China arms control (though some other features of the CFE Treaty concerning transparency and advance notifications of exercises and troop movements may be of greater utility, as we consider subsequently).[99]

Mutual notification of major weapons tests could be useful.[100] This would, among other things, reduce the odds of unpleasant surprises such as the recent experience of then Secretary of Defense Robert Gates, on a visit to China, having his visit "celebrated" by the test of a Chinese stealth aircraft. And it could help prevent unintended signals from being sent during a crisis or conflict. In some cases, it may possible to combine notification with agreed procedures on monitoring at least some forms of tests (e.g., rocket launches, discussed in chapter 7). This is an example of one of our core concepts: transparency.

From Air-Sea Battle to Air-Sea Operations

Despite all these challenges, there are opportunities for progress, most notably in adapting the core operational concepts used by each side in the Western Pacific. The emerging U.S. concept of Air-Sea Battle draws on sound operational concepts and is based on a compelling objective: ensuring important U.S. access to international waterways and areas around key allies. But by focusing on the war-fighting dimension (air-sea *battle*), important elements of the concept raise questions in Chinese planners' minds about whether the true U.S. objective is to assure an American capability to deliver an overwhelming preemptive, knockout blow to China's defenses. Such a perception (as we discuss in chapter 6) creates dangerous crisis instability and reinforces Chinese tendencies toward policies (such as anti-access/area denial efforts [A2AD]) that can fuel a destabilizing arms race. Air-Sea Battle, recast as Air-Sea Operations, should be reoriented to focus on its core objectives of war prevention, maintaining freedom of navigation and access to international waterways, and honoring commitments to allies—thus achieving the twin goals of providing strategic reassurance to China while communicating strategic resolve to defend core U.S. interests. That would encompass planning for war, to be sure, but also normal peacetime presence missions, handling disasters, addressing crime on the seas such as piracy, posturing for deterrence, exercising with allies, positioning for crisis response, and indeed even cooperating with China in some activities.

Two more modifications to the commonly perceived concept of Air-Sea Operations are also in order. As discussed more fully in the chapter on contingencies, Air-Sea Operations needs to be revised to reduce its emphasis on preemptive or even early campaign action against targets on the Chinese mainland in the event of war. This is a delicate line to walk, because the important goal of preserving access to international air and maritime domains near China's shores will not be achievable if the Chinese mainland is indefinitely granted sanctuary in a future conflict. But at the same time, rapid escalation to include attacks against such targets risks general war and is far more dangerous than some have recognized to date.

Similarly, careful attention needs to be paid to the interaction between the United States and its allies. For example, some Japanese are promoting a concept of "dynamic deterrence" and advocate development of systems, such as medium-range ballistic missiles, which can be seen as provocative, particularly in the context of deepening Sino-Japanese mistrust.[101] While the United States and Japan have a powerful interest in dissuading China from efforts to seize territory now controlled by Japan, it is important to focus on the defensive measures that demonstrate resolve without contributing to crisis instability. Small-scale training in amphibious operations could fit within this kind of framework, provided it not be seen as prejudging the appropriate Japanese and American counter to any given crisis that might develop, since in some cases nonmilitary instruments could be the optimal initial response by the allies.

More broadly, the right answer is not to expect U.S. and allied military forces to operate in harm's way without defending themselves but instead to look for indirect or asymmetric ways for the United States and its partners to respond to possible Chinese aggression that lower the risks of escalatory dynamics while still ensuring protection of core interests, as discussed further in the chapter on possible military contingencies. This approach also places a premium on resiliency, including developing military systems and command and control that can absorb strikes and still function, to reduce the perceived need to strike hard and strike first in any major crisis. Among other things that could mean more hardening of aircraft shelters and related fuel and maintenance facilities, acquisition of aircraft capable of operating from damaged runways, and communications systems tough enough to function even when suffering intense jamming or other attack.

The second and related change is this: Air-Sea Operations needs to move beyond a strictly Air Force and Navy concept. The process is beginning in today's Pentagon but only slowly; it should accelerate. This proposal is not intended simply to be ecumenical. Rather, it is because the other services including the Coast Guard have important contributions to make. No Army plan to spearhead an invasion of mainland Asia is needed or appropriate. But one set of changes would entail involving the Marine Corps, with its naval affiliations and expeditionary traditions, preparing for possible defense of Navy and Air Force assets and installations in the broader Asia-Pacific region. Perhaps it will be necessary, in a future conflict, to help establish and secure bases in the Indonesian or Philippine archipelagos or to help defend existing bases on Okinawa and Guam against special-forces attack from a hostile adversary. Creating such a ring of military capabilities in defense of national territory and the territories of friends and allies is not advisable now, as we discuss in the chapter on basing, but it could become the wisest long-term response to a China that becomes hostile someday. That would not only increase net American capabilities in the region and enlarge the coalition operating against a belligerent China should Beijing move in such a direction but also require China to attack a number of countries in order to neutralize U.S. military capabilities in the region—a potentially useful inhibition against such PLA attack. And it would be deescalatory, as a way of reacting to possible future Chinese aggression, without being irresolute or weak. Such planning under the concept of Air-Sea Operations should include allies, too—in a way that Air-Sea Battle thinking has largely failed to do to date.

Indeed, within limited realms, Air-Sea Operations can and should also include the PLA. That cannot extend to integration of computers, air defenses, and related systems at this time, of course. But there is a potential for some cooperation nonetheless, to drive home the point that major American initiatives in the Pacific (and beyond) today are not intended to be at China's expense. Natural avenues for improved collaboration include counterpiracy, counterterrorism, and counternarcotics operations, among others.

Just as Air-Sea Battle should be adapted to reduce the risks of crisis instability and a counterproductive arms race, China, too, should take steps to reduce the dangers associated with its modernization of capabilities that can threaten U.S. access to international waterways and America's ability to meet its security commitments to its East Asian allies. These probably begin with its missile force near Taiwan, which should be restrained and reduced, but extend as well to the pace of China's modernization of its antiship missiles and advanced submarines. It is unrealistic for the United States to expect China to stop all modernization. But in keeping with our previous argument that China might consider soon slowing its rate of military spending increases, the PLA might consider capping the rate at which new systems are built and deployed at roughly current levels. And as we discuss in subsequent chapters, the ways in which China employs its capabilities in the South China Sea and East China Sea also merit careful reconsideration.

CONCLUSION

The gap between U.S. and Chinese military spending and more gradually the gap in military capabilities are certain to narrow in the coming years. This fact is bound to create anxiety among U.S. and allied military planners and may over time trigger heightened security competition between the United States and China. While some of this competition is inevitable, there is a danger that the action-reaction dynamic will make both sides poorer and less secure. This chapter suggests a modest framework for restraining an uncontrolled overall arms race, by focusing on the elements of modernization that each side requires for its security, while reducing the degree to which pursuing those goals could threaten the other. Rather than enter into formal conventional arms control arrangements, each could begin to elaborate transparently its security strategy, explain how that strategy is consistent with its concrete modernization programs, and identify "red lines" or at least "red zones" that would trigger counter-moves—as well as areas of unilateral restraint by the other that would call forth reciprocal restrained responses on its own part. Some tacit degree of mutual restraint may be achievable in the domains of offensive conventional missiles, on the Chinese side, and arms sales to Taiwan, on the U.S. side. Continued restraint from China in creating amphibious assault capabilities and fielding advanced antiship missiles might be mirrored by U.S. decisions to limit deep-strike offensive conventional weapons, and by contrast a lack of restraint would have to be expected to elicit likely countermoves by the other side. In addition, the United States should re-cast its Air-Sea Battle concept to a less threatening and more inclusive concept of Air-Sea Operations and focus more effort on resiliency to avoid the need for premature escalation. At the same time, China needs to adapt its A2AD strategy, capping its pace of modernization in areas such as advanced submarines and antiship missiles.

It will be challenging to achieve all this. There is no simple algorithm for mutual arms restraint that can easily be applied to the geographic and technological context of U.S.-China security relations. Parity was the cornerstone principle of U.S.-Soviet nuclear arms control. But parity is not a useful guide to policy at a time when two nations' security needs are very different, when military technology is changing fast—and when the availability of asymmetric responses makes numerical parity a poor proxy for stability.

But there are important elements of reassurance even in this uncertain picture. For China, while the scale of American defense spending and capabilities (combined with that of U.S. allies and partners) may appear troubling, it can recognize that much U.S. defense capability is intended for other parts of the world. In addition, the United States is cutting, not increasing, military spending even as it talks of "rebalancing" toward Asia. U.S. global decline may not be imminent or inevitable, but American restraint, fueled by fiscal and political burdens, is already under way. Beyond that, the international order that U.S. military force has helped uphold for decades still serves China's core developmental and economic interests.

For America, China's rise is impressive and even foreboding. But in assessing the appropriate security response Americans need to remember that China is still a developing country, ranking roughly in the middle of all nations in per capita GDP, and facing enormous demographic, environmental, and other challenges in the years ahead. While its military budget is growing fast, it remains modest as a percent of GDP—and just as significant, since its rise has been so recent, it has not yet been able to procure a major inventory of modern equipment. Nor does its military have much experience in complex combat operations; in fact, it has virtually none, largely because the nation has not sought out foreign wars.

China's much-touted anti-access/area denial capabilities seem threatening. But seen from Chinese eyes, what Americans tend to describe as its anti-access and area-denial initiatives are largely a way of applying modern technologies to improve the defense of regions near Chinese shores as well as vital command and control capabilities. Because the intentions behind the Chinese approach are inherently ambiguous given the potential offensive use of these technologies, China needs to take steps to give credibility to the defensive character of its objectives by adapting the scale and pace of its associated modernizations.

6

———◈———

Military Contingencies: Enhancing Crisis Stability

Militaries tend to be offensively minded. Aware of the potency of preemption and surprise attack and inclined to bolster morale by cultivating an attitude of confidence and assertiveness among officers and enlisted troops, they often prefer to go for the knockout punch—and to do so early. Governments waging war tend to be offensively minded as well, even when history shows that hopes for short, quick, decisive wars usually prove unwarranted.[1]

This basic tendency of militaries was less prevalent in most of the Cold War, when both the United States and the Soviet Union typically sought to avoid conflict with each other. Nuclear dangers pushed them toward proxy war rather than direct conflict and led to caution in the handling of most crises. Even limited direct wars could have produced risks of inadvertent escalation and great pains were taken to avoid them.

Since the Cold War ended, however, the United States has reverted to the more classic ethos of military organizations and become more offensively inclined. The bombing campaign of Operation Desert Storm, as well the "shock and awe" salvos in the opening days of the second Iraq war followed a few short weeks later by "Thunder Run" in Baghdad itself, have typified the U.S. military's understandable interest in striking an enemy hard and with minimal warning. To be sure, this has not always been true over the last two decades, but an offensive mentality has prevailed more often than not. And while it is at least possible that U.S. war plans for contingencies involving China reflect some degree of appropriate caution, these war plans are not widely understood even within the American government, given classification concerns. Whatever their current nature, moreover, they could be revised quickly in the event of an actual crisis or war—just as was the case before the invasion of Iraq in 2003, when the Desert Crossing plan developed over previous years under earlier Central Command (CENTCOM) commander General Tony Zinni was largely jettisoned and replaced with a different approach.[2] Because such changes are always possible, it is important to develop as broad an understanding as possible of the risks of escalation in advance of any actual U.S.-PRC confrontation rather than to depend entirely upon the choices of a small cadre of military planners as well as a handful of top civilian officials running government at that time, should a major crisis or war ever occur.

Watching recent American experiences, Chinese officials have adjusted their own thinking, too. They have become more oriented toward rapid and decisive offensive military operations, with a much greater premium on "informatization" of joint capabilities through improved reconnaissance, command and control, and precision-strike technologies.[3] This has been a follow-on to the 1990s Chinese concept of waging "local wars under high-tech conditions" that began the conceptual shift away from large armies and attrition warfare.[4] Present Chinese military doctrinal writings focus on the importance of seizing and holding the initiative, at least in the employment of conventional weapons.[5]

This perspective, however, poses serious risks for any future conflict scenarios in which the United States and China might find themselves at loggerheads. Dreams of rapid decisive victory by both countries should be seen as just as unrealistic as they were ultimately found to be by the major parties to the world wars of the twentieth century, and to most other wars in history.[6] It is no exaggeration to say that in a major war between the United States and China there would be no winners, among other reasons given the prospect that one side might resort to nuclear weapons before accepting defeat.[7] Considerations of deescalation and conflict termination should be as high as, if not higher than, the priority for victory in any classic sense, should such scenarios occur. This is especially true because the stakes in many of the scenarios that could trigger a U.S.-China conflict are unlikely in themselves to constitute vital interests for either country in any proper sense of the word.[8] Demonstrations of resolve can be important to maintain credibility, but the abstract fear of dominoes falling does not require that every perceived provocation be fully rebuffed by force. Moreover, both sides would have to bear in mind that any initial successes they might achieve due to a bold, innovative plan would likely represent just round one in what could easily become a prolonged series of military engagements—and a new cold war. Any military operation therefore needs to be scrutinized not only for its short-term effects but for what could happen next in a multimove "game."

The dangers of escalation out of any limited use of force between the United States and China are far more akin to those of the U.S.-Soviet relationship in the Cold War than they have been in most recent American military campaigns. Escalation could result in part inadvertently. For example, military operations by one country to attack the other's command and control capabilities relevant to a limited conventional engagement could create the impression of a general strategic strike that might imperil the attacked country's nuclear forces or leadership, producing a "use them or lose them" situation.[9] Escalation could also occur if one side killed a number of the other's military personnel, perhaps even by accident, but thereby making it hard for the aggrieved state not to retaliate. Emotions, time pressures, and miscommunications could also play a role. In short, any conflict between nuclear armed states would likely create threats that "leave something to chance" in Thomas Schelling's memorable phrasing, dangers that cannot confidently be contained within specific parameters.

Accordingly, both countries need to look for ways to emphasize nonmilitary responses to various possible provocations or perceived provocations by the other. This rule of thumb is especially important, among other places, over disputes in the South China Sea and East China Sea. Should nonmilitary responses fail and force be used nonetheless, both countries need to look for ways to minimize their employment of firepower and seek to signal to the other an interest in rapidly constraining and then ending the conflict. This admonition has particular relevance with regard to crises over Taiwan. Finally, they should even look for ways to collaborate when feasible. Korea contingencies are an obvious case in point here.

The emotion-charged historical background of many disputes in East Asia increases the chance of dangerous escalation, for it can be hard for leaders to act cautiously in a crisis even over symbolic matters. Disputes such as the competing claims over the Senkaku/Diaoyu Islands belong very much in this category.[10] An added complication is the uncertainty over how the Law of the Sea Treaty applies in determining exclusive economic zones around such barely habitable and currently uninhabited land formations, meaning that the potential economic stakes associated with this sovereignty question are imprecise.[11] That situation further fans anxiety and inhibits compromise.

There are reasons for optimism, to be sure. China's military and territorial aims, while not necessarily peaceful or acceptable to its neighbors, do not appear to be infinitely elastic. This calls for a more sophisticated approach to deterrence that includes a long-term perspective recognizing both the importance of resolve and the need for patience in the handling of any crises that might occur, as well as a consideration of the full range of tools available.[12]

Ultimately this requires an exercise of judgment. Even as the United States remains well ahead of China in objective military capabilities in the years ahead, China may feel it can close the gap enough that its disproportionate interest in certain issues—most notably Taiwan—could provide it an overall edge in a showdown with Washington. A sense that its time has come, and that America is in decline, could reinforce these ways of thinking. China could possibly raise the costs and risks of intervention high enough that the United States would choose not to intervene or at least not to escalate in a given crisis. Believing this, whether true or not, China might act in assertive ways that raised the risks of direct conflict.[13] And the implications of whether, and how, the United States responds can have ramifications not just for the dispute at hand but for China's overall assessment of America's resolve to defend its interests more generally.

In this respect, the Obama administration's decision to "rebalance" toward East Asia is perhaps even more significant as an expression of intentions and as a reflection of the level of U.S. national interest at stake than a statement about force deployments. It seeks to convey to both China and U.S. allies not to underestimate America's determination to respond to challenges when U.S. vital interests, including its alliance commitments, are at stake. Such a posture can help prevent war in the first place. As a recent Center for Strategic and International Studies report put it, "the top priority of U.S. strategy in Asia is not to prepare for a conflict with China; rather, it is to shape the environment so that such a conflict is never necessary and perhaps someday inconceivable."[14] But the same sense of commitment that can contribute to deterrence can also lead to escalation in a crisis. Thus managing the U.S.-China relationship must place a heavy emphasis on crisis stability and well as arms race stability.[15] This chapter discusses the need for both in the context of some of the most likely contingencies involving the United States and China that could trigger the use of force as well as what might be done to make them less dangerous should any ever happen.

KOREA

Although another all-out Korean war seems unlikely, events in recent years on the Korean peninsula, including the North Korean sinking of the Korean frigate *Cheonan* and its shelling of Yeonpyeong Island in 2010, demonstrate that even relatively small incidents run the risk of triggering a wider conflict. North Korea's third nuclear test and its aftermath in early 2013 further highlight the dangers. Although most of the focus is on the consequences of the two Koreas clashing, there is a real risk of direct U.S.-China conflict should any such contingency begin, largely through inadvertence combined with possible organizational proclivities to escalate on the part of American and Chinese militaries.

Consider how a Korean scenario could unfold. According to public reports about the so-called 5027 war plan, North Korea might initiate another attack on South Korea, presumably without Chinese help, which would lead to a South Korean and American military response.[16] The North Korean attack might not begin as the earlier one did in 1950 but could grow out of a more limited exchange of lethal force—for example, something like North Korea's 2010 *Cheonan* sinking in which forty-six South Korean sailors died but in this case followed by a South Korean retaliatory strike. South Korean military rules of engagement issued after the 2010 incidents, as well as political realities, make it far more likely that a subsequent North Korean provocation would be met by a South Korean retaliation.[17] Such dynamics could lead to all-out war—not as their most likely outcome but as a possibility. It is also at least possible, even if less likely than in the nuclear crisis of 1994, that if North Korea moves forward to construct a new nuclear reactor suitable for producing large amounts of plutonium or begins to deploy nuclear-capable long-range ballistic missiles, the United States and South Korea would preemptively destroy the threatening assets. South Korea's decision to pursue longer range ballistic missiles, although designed for deterrence, expands the options available.

That could lead to possible retaliation against them by the Democratic People's Republic of Korea (DPRK).[18]

Alternatively, as apparently envisioned in public reports about the more recent 5029 plans developed by Combined Forces Command in Seoul, North Korean collapse or another type of internal chaos could create a situation of unrest adequate to justify an intervention by Republic of Korea (ROK) and American forces.[19] This might occur largely out of fear that the DPRK's nuclear materials could wind up in the wrong hands. The odds of such an outcome may have increased in the aftermath of Kim Jong-Il's death, depending largely on how well his inexperienced son Kim Jong-Eun is able to establish his hold on power.

Either one of these scenarios could lead to a major conflict. Large elements of North Korea's million-man armed forces, and ultimately many reservists, would be pitted against South Korea's half-million-strong active-duty military, the nearly thirty thousand American troops in Korea, and a similar number of American troops from Japan. Over time, Korean reservists and U.S. reinforcements would enter the fray as well. The latter might ultimately number in the hundreds of thousands, depending on the course of the conflict. The presumed goals for Combined Forces Command would be to eliminate the North Korean threat to South Korea in general and Seoul in particular in the first instance, to neutralize the North Korean Army, and to control the territory and population centers of North Korea with an eye toward restoring order while also securing weapons of mass destruction (most important, North Korea's nuclear materials). These goals would be most realistically achieved by also overthrowing the North Korean government; it is difficult to believe that, twice the victims of that regime (according to this scenario), Washington and Seoul would be willing to leave it in place and risk a third tragedy. But overthrow scenarios complicate and raise the stakes greatly for China.

So how would China, North Korea's only treaty ally, likely respond? The presumption among many American analysts has been that, recognizing North Korea as the chief source of the conflict, China would do everything possible to limit its own involvement. Why implicate itself in the mistakes of the world's last bastion of Stalinism? Why risk direct war with the United States? The idea that today's People's Republic of China would behave in a manner analogous to what Mao had done in the early days of the Cold War, and during the ideologically intensive period right after the Chinese revolution, would seem implausible.

However, there are reasons to be concerned that China would not simply stand by. Fearing refugee flows and perhaps the leakage of nuclear or chemical materials from the DPRK, China might wish to seal its border with North Korea. And if protecting the border were the goal, doing so from a forward position could strike many Chinese military minds as sound policy.[20] Creating a buffer zone fifty or one hundred kilometers into North Korea may appeal. In short, there are reasons to think the PLA might wish to intervene in a Korea contingency.[21]

Chinese decision making would also be influenced by assessment of the longer-term consequences of North Korea's collapse. Beyond concerns about border security, Chinese leaders could be thinking about postconflict force dispositions and political arrangements on the peninsula. Expecting that the United States might try to retain forces in Korea even after reunification and stabilization efforts were complete, they might seek to establish leverage against that possibility. This scenario is particularly credible in light of two Chinese perspectives: first, that an American military presence on the Asian mainland (particularly on China's border) poses an unacceptable threat to China's security, and second, that continued U.S. presence interferes with the long-term Chinese interests of creating a greater sphere of influence in the Western Pacific, harkening back to an era where Korea was a "tributary" state.[22]

Creating a fait accompli of tens of thousands of Chinese troops on Korean territory might seem a good bargaining chip in this context. Beijing's argument, explicit or implicit, might be that it would of course be willing to remove its troops from Korean soil once the peninsula was again stable—provided that the United States agreed to do so as well. Such a motivation might lead China to seek to deploy its forces farther southward than might be required for a border-related operation, and perhaps to employ larger numbers of troops than it otherwise would. It is also possible that China would hope to retain some kind of North Korean state after hostilities as a buffer between itself and the United States and Republic of Korea, even if it recognized that such a North Korean state could require a new government.

This competing set of interests and the actions they might engender could be a prescription for disaster. That is especially true in light of the fact that the American and Chinese militaries have had very little contact or discussion about Korea over the years. Some in both South Korea and the United States could be expected to call for firm, even forceful response by Combined Forces Command to such a Chinese encroachment.[23] Inadvertent escalation due to miscommunication or the assertive actions of local commanders could also result. Even if top-level political leaders did not advocate or authorize it, any ambiguity they conveyed in their orders might allow it to happen.

For those doubting this possibility, it is worth remembering how American and Russian troops nearly came into conflict in Kosovo in 1999, notably in their race to Pristina airport, when the stakes were much lower than they would be in Korea.[24] And once initial shots were fired, escalatory pressures would grow rapidly. Without advance planning or real-time coordination, both sides could have trouble ascertaining the motives and intentions of the other. Both sides' militaries would have a strong incentive to secure Yongbyon, the site where North Korea has produced nuclear materials over the years and may still store fissile materials or weapons. Would the operation become a race to Pyongyang? Would Washington and Seoul sense a move by Beijing to try to save the Kim regime? Whatever Washington and Seoul thought, how would field commanders behave within the "fog of war"?

To be sure, cooler heads might prevail, given the downsides of escalation, but this cannot be assumed. American and South Korean forces would be deadly serious about their mission, since defeating the North Korean military quickly would be crucial for saving lives in Seoul and since ensuring the security of North Korean nuclear materials would rank as a vital interest for the United States. Any Chinese interference that was perceived as even slowing down pursuit of these two goals could be viewed as a hostile action meriting response by American and South Korean commanders.

China, in turn, despite its growing dissatisfaction with the Kim regime, might feel obliged to honor its treaty commitment to the DPRK—if only as a demonstration of its resolve (not unlike how America has seen many conflicts in places that otherwise seemed relatively unimportant, especially during the Cold War). It is not obvious that under either a 5027 or a 5029 scenario, Chinese leaders would immediately assume that the inevitable and desirable outcome should be the forceful reunification of the entire peninsula under South Korean rule. Certainly it has been opposed to other "regime change" operations in the past. American and South Korean leaders would surely not seek to start a war with North Korea out of the blue, given the enormous destruction that any such conflict would wreak. But with Chinese memories of American preemption doctrine as well as the overthrow of Saddam Hussein (and Mohammar Qaddafi) still fresh, Chinese military leaders might not be so sure themselves. Regardless, once a conflict broke out, China might seek (as in 1950) the restoration of the status quo ante—and view its ability to reach Pyongyang first, before Combined Forces could do so, as a necessary precondition to achieving this goal.

For a Chinese military that has not gone to war in a generation, it is possible that the dangers of combat might be downplayed or underappreciated. As scholar Andrew Erickson has said, the modern Chinese military has not gone through its own version of a "Cuban missile crisis"—meaning its operational concepts have not been tempered by deeply unsettling and frightening experience.[25] Overconfidence could result. So could an inadequate appreciation of the dangers of war, or a hope that new technologies will permit shorter and more decisive wars than in the past—a tendency of many militaries and many leaders over the generations, as historian Geoffrey Blainey and others have documented.[26]

Exacerbating this potential problem could be the improvement in Chinese weaponry, command and control, and logistics. For a PLA that has generally not been capable of sustained power projection previously, parochial and bureaucratic self-interest could make some Chinese military leaders anxious to test, and demonstrate, their newfound capabilities for sustaining forces in complex operations abroad. The danger of this adverse outcome is exacerbated because neither China nor the United States has any real sense of the likely goals or strategy of the other side in the event that crisis along the various lines described unfolds.

Beyond counseling caution on both sides, all of these considerations suggest that Beijing and Washington should try to coordinate closely before as well as during any future Korea crisis. The United States and the Republic of Korea should consider that a Chinese role in a future Korea scenario can in fact be *helpful* rather than threatening.[27] It could lower the risks of inadvertent war. It could also reduce U.S. and ROK troop requirements for stabilizing the northern part of North Korea. China, too, has much to gain from prior coordination with the United States, although this would need to be highly confidential, given the anxiety this kind of dialogue would likely cause in Pyongyang.

Such coordination could focus initially on the common interest in stabilizing the North Korean territory and population and securing its weapons of mass destruction. Given likely Chinese concern over the possibility of U.S. troops stationed on its land border, the United States could also agree to keep any future American forces south of the 38th parallel once the conflict was over and to reduce their number and capabilities relative to prewar totals, drawing on the model adopted in the postunification arrangements for Germany in NATO.

Some details of postwar arrangements would have to be worked out after the conflict, of course, and aspects of them could prove a contentious issue in U.S.-China relations. But the political negotiation that would inevitably ensue is far less dangerous than the risk of military miscalculation in a crisis brought on by a North Korean provocation or political collapse.

One corollary to the above is that the political leaders and the militaries of the United States and China need to establish channels of communication that facilitate rapid contact in a crisis. Here the PRC needs to rethink its past reluctance to engage fully with the American military in particular. The two countries have had since 1998 a communications hotline for political leadership—but not for uniformed military leadership. The two sides also have a Military Maritime Accord dating to 1998 encouraging consultation and transparency on each country's respective activities—but not on operational rules of the road per se and not on specific tactical movements or operations. It would be desirable to establish a formal military hotline patterned after the 1963 U.S.-Soviet precedent.[28] At a minimum, the two countries should each possess a much more complete set of contacts for the other's top military leaders to facilitate rapid communication in crisis circumstances.

If China remains reluctant to discuss specific contingencies about Korea in advance, the conversations could be conducted more generically, perhaps using war games about imaginary places that are designed to sensitize both sides to dangerous situations where their forces could come into proximity with each other and where coordination and communication could be essential. Track 1.5 discussions involving independent scholars as well as government officials in their "personal roles" rather than "official roles" could also facilitate mutual understanding of the potential risks associated with a Korean conflict, as well as tools for managing the crisis.

TAIWAN

Scenarios involving the United States and China over Taiwan receive the greatest amount of scrutiny of any in the bilateral relationship and are widely recognized as the most dangerous as well. Some suggest that recent political developments both in Taiwan and on the mainland have reduced the risk of conflict. But in fact aspects of Taiwan contingencies may be even more dangerous in future years than many realize. The evolving military balance between China, Taiwan, and the United States, combined with specific force modernization and war-fighting strategies being adopted by both major powers, could increase the risk that a crisis turns into a direct U.S.-China conflict and perhaps even major war.

At its core, avoiding conflict over Taiwan is primarily a political challenge. But the decisions that each side makes over its military strategy and force posture can both exacerbate the difficulty of managing the overall political relationship (because they undermine each side's confidence in the other's underlying intentions) and create greater risks of escalation if a crisis emerges. In particular, to the extent that the United States focuses its military strategy on holding at risk key Chinese national assets and China counters by asymmetric threats to crucial U.S. capabilities, the stage may be set for a crisis with implications far beyond Taiwan itself.

While cross-strait relations are presently calm, Chinese and American analysts and officials share the view that China's overall power relative to Taiwan is growing.[29] That could make for a greater assertiveness by Beijing in the future, especially if it senses American disengagement or lack of resolve. The prospects for conflict could also increase as result of domestic developments either on the mainland or on Taiwan—for example, if a political or economic crisis in the PRC leads the Communist Party leadership to turn to nationalism to shore up the party's support or if political pressures from the mainland stoke independence sentiment on Taiwan.

Chinese leaders also resent America's role in continuing to sell arms to Taiwan, viewing the continued arms sales as a violation of prior commitments (and thus an indication of America's untrustworthiness). They also tend to interpret U.S. motives as part of a broad containment strategy, including what they perceive as an American desire to maintain Taiwan's capacity to serve as a permanent "aircraft carrier" in the Western Pacific close to Chinese shores and a barrier to China's open ocean access.[30] Although their dissatisfaction has to date been expressed only through political gestures, it is conceivable over time that China might up the ante to pressure the United States to halt these sales.

The current stability in the China-Taiwan relationship is a product of a number of factors, including the mutual economic interdependence between the two. But a critical component has been U.S. policy—with its opposition to unilateral change of the status quo by either side, combined with an implicit threat to intervene if China uses force to achieve unification.[31] That policy has served to deter China, even in the period after the recognition of China and termination of the formal American security treaty with Taiwan. The Taiwan Relations Act helped sustain the image and reality of an ongoing American commitment to Taiwan's security. Subsequent actions have buttressed America's intention to resist coercion of Taiwan, particularly the Clinton administration's decision to dispatch two aircraft carriers to the waters around Taiwan following China's missile-firing exercises in 1995–96.[32] This basic approach has been criticized by some as too ambiguous, but it is a measured expression of American resolve, requiring Beijing to take seriously the risk of U.S. intervention without encouraging risk taking by Taiwan. The strategy has sustained stability, but as with many deterrence strategies, it nonetheless holds serious risks if a political crisis should escalate in the future.

If a crisis were to begin, Taiwan could need U.S. help even more quickly than in the past. Should American armed forces become involved, however, dangers would intensify. In order to protect one's own forces and send messages of resolve intended to force the other side to back down, both the United States and China could choose to pursue aggressive warwinning strategies early on.

An attempted Chinese invasion of Taiwan continues to appear unlikely. Amphibious assault remains a daunting proposition in the modern age. Despite the close proximity of China and Taiwan, a PLA invasion would be severely challenged by Taiwan's large land armies, developed beach defenses, and links to American reconnaissance platforms, combined with trends in technology that render large objects like ships quite vulnerable when approaching shorelines. It is worth remembering that the American military eschewed any attempt to mount an amphibious assault on Kuwait's coastal regions in the 1991 Desert Storm mission against Saddam's Iraq, even when willing to plow directly through Iraqi prepared defenses on land. The British seizure of the Falkland Islands in 1982 is also instructive; it was a successful amphibious assault, but only against sparsely defended islands hundreds of miles from the Argentinian mainland. Moreover, any failed invasion attempt would likely result in the loss of tens of billions of dollars of assets, thousands of Chinese lives, and an enormous amount of face, as it would be difficult to deescalate gracefully from any such attempt. China has built up its amphibious forces in recent years, by perhaps one to two divisions in all. But they remain undersized for this mission by perhaps a factor of five to ten, relative to what might be required for the PLA to have a reasonable prospect of success, and its lift capabilities have not increased as much as its amphibious-oriented force structure.[33]

For these reasons, China is more likely to contemplate a limited use of force focused on disrupting Taiwan's economy, isolating the island, and coercing Taiwan's leadership. (It could also seize the nearby and far less important Kinmen or Matsu islands, an option that has reportedly been discussed even as recently as the 1990s by Chinese officials, though it would be less consequential than any type of attack on the main island of Taiwan itself.)[34] Perhaps beginning with cyber attacks, designed to interrupt Taiwan's economy and sow panic and weaken military command and control, it could then threaten shipping on which Taiwan's economy so crucially depends. Here, the difficulty of defending large assets in an era of precision warfare would be Taiwan's dilemma, not China's. And China could turn up or down the pressure as a function of the American and broader international response. It might not even need to sink any (or at least not many) ships to have dramatic effects on Taiwan's economy.[35]

If China were willing to go further and carry out precise attacks against key airfields and other important fixed assets on Taiwan, it could truly establish a leg up in the conflict with relatively limited loss of life or damage. Indeed, a recent rigorous RAND study has concluded that because of China's improved missile forces and other capabilities, "the air war for Taiwan could essentially be over before much of the Blue [Taiwan and U.S.] air force has even fired a shot."[36]

The United States might choose to involve itself in such a conflict. The decision would in part depend on the circumstances that led to China's decision to use force, naturally. But experience in past Taiwan crises, and broader questions about U.S. resolve to demonstrate its opposition to the use of force to resolve territorial disputes, suggests that a strong reaction would be likely. Although this might initially focus on diplomacy, fast-moving events might impel the United States to take more direct action. It could seek to work with any surviving elements of the Taiwanese Navy to break the Chinese blockade. But even this counterblockade mission would be hard, given China's growing ability to threaten the U.S. fleet with advanced submarines and antiship cruise and ballistic missiles as well as its ability to threaten land-based airfields that would be crucial in any such conflict.

If the United States intervened, China would have an incentive to strike not only U.S. warships but airfields in Guam and possibly U.S. forces in Japan as well. The United States would itself have a strong incentive to attack Chinese submarine ports, antiship missile launcher sites, and airfields.[37] What seemed a tactical engagement, with the greatest initial danger involving the possible sinking of a naval vessel or two, could quickly spiral into direct attacks on the territory of the major parties to the conflict. This situation would thus pose a true dilemma. Even a successful tactical escalation—say, the United States sinking some of China's best submarines in port—would put enormous pressure on China to up the stakes. Accepting defeat seems unlikely. China could well escalate or respond massively in some other way. And even if China did not do so, the outcome would likely be a protracted cold war between the two countries rather than a true peace that would shape the course of Sino-U.S. relations for generations. China might build up its military and plan a future war during such a period. Maintaining a low-level harassment campaign against Taiwan indefinitely would be another possible Chinese response.

The challenges could work in the other direction, too. While Taiwan might be inherently less central to American security interests than to Chinese interests, an American acquiescence in China's use of force or a U.S. defeat would call into question U.S. credibility and capability throughout the broader region, meaning that U.S. leaders might feel compelled to take extraordinary steps to prevent it. Perhaps no one would invoke a domino theory per se. But many would worry that a Chinese defeat of the United States even over a limited issue like Taiwan portended the changing of the guard in terms of East Asian security leadership—and could have a significant impact on the calculations of actors dependent on a U.S. security guarantee. Knowing this, American officials would have a very hard time backing off the engagement itself, once initially involved. In short, it would be difficult to control this kind of conflict if it began because it would be difficult for either side to accept defeat.

It is not hard to see why escalatory measures could become appealing to either military. For the United States trying to help break a possible Chinese blockade of Taiwan's shipping lanes, for example, China's submarine threat would be daunting. Such ships are very hard to find in open waters, especially modern vessels like the Kilo-class submarines that China has purchased from Russia and comparable models it has begun to produce at home. And once they fire either torpedoes or antiship missiles at close range at U.S. warships, their chances of striking and severely damaging such a ship are uncomfortably high—perhaps in the range of 25 to 50 percent per engagement, based on historical precedent and the best available unclassified data.[38] Clearly American warships cannot countenance too many tactical engagements of this type. Once a warship or two has been damaged, the case for going to the source of the problem and sinking the Chinese submarines when they return to port for refueling and rearming would probably prove compelling to many, as this would provide the only predictable moment of vulnerability for the submarines.

A similar calculus might apply to the locations where China could deploy its DF-21 ballistic missiles equipped with homing antiship munitions. Missile defenses would likely intercept some but not all such missiles while in flight. It is not known if American countermeasures could defeat the homing sensors in these munitions. If they could not do so dependably, the only recourses would be to preempt the missiles before launch, blind the satellites trying to locate the American vessels so as to cue the antiship missiles, or operate U.S. ships farther away from shore. A conservative American military planner would probably try to do all three of these things, including interference with the satellites. But going after the missiles before launch would probably seem prudent as well, with the lives of U.S. sailors and the success of the counterblockade mission potentially hanging in the balance.

For its part, China would have incentives to strike those relatively few big assets that the United States would require to carry out such operations. U.S. ships and airplanes would be on that list; land bases on Okinawa, other parts of Japan, other regional states, and Guam could be as well. But strikes against Japanese and American territory could prove far more escalatory than Chinese officials had originally calculated, and errant missiles could kill innocent civilians as well as military personnel. Again, the dangers of escalation would be substantial. This situation would create strong incentives for preemption and high dangers of escalation.

"Use or lose" pressures could also arise from the perceived vulnerability of reconnaissance and communications systems. Both countries might fear that they would lose their eyes and ears over the battlefield as war progressed and feel some military urgency about attacking the other side's key assets while they still had the capacity to do so.

Dangers could get even worse. As the conflict escalated into a direct U.S.-China confrontation, military planners could consider targeting nuclear forces as well as command and control capabilities. At the extreme, American planners, perhaps partly out of intellectual inertia from earlier eras when Chinese nuclear forces were particularly small and vulnerable, might think about preempting China's nuclear capabilities fairly early in a future war so as to deny China escalatory capability down the road. But that very act could create a "use or lose" mentality among some Chinese leaders. Indeed, there are indications that Chinese military planners are debating how they should respond to any such future U.S. strikes (and whether their nuclear no-first-use pledge should still apply in such a scenario).[39] Even more likely, in an effort to weaken China's central air defense networks as well as its ability to use satellite systems for reconnaissance and targeting of carriers, the United States might attack (by kinetic or cyber means) central Chinese command and control. Even if the American purpose in doing so was tactical, such command assets might be co-located with strategic command networks including those that direct nuclear operations. In other words, an American effort to reduce China's tactical conventional capabilities near Taiwan could lead to attacks against central Chinese assets that Beijing might mistake for attacks on its nuclear infrastructure.

For its part, China has less ability to strike comprehensively against the American homeland. For this reason, it seems apparent that Chinese planners are focusing on asymmetric responses, such as attacking U.S. central satellite capabilities and perhaps command assets associated with Pacific Command in Hawaii (as well as facilities on Guam and in Japan). This could also involve cyber attacks against U.S. command and control assets. Escalation could result, as each side mistook tactical attacks by the other as broad strategic threats.

It is important to think about the remote possibility of deliberate nuclear escalation in this context as well. To be sure, no preemptive all-out nuclear attack would likely be contemplated by either side against the other. But if, for example, China were losing the conventional battle, and also fearing a possible American attack against its nuclear assets (perhaps with conventional weapons), Beijing might decide to take a desperate step that nonetheless seemed an acceptable risk under the circumstances, such as launching a demonstration attack with one nuclear weapon—partly to shock America into backing off from the original conflict, partly to suggest what could happen if the United States in fact did attempt a comprehensive counterforce attack against Chinese nuclear forces. In narrow military terms, China would have a logical basis for acting this way, since it might consider the complete elimination of its nuclear forces by American preemption to be entirely unacceptable, yet also wish to avoid large-scale nuclear war. By conducting a limited nuclear attack first, it would be making a threat in nonverbal fashion—communicating a desire to limit the conflict at the same time it underscored that it could not be pushed around. American strategists used to think in such terms when contemplating U.S.-Soviet strategic exchanges and it is perhaps time we got back into the habit in regard to China.

Dangerous dynamics could develop in other ways, too. Suppose, for example, that in pursuing Chinese attack submarines into their ports and seeking to sink them there before they could again threaten U.S. aircraft carriers and other ships near Taiwan, the U.S. Navy sank China's only ballistic-missile submarine. This might well happen by mistake. But how would China know that? It might see such a strike as the opening salvo in a more comprehensive campaign against its nuclear forces. Good communications might be able to prevent such perceptions from snowballing out of control, but then again, would China believe an American commander who declared such a sinking to be unintentional? Dangers would be especially worrisome among officers who did not routinely interact with each other, since there would be little basis for personal trust.

Apart from its inherent dangers, a military solution to a future Taiwan crisis would likely be no solution at all. For example, even if the outcome of a future war were an independent Taiwan, avoiding forceful reunification in the process, China would be unlikely to concede the issue permanently. More likely it would bide its time, rethink its basic strategy, undertake a military buildup, and pursue a different and perhaps more forceful course than what has been seen in recent periods. This is just one more reason why, in any future crisis, it would be important to avoid war in the first place—or, if it proved infeasible to do that, to limit it and end it as soon as possible. For example, in the unlikely but not impossible event that Taiwan unilaterally declared independence in the future, Washington should try to persuade China not to use force but instead to take several other steps. Elements would include a commitment by Washington not to recognize Taiwan as independent, to suspend arms sales (and maintenance of existing weapons previously delivered to Taiwan), and perhaps to impose sanctions on Taiwan if it did not change course.

If conflict did erupt, for example through a Chinese decision to blockade Taiwan followed by a U.S. decision to undertake convoy escort operations to keep Taiwan afloat economically, American officials should adopt strategies that avoid escalation. Even if a U.S. ship were damaged, even if Chinese submarines remained active in nearby waters, it could be better to conduct tactical antisubmarine warfare locally rather than to attack Chinese naval bases, at least for a time. This would admittedly raise the immediate risks to U.S. forces in the vicinity, but it would be doing so in the interest of reducing the even greater risks associated with general war.[40] For their part, Chinese military leaders should recognize the huge dangers of attacking a large American ship or a major base used by U.S. forces in the region. Rather than escalate, Chinese leaders need to consider both military and nonmilitary steps, such as direct economic sanctions on Taiwan businesses and third-party sanctions, as well as diplomatic and political measures, designed to sustain pressure on the putative independence efforts of Taiwan.

Over time the United States might shift its own thinking on Taiwan contingencies more fundamentally, away from the classic approach it used when the United States had uncontested dominance of the Pacific. Rather than direct defense of Taiwan, an indirect approach might be better.

Militarily, the United States might think less about breaking a blockade, with all of its associated dangers including the likely need to attack Chinese mainland targets to reduce threats to U.S. military assets, and more about controlling sea-lane access into China as a response to any Chinese blockade of Taiwan. As James Dobbins and Andrew Krepinevich have recently put it, this would reflect a change in underlying strategy from one of deterrence by denial to deterrence by punishment.[41] Another proponent of a similar concept, T. X. Hammes, describes it as a policy of "offshore control" (as contrasted with offshore balancing).[42] As one indication of its dependence on the sea and sea-lanes, China is now the world's largest oil importer, and most of its foreign oil comes by ship.[43] Even as pipelines are built on land in future years, China will remain vulnerable to attacks against the oil transport infrastructure on which its economy depends.

Threatening these lifelines of China's economy should not be done lightly, of course. Indeed, concerns about such a hypothetical blockade likely rank high on the list of geostrategic fears of current Chinese leaders, and the prospect of such an approach itself will lead China to focus on developing its own blue-water capabilities.[44] That said, posing temporary and partial threats to these trade routes would be a more proportionate and less risky course than attacking the Chinese mainland or Chinese forces. Such an action could be threatened before it was initiated, and initiated in a limited fashion before being attempted in a more comprehensive way, further improving the odds for diplomatic intervention and resolution of the crisis before the conflict escalated to major combat operations. Better yet, over time, the United States and its allies could explore economic sanctions strategies that would have similar effects as such naval operations. This would be akin to how the United States helped protect Georgia from Russian threats in 2008, when tanks were headed in the direction of Tbilisi. Rather than rattle sabers, President Bush warned Russian leaders that were President Saakashvili overthrown, U.S.-Russia relations could not thereafter be the same, implying at least the possibility of economic reprisals.[45] There is of course no guarantee that any such sanctions would quickly, or even eventually, change Chinese behavior. But they would make China pay a price and could be gradually transformed into long-lasting strategic sanctions targeting high-technology trade that could over time reduce China's economic advancement. They could also be accompanied by more robust basing measures in the Western Pacific for U.S. forces, and perhaps military buildups by the United States and its allies, too—with all these measures gradually and collectively approaching something like a containment strategy. Even though there are risks to this approach as well, including Chinese countermoves to damage the U.S. economy, the importance of demonstrating resolve, while avoiding counterproductive escalation, suggests that developing this menu of responses and communicating U.S. determination to China are imperative.

ISLANDS, SEAS, AND SEA-LANES

The third major category of potential military contingencies involving the United States and China relates to contested areas of sovereignty between China and its neighbors, generally in maritime areas to China's south and east. There are many sources of conflict: disputed uninhabited islands; resources in the seas and seabeds where claims overlap, including fishing grounds and hydrocarbon deposits; and the open waters of the South China Sea itself, where China has asserted extensive if somewhat ambiguous claims.

These disputed islets and surrounding areas have led to numerous military flare-ups in the recent past. Prime examples include those involving the Scarborough Shoal, contested recently by the Philippines and China; the Senkaku/Diaoyu Islands, claimed by China and Japan; and the Paracel and Spratly island chains in the South China Sea. (The Paracels are claimed by Vietnam and China; various islands of the Spratlys, further south, are claimed by China as well as Malaysia, Brunei, the Philippines, and/or Vietnam.)[46]

As its power has increased in recent years, China has become more assertive about its claims to those islands and resources. Chinese ships entered into Japanese territorial waters or otherwise took provocative actions in late 2004, in September 2005, October 2008, November 2008, June 2009, March 2010, April 2010, and September 2010. Japan reported that it had conducted 306 intercepts of Chinese aircraft in 2012 around its islands, up from just two intercepts in 2003.[47] A Chinese vessel also cut cables attached to a Vietnamese surveying ship in 2011.[48] The pace of activity further accelerated with several incidents between China and the Philippines over the Scarborough and Thomas shoals and with Japan over the Senkaku/Diaoyu Islands in the last two years.[49] Some increase in close passages is perhaps inevitable in light of the improvement of the PLA Navy and thus its greater desire to operate farther from Chinese coastal waters.[50] But some of it appears to be deliberate action designed to signal increased Chinese resolve to secure its claims. And in early 2013, there were allegations, denied by China, that a PLA Navy vessel had trained a radar on a Japanese warship.[51]

Although China's official sovereignty claims seem limited to the islands (and the associated maritime rights under the UNCLOS or Law of the Sea Treaty that accompany territorial claims), on occasion some have hinted that China actually claims sovereignty over the waters themselves within China's so-called nine-dash line that encompasses most of the South China Sea. China's assertive actions have led not only Japan but Vietnam and the Philippines and Singapore to tighten collaboration with the United States on security cooperation activities.

Part of China's assertiveness in this area may be due to bureaucratic and political confusion, internal rivalry, and muddled lines of authority within Chinese government decision-making circles. Indeed, the situation has been described by the slogan of "nine dragons stirring up the sea" to refer to the multitude of relevant actors within the PRC system.[52] But recently the central leadership has tightened its organizational control over the disparate elements, thus suggesting that the actions are reflections of decisions at the highest levels of government.[53] China has sent troops to disputed islands in recent times, while also pursuing a diplomatic strategy at the 2012 ASEAN Regional Forum to prevent serious discussion about a multilateral code of conduct on how to handle disputes in this region.[54] China has insisted that it wants to handle issues bilaterally, where it can more easily pressure smaller nations, and likely wants to play for time, allowing its absolute and relative power to grow.

While taking no position on the underlying sovereignty disputes, the United States insists on preserving international transit rights through which so much trade passes, in accordance with Law of the Sea principles. It also expects peaceful resolution of disputes. With respect to the Senkakus/Diaoyus, the United States has asserted that irrespective of the merits of the sovereignty claims, because currently Japan has administrative control of the islands following the U.S. transfer of control in 1971, they fall under Article V of the U.S.-Japan security treaty of 1960. The treaty commits each side to "act to meet the common danger," although the language is ambiguous as to what steps would satisfy that obligation.[55] The language is similar to the comparable commitment in the U.S.-Philippines security treaty,[56] but each is sufficiently flexible to accommodate a range of U.S. responses depending on the circumstances and the perception of interests at stake. The Obama administration reaffirmed American interests and perspectives on the relevant issues at various points, including by then Secretary of State Hillary Clinton during the ASEAN Regional Forum in Hanoi in July 2010.[57]

The waters of the Western Pacific region are not the only places where these kinds of disagreements exist in the world today. Resources in the eastern Mediterranean are claimed by Israel, Turkey, and Greece; giant gas fields in the Persian Gulf produce a degree of ongoing contention between Qatar and Iran even though an international demarcation line does exist. But it is indeed in the Western Pacific where the issues have come to a head most acutely. There, growing populations place major demands on fisheries, new technological capabilities provide the means to develop seabed resources in contested areas, and shifting military balances raise the concern that China may seek to wield its newfound power in support of its own claims.[58]

At first glance, it seems inconceivable that the stakes involved would justify a major military conflict between the countries of the region, let alone between the United States and China. Virtually all disputed islands at issue are uninhabited—and also uninhabitable for practical purposes. That means a legal case can be made that even though it has not been the position of parties to date, the Law of the Sea Treaty does not automatically grant resource exploitation rights to whoever controls the islands, in light of Article 121 of the treaty—or at least that it is not wise to apply the treaty in this kind of case.[59] The sea-lanes through the South China Sea are busy and convenient but hardly the only way to reach Japan and Korea given that the whole Western Pacific Ocean lies just to the east. Fisheries are valuable, but fishery issues are faced around the world and are not acute only in this region—and moreover, the parties have reached serious accords on sharing fishing grounds.[60] Hydrocarbon resources may be highly valuable, it is true—and this may wind up being the most substantive issue. Cautious and probably the most realistic estimates put recoverable oil and gas reserves at the likely level of several hundred thousand barrels per day (of oil equivalent), though some Chinese estimates reach into the range of two million barrels a day or more.[61]

The islands themselves are nearly worthless from an economic standpoint. Indeed, a solution that allowed various countries to maintain indefinitely their respective claims of overlapping sovereignty but disentangled questions of island sovereignty from those of jurisdiction over nearby resources holds obvious appeal. This is the approach that has largely characterized handling of the issues from the time of China's normalization with its neighbors—beginning with Deng Xiaoping's suggestion to Prime Minister Tanaka that China and Japan "shelve" the dispute to be solved by future generations to the more recent agreement for joint exploration in 2008.[62] The recent agreement between Japan and Taiwan over fishing rights in the vicinity of the Senkakus suggests that this path remains available.[63]

Despite the limited stakes, and the availability of diplomatic avenues to manage these disputes, powerful factors in all the countries in the region are raising the risk of direct confrontation. With this perspective in mind, we turn to a consideration of some possible conflict scenarios involving territorial disputes in the East and South China and how to manage the potential risks those scenarios pose.

Conflict over Disputed Islands

Consider first the possibility of another China-Japan confrontation over the Senkaku/Diaoyu Islands, but this time a situation in which casualties are suffered. Recent incidents suggest how a conflict might unfold. In 2010, Japan arrested a Chinese skipper who had been aggressive around the islands and brought him to trial in Tokyo, at which point Beijing escalated and cut off shipments of rare Earth metals for a time. Similar though somewhat less testy dynamics occurred during standoffs in 2012. Then, in another escalation, a Chinese aircraft flew through Japanese-controlled airspace near the islands in December 2012, and as noted a Chinese military vessel allegedly painted a Japanese naval vessel with a fire-control radar. These close encounters could quite plausibly result in someone being killed, which would greatly increase the pressure to respond to the escalation.[64]

China's recent efforts to contest Japan's exclusive administrative control of the Senkakus/Diaoyus, including its decision in 2013 to declare an Air Defense Identification Zone in the area—and Japan's determination to resist de facto joint control—mean the dangers of a military clash have increased. Moreover, Japanese officials have gained U.S. acknowledgment that the Senkakus/Diaoyus fall under Article V of the U.S.-Japan mutual security treaty, obligating the United States to act in the event of an attack. In case of a Sino-Japanese conflict over the islands, Japan will likely seek U.S. involvement—including military action. This would pose a dilemma: going to war over a relatively insignificant territorial matter or raising doubts about the credibility of U.S. security commitments and risking the weakening of deterrence, emboldening China to act more forcefully in other territorial disputes or other crises.

For this reason, all three parties (the United States, Japan, and China) need to consider how to manage and prevent an escalatory spiral, blending resolve and prudence. To demonstrate resolve, both Japan and the United States need to communicate clearly to China that forceful efforts to alter the status quo on the Senkakus/Diaoyus are unacceptable and will be met with an appropriate response.

If deterrence fails, it will be important for the United States to demonstrate its reliability under the U.S.-Japan Security Treaty. That does not necessarily mean that the United States needs to be directly involved in the response. Japan should take into account the need for crisis deescalation as well as deterrence in determining what it will ask of the United States. Even though the treaty may be applicable, that does not mean that Japan must ask the United States for military involvement. For example, the United States and Japan could agree that should China try to establish a physical presence on the islands, Japan would quarantine the islands to prevent resupply, and the U.S. role would be to provide logistical support but not armed combat patrols. Consider the case of the most recent provocations on the Korean peninsula (*Cheonan* and Yeonpyeong) where Seoul did not ask the United States to retaliate—but the United States and ROK did increase their coordination on responding to possible future provocations, including in expanded military exercises. This could provide a model for the United States and Japan with respect to the Senkakus/ Diaoyus.[65]

There are other options for imposing costs, including diplomatic measures and "horizontal" moves such as deepening security ties and expanding basing arrangements with others that have territorial disputes with China. Economic sanctions are also available. Although they risk retaliation in kind by China, they also offer greater opportunities for deescalation than would military measures.

China, too, has a responsibility to avoid actions that would evoke an escalatory response. Given China's confidence in the basis of its sovereignty claim, it could pursue judicial or arbitral solutions. At a minimum, it can avoid assertions of sovereignty with military vessels or aircraft, especially armed platforms.

Similar arguments would naturally apply to any skirmishes that might result over the Paracels, Spratlys, or Scarborough Shoal. To the extent that countries involved are not U.S. treaty allies (e.g., Vietnam), the United States will have more flexibility in calibrating its response. In the case of the Philippines, a U.S. treaty ally, the circumstances would be more similar to the Senkakus/Diaoyus scenario discussed above. The problem was well illustrated in the 2012 confrontation over Scarborough Shoal. U.S. efforts to facilitate a deescalation of tensions led to discord when China subsequently failed to honor the agreement to withdraw from the shoal.[66]

The challenge for the United States is to demonstrate resolve through nonmilitary responses where possible but to lay the groundwork for effective response if diplomacy fails. The purpose should be both to restrain provocations by claimants other than China and to deter coercion of others by China. Agreed principles along the lines of the code of conduct proposed but not adopted at the 2012 ASEAN Regional Forum can help establish bright lines for acceptable and unacceptable action. The code would have called on claimants to pursue their claims peacefully in keeping with international law including the Law of the Sea, to allow ASEAN a role in the process, and to ensure freedom of navigation. Agreements limiting the deployment of military forces in the region could permit assertions of sovereignty without risking confrontation. Adherents could also adopt a specific set of agreed measures on dispute resolution and response. ASEAN "independence" relative to both the United States and China makes this an attractive option.

An agreed code of conduct is important not only for setting the rules of the road but for creating a context for enforcement of those rules that poses less danger of uncontrolled escalation if the rules are violated. Enforcement action, multilateral if possible, would be critical to give meaning to the rules but would be less likely to lead to an escalatory spiral since the action would have followed from principles agreed to by all the parties in advance. In this case, there would be significant pressure on the violator to find a way out rather than up the stakes. Even if the agreed code did not contain explicit enforcement mechanisms, the United States could also announce unilaterally steps that it would take for violations of the code.[67]

Disputes over Seabed Exploitation

Many of the most direct confrontations between states in East Asia in recent years have come over efforts to explore for undersea natural resources. Thus far, these have not seriously escalated, but as the confrontations grow, and diplomacy fails to find a solultion, the pressure for more direct response is growing not just on the parties involved but also on the United States. In considering American options, it is again important to consider how to blend resolve with sound crisis management. After an event concerning disputed seabeds, which might involve, for example, a Chinese attack on Filipino assets, such as future oil or gas wells, the United States acting with the Philippines might have several options. The United States could agree to provide joint military protection against any future similar incidents, putting the burden on China to raise the stakes by penetrating a security perimeter and perhaps even firing at U.S. or Filipino naval vessels. The United States could also consider commensurate economic sanctions on trade with China designed to exact a roughly comparable economic price from China to whatever gain it felt the seabed resources might provide it—or perhaps a 50 to 100 percent higher price, to be sure that Beijing saw no advantage in its actions (even if the sanctions hurt other countries just as much as they were injurious to China).

The optimal American and allied response would of course be context specific. To discourage further Chinese adventurism, the natural American recourse beyond economic retribution would be a tightening of security ties with regional states. That could begin with greater joint exercises and increase gradually toward a permanent American military presence with combat units (if desired by both parties) in the Philippines or Vietnam.

Restricting Maritime Rights in the South China Sea

The nature of China's maritime claim to the South China Sea remains ambiguous. While official statements from Beijing suggest that its position is derivative of its sovereignty claims over disputed islands, some more expansive statements suggest that the South China Sea constitutes Chinese territorial waters.[68] While this situation seems unlikely to come to a showdown, China's claim could in theory pose the most direct challenge to the United States, since Washington has a strong stake in assuring access to and free flow of navigation through what it considers international waters, including rights in other nations' exclusive economic zones under the Law of the Sea. Clearly the United States would not accept a Chinese "closure" of the South China Sea, even if the closure applied only to military vessels. But the types of escalation that might be considered by the United States should China seek to restrict access would need to be very carefully considered. Again, deescalation and conflict termination would need to be given as high a priority as demonstrations of resolve and a tactical victory.

With this in mind, consider several possible scenarios. First, what if a U.S. ship were actually fired upon? How might the United States demonstrate its resolve to vindicate its maritime rights while avoiding wider U.S.-China conflict? Of course, the ship captain would be expected to defend the lives of the crew, but it would be important to have rules of engagement (ROE) in place to ensure that the response adopted was the minimum necessary for crew safety (e.g., if the hostile fire was warning, rather than directly aimed at, the U.S. vessel, a direct attack on the firing ship should be avoided). This would not be the time or place to make broader political statements about demonstrating resolve to defend U.S. interests. Rather, the United States might return in force days or weeks later, with a larger armada, harder to challenge and clearly capable of escalation dominance over any small number of Chinese vessels. But such an approach would create an opportunity for a diplomatic resolution while the enhanced U.S. forces steamed to the region, backing diplomacy with a show of resolve should diplomacy fail. This show of force could be reinforced by economic measures as well.

Of course, China might persist even in the face of this response. China might tolerate an American armada sent to reassert U.S. prerogatives in the area but then carry out another attack down the road against another lone American ship. Or perhaps it would even fire at the armada from the safety of its shores, using ballistic missiles with antiship munitions or cruise missiles.

Given the nature of modern weaponry and the growing capabilities of Chinese naval and air power, it would no longer be automatic and easy for the United States to prevail in any maritime engagement. Were a series of skirmishes to escalate, with neither side backing down, American vessels could quickly be put at serious and protracted risk. The only decisive way to address such threats would be to attack Chinese ships and planes and missile launchers in their home ports and bases in southeastern China. That would mean a form of general war, raising all the dangers we laid out in earlier scenarios involving a Taiwan conflict. Even if the United States and its allies prevailed in a large-scale maritime engagement in the South China Sea, the long-term implications for U.S.-China relations would be chilling and could set the stage for an even more cataclysmic confrontation in the future.

Rather than have to risk an escalation that could involve submarines and shore-based aircraft—and thus lead quite possibly to attacks on parts of the Chinese mainland—the United States and its partners need to use their own leverage against China's dependence on maritime trade. They could implement restrictions on China's access to key waterways, perhaps in the Gulf and Straits of Malacca. This could be accompanied by military buildups in the region and tightened security agreements (potentially including basing in countries like Vietnam and the Philippines) together with other economic sanctions designed to stay in effect until Beijing reversed the decision—and calculated to cost China substantially more than it could expect to gain from, for example, developing South China Sea seabed resources unilaterally. On the diplomatic front, Washington could abandon its previous neutral position on sovereignty issues in the South China Sea, siding against China. And if China limited its denial of access to non-U.S. ships (e.g., ASEAN or Japan), Washington could offer to reflag or escort, drawing on experiences in the Persian Gulf in the 1980s.

Over time, if such Chinese provocations continued, the American and allied calculus on the desirability of using force might change—and the buttressed U.S. military capabilities in the region would constitute an implicit threat in that regard. But this process of horizontal denial of shipping freedom against China, increased deployments, and basing and economic reprisals would also allow for an opportunity to avoid direct military engagement while seeking a diplomatic reversal of unacceptable restrictions on international freedom of navigation.

CONCLUSION

This chapter has considered a set of scenarios, of varying degrees of plausibility. None is unthinkable—and were any of them to occur, the risks of serious U.S.-China war could be far greater than many now appreciate. The United States needs to find a new paradigm for thinking through such scenarios. Traditional offshore military dominance, even right up to China's very shores, juxtaposed with escalation dominance in any contingencies does not necessarily serve U.S. interests—and could lead to unwanted escalation out of proportion to the triggering event.

At each turn in possible military engagements that could bring American and Chinese forces into close proximity, the dangers of escalation, inadvertent or intentional, need to be understood and incorporated into U.S. contingency planning. The United States needs to find ways of demonstrating resolve without risking general war unless absolutely necessary. In some scenarios, this could mean greater deliberateness and tactical patience—and indirect rather than direct responses to certain possible provocations—than might have been the expectation previously. Conflict termination and escalation control must now vie with the Powell doctrine on overwhelming force, as well as the modern American military's preference to achieve escalation dominance and employ it early and emphatically in war. Sarajevo 1914—or at least the caution of Cold War dealings with the Soviet Union—should be on planners' minds as much as Munich 1938 or Kuwait 1991.

The scenarios we have examined are in the first instance lessons for Washington. But China also needs to understand that for the United States there are real red lines that will call forth a response—both unilateral actions by the United States and cooperative measures with partners. China needs to develop reciprocal commitments that will allow it to retain its formal positions as deemed necessary in Beijing—particularly with respect to sovereignty claims that are highly emotional but have little practical significance—without risking military confrontation. It should also understand that the failure to clarify the nature of its claims and the limits of the tools it seeks to employ will call forth reciprocal measures from the United States, ultimately up to a fundamental change of strategy that would embrace a more confrontational relationship. China's late 2013 decision to implement an Air Defense Identification Zone around contested areas in the East China Sea—whatever its intended rationale—raises legitimate questions in others' minds about China's long-term intentions. At a minimum, this decision increases the risks of accident or miscalculation. Chinese leaders need to understand the risks of escalation even in seemingly minor actions and skirmishes.

In particular, China needs to understand the consequences of its unwillingness to renounce the use of force to resolve its territorial disputes. What may appear to Chinese leaders as a policy necessary to deter provocations by others could easily become a cocked gun pointed at China's own head in a crisis. China needs to develop a set of options (both unilateral and, where possible, with the United States) to deter (or if necessary respond to) provocative actions by others (such as a unilateral movement by Taiwan toward independence) with firm but nonmilitary means. This evolution will take time in the best of circumstances, but it is necessary if China hopes to reassure the region about its long-term intentions.

Meanwhile the United States and its allies need to prepare their own options for meaningful and effective response that will impose real costs on China without resort to military escalation if possible. They need to employ measures that leave room for China to back away from confrontation rather than escalate. Developing these tools is especially critical for contingencies involving disputed islets and maritime resources, where the stakes for all are modest in comparison with the risks of war.

7

―――❖―――

The Strategic Domain: Nuclear, Space, and Cyber

Nowhere are the dangers of U.S.-China security competition more acute or the opportunities so great for managing them than in the area of so-called strategic systems—nuclear weapons, national missile defense, and high-level command and control capabilities including space and cyber assets. These systems are called strategic precisely because in contrast to most battlefield capabilities, they are fundamental to national survival from a security perspective—and conversely have the ability to challenge the survival of opposing regimes.

Strategic stability was of course a preoccupation of managing the U.S.-Soviet competition, and although neither the United States nor China is comfortable with Cold War analogies, parallels do exist: strategic force posture and doctrine profoundly shape the character of the bilateral relationship, and managing them is fundamental to a stable relationship between the United States and China. On the political level, each side is likely to interpret efforts by the other to change meaningfully the existing strategic balance as powerful evidence of hostile intent. On the military level, an effort to achieve superiority will trigger efforts both to reduce vulnerability and to put the other at risk. Competition in strategic systems lies at the core of the security dilemma, and any attempt to mitigate that dilemma must therefore address the strategic competition directly.

As the U.S.-Soviet experience demonstrates, it is possible to enhance strategic stability even in circumstances where two sides consider themselves adversaries. It would seem even more promising in the case where both sides profess to pursue a cooperative relationship.[1]

To date, the U.S.-China strategic competition has been remarkably muted. Despite the overwhelming U.S. offensive nuclear advantage, China has only slowly increased the size of its arsenal, and much of its modernization has focused on survivability rather than enhancing its offensive potential (although of course the pursuit of survivability can create offensive capabilities as well). Its official policy, further, is that it will respect a moratorium on the production of fissile materials for weapons, preventing significant expansion of its nuclear arsenal.[2] On the American side, there has been a de facto constraint on the deployment of missile defenses that would negate China's retaliatory capability, although the United States has never formally acknowledged a doctrine of mutual vulnerability vis-à-vis China as it did with Soviet Union (as embodied in the ABM Treaty).[3]

But recent developments are worrisome. There is some evidence that China may be accelerating its nuclear modernization. On the missile defense side, the United States and its allies are enhancing their capabilities, focused on North Korea and Iran but with implications for China as well. In space, recent advances in China's antisatellite (ASAT) capabilities (both in terms of dedicated weapons and as an implication of its overall space program) could foreshadow enhanced instability in that realm. And there is increasing concern that offensive cyber could be a strategic arena as well, as implied for example in former Secretary of Defense Panetta's warning about a cyber Pearl Harbor.

And while both sides are respecting nuclear testing moratoria at present, neither has ratified the Comprehensive Test Ban Treaty, calling into some doubt the potential durability of their commitments to restraint.

What are the opportunities here for strategic reassurance? Can anything be done to help each side understand the other's intentions in the strategic arena that avoids worst-case imaging? How can the two sides restrain their competitive dynamics, or at least make them less dangerous than they might otherwise be, without compromising their own security?

Nuclear Arms and Missile Defenses

The basic nuclear philosophies of China and the United States have been radically different over the years. China was two decades behind the United States in obtaining nuclear arms and challenged their potential utility in the early Cold War years under Mao. Even after its first nuclear test in 1964, it sought only a modestly sized arsenal as a minimal survivable second-strike force. The United States, by contrast, engaged in a major nuclear competition with the Soviet Union. It developed single integrated operational plans for nuclear war that envisioned massive attacks against the Soviet Union and, ultimately, its allies as well—to include China at various periods.[4] (There was even serious consideration of a preemptive strike against China's nascent nuclear infrastructure during the Johnson administration.)[5] Nuclear threats were issued at China by Washington over early Cold War crises in Korea and Taiwan, and China's own development of a nuclear arsenal was in part a response.[6] Some early proposals for American missile defense systems also focused on the China threat. The United States purportedly discussed Taiwan Strait contingencies in its formal nuclear force planning in the early George W. Bush administration.[7] And still today, both focus on each other in their planning.[8]

The increasingly vigorous pursuit of American theater missile defenses starting in the 1990s, though a response initially more to the SCUD attacks of Operation Desert Storm with Iraq, also factored into the equation—as did China's extremely rapid buildup of short-range and conventionally armed ballistic missiles aimed at Taiwan. In short, while the U.S.-China strategic competition has never had the existential quality of the U.S.-Soviet Cold War experience, it has become increasingly complicated in recent years and increasingly fraught.[9]

The Federation of American Scientists has estimated that China has about 240 nuclear warheads, with 55 to 65 that can be carried on long-range missiles able to reach the United States.[10] (There are some concerns that China has hidden away a larger force. While we know of no compelling evidence to support this hypothesis, its very existence is an argument in favor of greater transparency.)[11] China's arsenal has been steady in size for three decades, though the PLA is moving toward a more mobile and survivable force. It has no substantial missile defense capabilities (though it has begun a nascent missile defense program). There are scholars and policymakers who worry about a Chinese expansion of its arsenal in the years to come—based on developments of multiple independently targetable reentry vehicle (MIRV) missiles with multiple warheads, suspicions about underground tunnels that could harbor more nuclear assets, improving Chinese submarine capabilities, and other factors.[12] But on balance, the weight of evidence would suggest that China's force posture and doctrine remain focused on "minimum deterrence"—a modest survivable

TABLE 7.1. United States and China nuclear forces comparison

Type	No.	Year deployed	Warheads x yield (ktons)	Range (km)	Deployed
United States, 2012					
ICBMS					
LGM-30G Minuteman III					
Mk-12A	200	1979	1–3 W78 × 335 (MIRV)	11,300	250
Mk-21/SERV	250	2006	1 W87 × 300	13,000	250
Total	450				500
SLBMS[a]					
UGM-133A Trident II D5	288				
Mk-4		1992	4 W76 × 100 (MIRV)	12,000	468
Mk-4A		2008	4 W76–1 × 100 (MIRV)	12,000	300
Mk-5		1990	4 W88 × 455 (MIRV)	12,000	384
Total	288				1,152
BOMBERS					
B-52H Stratofortress[b]	93	1961	ALCM/W80–1 × 5–150	14,080+	200
B-2A Spirit	20	1994	B61–7/-11, B83–1	11,100+	100
Total	113				300[c]
NONSTRATEGIC FORCES					
Tomahawk SLCM	n/a	1984	1 W80–0 x 5–150	1,200 km	0[d]
B61–3,-4 bombs	n/a	1979	0.3–170	Gravity bomb	200[e]
Total					200
TOTAL DEPLOYED					~2,150[f]
RESERVE					~2,800
TOTAL STOCKPILE					~5,000[g]
China, 2011					
LAND-BASED BALLISTIC MISSILES					
DF-3A	~16	1971	1 x 3,300	3,100	~16
DF-4	~12	1980	1 x 3,300	5,400	~12
DF-5A	~20	1981	1 x 4,000–5,000	13,000	~20
DF-21	~60	1991	1 x 200–300	2,150	~60
DF-31	10–20	2006	1 x 200–300?	7,200	10–20

(continued)

TABLE 7.1. (continued)

Type	No.	Year deployed	Warheads x yield (ktons)	Range (km)	Deployed
China, 2011 (continued)					
LAND-BASED BALLISTIC MISSILES (continued)					
DF-31A	10–20	2007	1 x 200–300?	11,200	10–20
Total	~138				~138
SUBMARINE-LAUNCHED MISSILES					
JL-1	(12)	1986	1 x 200–300	1,000	n.a.
JL-2	(36)	?	1 x 200–300?	~7,400	n.a.
AIRCRAFT[h]					
H-6	~20	1965	1 x bomb	3,100	~20
DH-10[i]	?		?		
Others?	?	1972–?	1 x bomb		~20
TOTAL[j]					~240

Source: Hans M. Kristensen and Robert S. Norris, "US Nuclear Forces, 2012," *Bulletin of the Atomic Scientists*, May 2012, p. 86, http://bos.sagepub.com/content/68/3/84; Hans M. Kristensen and Robert S. Norris, "Chinese Nuclear Forces, 2011," *Bulletin of the Atomic Scientists*, November 2011, p. 85, http://bos.sagepub.com/content/67/6/81.

[a] Two additional submarines with 48 missile tubes (total) are normally in overhaul and not available for deployment. Their 48 missiles are considered part of the responsive force of reserve warheads. Sometimes more than two submarines are in overhaul.

[b] The figures shown for aircraft are total aircraft inventories. Primary mission aircraft include 44 B-52s and 16 B2-As.

[c] The pool of bombs and cruise missiles allows for multiple loading possibilities depending on the mission. The air force has 528 ALCMs, of which 200 are deployed at bases with nuclear-certified bombers; 100 gravity bombs are operationally deployed only with the B-2.

[d] The Tomahawk is in the process of being retired.

[e] Nearly all of these are deployed in Europe. (Another 300 bombs are in storage in the United States, for a total inventory of 500 nonstrategic bombs.)

[f] The U.S. government does not count spares as operational warheads. They are included in the reserve, which is estimated to contain approximately 2,800 warheads, for a total stockpile of approximately 5,000 warheads.

[g] In addition to the warheads in the Defense Department stockpile, an additional 3,000 warheads under custody of the Energy Department await dismantlement.

[h] China is thought to have a small stockpile of nuclear bombs with yields between 10 kilotons and 3 megatons. Figures are for only those aircraft that are estimated to have a secondary nuclear mission.

[i] There is no clear confirmation that the DH-10 has nuclear capability, but U.S. Air Force intelligence lists the weapon as "conventional or nuclear."

[j] Though the deployed total line equals 178, we have included an additional 62 warheads produced for SLBMs or awaiting dismantlement, for a total inventory of approximately 240 warheads.

second-strike capability in the face of America's still-enormous nuclear force, growing American conventional precision-strike capabilities, as well as missile defenses.[13] That is certainly its history, and to date there is not a compelling case to suggest that China has decided to alter its overall approach to nuclear weapons modernization and doctrine.[14] That said, there may be some initial signs of a Chinese rethinking of some aspects of its nuclear policy. Perhaps out of concern that advanced American conventional munitions could destroy some of its nuclear forces, China did not repeat its usual pledge concerning no first use of nuclear weapons in its 2013 defense white paper although subsequent Chinese statements deny that the omission reflected a change of policy.[15] But the very fact that this omission stirred such concern demonstrates the necessity for China to take steps to enhance strategic reassurance with this respect to its nuclear strategy.

The United States possesses about 5,000 nuclear warheads, down 80 percent from Cold War highs. It has recently ratified the New START Treaty with Russia that will require it to lower its strategic or long-range total down to some 1,550 deployed warheads within several years, though it will not be constrained in its holdings of tactical or surplus warheads (and in fact its strategic force will be able to exceed 1,550 somewhat because of lenient rules on how weapons on bombers are counted). It has also been spending $10 billion a year on missile defenses in the last decade, and about half as much annually for the twenty years before that. It has now deployed substantial systems in Alaska and California, on Navy ships, and on land, and has recently taken steps to strengthen those deployments focused on missile threats from North Korea. The disparity in the two countries' capabilities in these realms thus remains enormous. The United States is also embarked on several initiatives to refurbish its nuclear weapons through the Department of Energy, but these are generally focused on ensuring long-term safety and reliability rather than improving performance or creating new capabilities.[16] In its 2010 Nuclear Posture Review, the Obama administration committed not to develop new nuclear warheads.[17] The administration has also recently adopted new guidance concerning nuclear weapons employment strategy, but it is unclear from the unclassified statement whether this has any implications for U.S. strategy toward China.[18]

America's principal partner for formal agreements on nuclear arms reductions in the years ahead will likely remain Russia. The huge gap between U.S. and Russian levels compared with China's has meant that the two could make significant cuts without worrying about the implications for strategic stability between them and China, and that remains partly the case. But as numbers on both sides come down, the arsenals of the medium-sized nuclear powers will take on increasing relevance to both U.S. and Russian force planning. Thus bringing a multilateral perspective to bear will be increasingly important to the prospects of follow-on agreements between the United States and Russia, quite apart from the potential benefits to bilateral U.S.-China relations.

The United States and China have already begun a modest engagement on nuclear stability. Under Presidents Clinton and Jiang, the two sides agreed not to target each other with nuclear weapons.[19] This agreement was largely symbolic, in part because there were no verification provisions associated with it and in part because even if weapons were "zero targeted," introducing targeting information in a crisis could be done quickly and nontransparently. The benefit of that agreement for stability is thus limited although there is positive symbolic value. The two sides have also established a hotline between the two capitals, although this is far less operational than the Cold War era U.S.-Soviet version. More recently, the two sides have agreed to include nuclear issues in the Strategic Security Dialogue, although there has been little substantive engagement on this issue to date. More promisingly, both sides have participated in track 1.5 dialogues on nuclear weapons including former senior officials knowledgeable about nuclear issues, offering an avenue for informed but officially deniable exploration of possible areas of agreement.[20]

As a first step in building strategic reassurance in the nuclear realm, in conjunction with the next round of U.S.-Russian nuclear arms control, China (and other medium nuclear powers) could commit not to increase the size of their arsenals.[21] While not strictly required to permit a U.S.-Russian accord at the levels now under consideration (President Obama sketched out a goal of roughly one thousand strategic warheads on a side in his Berlin speech of June 2013),[22] it would be helpful and would facilitate a subsequent multilateral arms control process in which all nuclear powers might reduce their arsenals. For now, the commitment of the medium powers not to augment the size of current arsenals could take the form of a politically binding promise rather than a formal treaty in this next phase of arms control.

This approach would not require agreement to intrusive verification from China, which has resisted sharing information at a time when its arsenal is so much smaller than America's and when its fears of a hypothetical U.S. first-strike capability against its forces may still exist (especially when American offensive nuclear capabilities are juxtaposed with missile defenses and conventional precision-strike systems).[23] As such, its value as strategic reassurance would be substantially less than a fully verified agreement. But it would still be a notable gesture that would make formal China's observed restraint in avoiding nuclear arms racing.[24] Equally important, evidence that China was increasing its arsenal following such a pledge would raise legitimate questions about China's intentions and justify an appropriate response by the United States in its nuclear posture and missile defense programs. In terms of process, this would not need to be done as bilateral "bargain" but as a unilateral step that could contribute to a virtuous cycle of cooperative restraint.

While China may question an arrangement that is predicated on allowing Russia and the United States to have more nuclear capability than it would be expected to possess, there are compelling arguments that are consistent with China's own legitimate security interests.[25]

Russia depends on nuclear deterrence to compensate for its modest conventional forces and long borders and sees nuclear weapons as important for prestige purposes—they provide the main basis by which Russia can still claim global superpower status. For its part, the United States maintains defense commitments to dozens of countries around the world, a number of which face possible nuclear threats from other countries. This extended deterrence is important to sustain U.S. credibility but also provides a significant benefit to China by providing reasons for some of China's neighbors (notably Korea and Japan) to forswear their own nuclear weapons program.

Moreover, the current balance of nuclear forces militarily—in which the United States has objective superiority but China has a reliable second-strike capability—should be acceptable to both countries. That is especially true if the United States, in partnership with Russia, continues to scale down its existing arsenal and continues to limit the role of nuclear weapons in both strategic doctrine and crisis management. Most alternative scenarios could be less stabilizing. If the United States tried to retain current nuclear levels indefinitely, China could well respond at some point and abandon its earlier restraint. Alternatively, if the United States undertook dramatic unilateral reductions to levels approaching the current Chinese arsenal, without clear assurances of China's own strategic plans, it would risk encouraging a Chinese buildup that Washington could then find necessary to counter. In addition parity could create anxieties among American treaty partners about the credibility of U.S. security guarantees. The net effect could be worse than if Washington had not made such a move in the first place. It is possible that an arms race could result from what was intended to be a commitment to deep nuclear cuts.[26] Therefore, any nuclear drawdowns would need to preserve *some* level of numerical advantage for Moscow and Washington, it would seem, at least for a time.

Greater transparency should be feasible across numerous domains of the strategic competition. Chinese officials and scholars often say that transparency is a luxury of the strong and that the weak must limit how much information they share about smaller and lesser nuclear capabilities as a matter of national security.[27] But that is more a reason to be careful about how transparency is defined and pursued than a reason to avoid it altogether. Transparency is an important adjunct to the kind of reciprocal unilateral gestures we propose here because transparency can reduce the risk of covert "breakout" from unilateral commitments, thus reducing the need for hedging while increasing the ability for timely response in the case of any aggressive action by the other side.

While China should share a good deal more information on its nuclear forces, the United States needs to recognize that it, too, has work to do in the area of transparency, especially given its disproportionate advantages in offensive nuclear weapons and precision-strike conventional ordnance. In order to sustain and reinforce Chinese restraints in the strategic sphere, the United States will need to pursue steps to reassure China, through transparency and perhaps through limits on fielding conventional long-range precision-strike capability (including ballistic missiles, bombers, and emerging technologies), to dispel Chinese fear that they could somehow effectively target PRC nuclear assets without the United States needing to resort to nuclear weapons in the process itself. (Where U.S. precision-strike capabilities could be relevant is in attacking Chinese command and control systems in populated areas that could not realistically or humanely be struck with nuclear weapons; that is another reason for not embarking on a major increase in American long-range strike assets as a possible manifestation of Air-Sea Battle thinking.) In the absence of some American reassurance with respect to long-range precision strike, China's likely response will be to accelerate not only its offensive nuclear capability but also its development of its own missile defenses and other asymmetric counters to the precision-strike capability, including cyber. The result will be not only to fuel an offense-defense arms race but also to increase China's incentive to act preemptively against U.S. strategic capabilities early in a conflict, thus contributing to increased instability and greater risk of such a conflict.

China has also often expressed concern about American strategic missile defenses.[28] In the absence of some understanding concerning planned U.S. missile defense capabilities, China is likely to resist even unilateral measures to restrain its offensive nuclear modernization.[29] The United States has been deploying X-Band radars and improved Standard Missile ship-based interceptors in Asia and has plans to do more in this regard.[30] There are good justifications for the United States to do this independent of defending against a potential Chinese threat, but from China's perspective the evolution of this missile defense architecture could be seen as threatening the reliability of China's retaliatory capability, particularly if long-range or strategic missile defenses grow significantly in size and scope.

There are possible measures that each side can take to address each of these concerns. China might be reluctant to adopt them until it modernizes its strategic forces, including possible deployment of at least some MIRVs on its missiles and perhaps some rudimentary missile defense capabilities of its own—giving it confidence that it has a technologically sophisticated arsenal.[31] But for this very reason, China would provide more substantial reassurance of its strategic intent were it to limit even this level of modernization, given the current survivability of its arsenal. A willingness to make such a unilateral commitment now would facilitate a reciprocal action by the United States in the missile defense realm. Indeed, former President Hu Jintao made a comment in this general vein at the United Nations in September 2009.[32] Rather than provide transparency on all of its nuclear forces, China could provide limited information—or begin simply with a pledge to cap its arsenal in the coming years.

Regarding missile defenses, the United States should provide more information to China on its current and planned missile defense deployments and not assume that simply asserting they are designed only for a North Korean threat will constitute adequate reassurance to Beijing. Taiwan and Japan might similarly provide public information on their missile defenses.[33] The United States is deploying many hundreds of ballistic-missile interceptors. But for the defense of American territory, only the midcourse interceptor system based in Alaska and California is currently relevant, with its complement of 30 interceptors (and new plans as of early 2013, in response to North Korea's third nuclear test, to increase that number to 44). It is deployed with a primary focus on the North Korean threat and a secondary focus on the Iranian threat. But Russia voiced considerable concern about a possible U.S. missile defense capability to be based in central Europe in six to eight years, at least before a key part of that plan was abandoned in early 2013, and Russia continues to seek further assurance on the future of U.S. missile defenses in conjunction with further rounds of nuclear reductions. For this same reason, China might also worry about potential future upgrades or expansions of existing American capacities.[34]

Both countries will need to develop an approach that takes into account the other's motivations for these deployments. The United States lost more troops from a SCUD attack in the 1991 Gulf War than from any other single incident in that conflict, and North Korea's ongoing nuclear and missile modernization efforts provide a basis for much greater American concern. But Washington's actual strategic defense deployments have been rather modest to date, which should be of some reassurance. For China, short- and medium-range missile deployments near Taiwan are viewed as a central element of deterring independence-oriented actions from the island but are in turn a motivation for the United States (working with Taiwan) to upgrade theater defenses.

Are there any arms control options here? Again, formal accords could be difficult to achieve, given the inherent asymmetries between offense and defense, and the role of third parties in the relevant strategic calculus of the two sides. But more limited measures could be helpful. It is doubtful that China would agree to ban all surface-to-surface ballistic missiles covered by the U.S.-Russian INF Treaty. But limits on future production and deployment might be possible, keeping only shorter-range missiles thereafter—and China certainly could scale back existing missile forces by as much as a factor of two or more. The United States could similarly promise to cap its missile defense force—if not the theater systems right away, then at least the longer-range capabilities like those in California and Alaska. Given the growing long-range ballistic-missile threat to the United States from other emerging nuclear powers (North Korea and Iran), the United States would be understandably reluctant to revive the ABM Treaty or anything similar. Current technology has its limitations and may need upgrading, as a recent National Research Council study reaffirmed, to provide an effective capability against even a very small North Korean or Iranian threat.[35] But the size of any such system need not pose a risk to the credibility of China's second strike capability.

Some of the ideas being discussed to address Russian concerns with U.S. missile defenses could also be relevant in the U.S.-China context. For example, an informal cap of 75 to 100 dedicated long-range interceptors through at least 2020 would be unlikely to interfere with any American needs or plans, as long as such a commitment did not include medium-range missile defense systems like the Standard Missile on Aegis-equipped ships. The United States could further declare that as a matter of policy its missile defense systems will not be sized or configured to threaten China's long-range nuclear deterrent.

NUCLEAR TESTING

Nuclear weapons development and testing has been an area where Beijing and Washington have demonstrated considerable restraint for two decades. It would be valuable for strategic reassurance that the situation endure. In particular, the two countries should continue their respective testing moratoria and continue not to develop new types of warheads with improved performance parameters. This subject is worthy of serious ongoing attention, as the continuation of the existing testing moratorium by the two countries (and others) should not be taken for granted just because it has been sustained over a long stretch. If either of the countries did test, it would not only put pressure on the other to do so but risk disruption to the broader relationship, as it would be taken as a potential sign of more assertive intent. Washington might see Beijing as trying to reach nuclear superpower status to create cover for its regional ambitions; Beijing might see Washington as working toward a disarming first-strike capability with, for example, an Earth-penetrating warhead design.

TABLE 7.2. United States and China nuclear weapons test detonations

Type	Devices
United States, 1945–1992	
Underground	934
Atmospheric	212
Underwater	5
Total	1,151
China, 1964–1996	
Underground	23
Atmospheric	22
Total	55

Source: Nuclear Explosion DataBase (NEDB), http://www.rdss.info/database/nedb/nedb_ent.html.

Note: Multiple devices were exploded in several U.S. tests. The total number of U.S. test events was 1,054. The following countries have also conducted nuclear tests: USSR/Russia (726), France (200), United Kingdom (45), India (6), North Korea (3), and Pakistan (6).

Beyond the moratoria lies the question of bringing into force the Comprehensive Nuclear Test Ban Treaty (CTBT). Ratification of the CTBT by the United States and China would be in their respective national interests and in the interests of their relationship as well. Because China and the United States are the only two established nuclear powers, out of the original five, not to have ratified the treaty to date, it could be a productive area for discussion—with the caveat that the United States would have to be careful not to promise ratification only to have the Senate reject the treaty. Another failed ratification effort might be worse than no attempt at all in its impact on China's (and others') understanding of U.S. strategic intentions.

It is possible that China would go along with CTBT ratification only if India and Pakistan committed to it as well. Renewed efforts should be made by both the United States and China to bring these two countries into discussions (indeed, they must ratify for the treaty to enter into force officially). Still, the complexity of the situation may also present an opportunity, if ratification could reassure even beyond the U.S.-China relationship. Working together, Beijing and Washington might catalyze a process that could yield broader benefits and underscore how their bilateral co-operation can produce multiple desirable effects for regional and global stability.

The merits of the case for the CTBT are strong. A high confidence in the long-term viability of the U.S. nuclear arsenal is possible without testing. To be sure, with time the reliability of a given warhead class may decline as its components age.[36] But at this point, the physics of warhead aging is much better understood. Through a combination of monitoring, testing and remanufacturing the individual components, and conducting sophisticated experiments (short of actual nuclear detonations) on integrated devices, the overall dependability of the American nuclear deterrent can probably remain very high indefinitely. Notably, in today's U.S. arsenal, the so-called plutonium pits are holding up better than anticipated. These are the spherical shells of fissile material that make up the first stage or primary of most U.S. nuclear warheads, along with associated conventional explosives, detonation mechanisms, and other key technologies. The pits may remain dependable for up to a century without having to be remanufactured. As the so-called JASON advisory group wrote in 2007, "Most primary types have credible minimum lifetimes in excess of 100 years as regards aging of plutonium; those with assessed minimum lifetimes of 100 years or less have clear mitigation paths that are proposed and/or being implemented."[37] A 2012 National Academy of Sciences report reached similar conclusions. The longevity of these pits is such that no near-term or even medium-term mechanism is needed to address any existing or expected problems.

The situation will not last forever, to be sure. Some argue that prior to ratifying any CTBT of indefinite duration, it would be important that the nation know how it could respond decades down the road when today's pits are no longer so robust. Part of the solution could be, of course, to re-make the pits. But that may not be completely reassuring. Pits, and weapons primaries more broadly, are very sensitive devices with only small error tolerances. If not remade to nearly exact specifications, the weapon that they are intended to drive can fizzle. The primary is the first part of a thermonuclear weapon, the part that depends mainly on fissioning of uranium-235 or plutonium to generate a nuclear yield. That initial yield then heats and pressurizes the warhead's "secondary" to the point where thermonuclear combustion of its hydrogen fuel results, generating the warhead's main explosive power. Because U.S. nuclear weapons in the Cold War were designed to be as light as possible to fit atop ballistic missiles and produce large yields, warhead designers tried to make the primaries light—which in turn meant that they used less fissile material than might have been otherwise preferred, lowering margins for error in the actual detonation of the weapon and the ignition of the secondary.[38] It is this kind of effort that drove a Cold War U.S. nuclear weapons design and testing effort that included, among other things, roughly a thousand tests generating nuclear yield between 1945 and 1992.[39] And it is such scientific realities that led observers such as Secretary of Defense Robert Gates in 2008 to say that the existing American nuclear stockpile could not be assumed to be dependable indefinitely.[40]

But there are other means of ensuring stockpile safety and reliability over time. Development of a simple, conservative weapons design or two based on existing concepts (thus, not "new warheads" or "modernized warheads") could be done without testing and could complement the existing inventory of warhead types in the future as needs require. Weapons designers tend to agree that very reliable warheads can be produced if performance criteria are relaxed. Indeed, some actually favor a smaller warhead yield for certain purposes, of perhaps the 10-kiloton magnitude.[41] Approaching the power of the Hiroshima and Nagasaki bombs, it would hardly be "small" or easily "usable" and thus should not raise fears that the nuclear threshold would be easily crossed as a result in a future conflict. But it could be a more credible deterrent, say, against relatively isolated military targets, than today's huge warheads. It could also lead to less use of toxic materials such as beryllium and safer types of conventional explosives (that are less prone to accidental detonation) than has been the case for some warheads in the past.[42]

In addition, the verification challenges associated with the CTBT are not insurmountable. The United States can, working with other countries, detect any nuclear weapons test even a fraction the size of the Hiroshima or Nagasaki bombs occurring virtually anywhere on Earth. Large nuclear weapons detonations are easy to detect. If they occurred in the atmosphere (in violation of the Limited Test Ban Treaty), they would be visible from satellites. It is for such reasons that no country trying to keep its nuclear capabilities secret has tested in the atmosphere in the modern era

(South Africa is the last country that appears to have done so). If the detonations were underground, they would still be straightforward to identify via seismic monitoring provided they reached a certain size. Any weapon of a kiloton power or above (the Hiroshima and Nagasaki bombs were in the 10-kiloton to 20-kiloton range) can be "heard" in this way. In other words, any weapon with significant military potential tested at or near its full strength is very likely to be detected. U.S. seismic arrays are found throughout much of Eurasia's periphery, for example, and even tests elsewhere could generally be picked up. The U.S. system is augmented by the globally distributed International Monitoring System. With 85 participating countries and more than 300 monitoring sites—which will ultimately include 50 primary and 120 auxiliary seismic stations—the system can generally detect nuclear tests of 0.1 kiloton (that is, 100 tons of high-explosive equivalent) or even less.[43] Indeed, even though it either "fizzled" or was designed to have a small yield in the first place, with a yield of no more than 1 kiloton and thus well below those of the Hiroshima and Nagasaki bombs, the October 2006 North Korean test was detected and clearly identified as a nuclear burst.[44]

The existing U.S. and international seismic systems are not sensitive enough to detect "microtests" (sometimes called hydronuclear tests) that would produce a nuclear yield equivalent to say 100 kilograms of high explosive. Such testing by sophisticated nuclear weapons states such as Russia or China cannot be ruled out at present.[45] The military utility of such tests, however, is doubtful and almost surely very limited.

What is the real importance of CTBT ratification? At present, the international consensus that nuclear weapons testing is not only unnecessary but unwarranted and indeed illegitimate is holding strong, as it has for nearly two decades. No established nuclear power has tested since France and China (both in 1996). Nor does any major power appear to be considering a change to its own moratorium. Despite setbacks, the failure of the CTBT to enter into force has not appreciably weakened the global norm against proliferation or testing. In fact, if anything, the opposite seems true. Sanctions against India and Pakistan in 1998 were milder and shorter-lived than those against North Korea in 2009 (and now 2013) or those aimed at Iran in recent times as it has advanced its nuclear capabilities even in the absence of testing.

Still, the current equilibrium is vulnerable to disruption. Like the United States, China has not ratified the CTBT, and some worry that Beijing might be tempted to try to vault into the ranks of the nuclear superpowers at some future date—or at least stay ahead of India and its nuclear modernization efforts. Either motivation, or concern about defeating a U.S. missile defense system or further solidifying its second-strike capabilities, could lead Beijing to reconsider its current restrained approach.[46] Indeed, in 2008 Secretary of Defense Gates asserted that both Moscow and Beijing were hedging; in his words, "China and Russia have embarked on an ambitious path to design and field new weapons."[47] Gates was presumably referring primarily to nuclear delivery vehicles rather than warheads. But Beijing may someday want to test and build actual new nuclear devices as a complement to new delivery vehicles. Thus Chinese ratification and implementation of CTBT would have important benefits in constraining China's modernization program and would offer considerable reassurance to the United States.

A CTBT would not, by the force of its own moral suasion, prevent countries from testing nuclear weapons. But countries on the UN Security Council, in the aftermath of a possible future nuclear test by a country like North Korea or Iran, could be more inclined to react strongly against such a transgression if a binding international accord prohibited it. Knowing that in advance, countries like Iran and North Korea might be even less inclined to test nuclear devices than they are now, should the test ban treaty be ratified. Put differently, CTBT ratification could help China and the United States make more common cause in dealing with a problem that has often divided them in the past, that of North Korea and its nuclear ambitions.

An added advantage of CTBT ratification is that it would represent an area of possible fruitful U.S.-China cooperation. This opportunity should be grasped. Indeed, there is even a case that Beijing and Washington could lead a movement to treat the CTBT as quasi-effective once they ratify, even though China's complex relationship with India might temper its willingness to do so if India had not. That is to say, with all five original nuclear states aboard, the treaty could be considered binding even if technically it had not yet cleared the treaty's formal entry into force threshold of also including other states with nuclear potential (notably Iran and North Korea). Other signatories to the CTBT would have to support the idea of course, but it could provide an opportunity for Beijing and Washington to cooperate and indeed spearhead a major multilateral initiative on an issue of considerable mutual concern.

All that said, in the United States at least, the issue would ultimately require a pragmatic calculation about the prospects of Senate ratification. And this would admittedly be daunting. It is true that 75 percent or more of all Americans, including a strong majority of Republicans, support a nuclear test ban. But that has been true since the 1960s and as such is not a great guide to predicting congressional action.[48] In October 1999, Congress voted down the treaty along mostly partisan lines. The final vote was 51–48 against; 19 more affirmative votes making for a total of 67 would have been needed for the treaty to enter into force. Numerous moderate or internationalist Republican senators voted against, including Senators Lugar, Warner, Domenici, McCain, Hagel, Snowe, and Collins; only Chafee, Jeffords, Smith, and Specter supported it from the GOP ranks, none of whom are in the Senate today.[49]

Some have argued that ratification might have been within reach in the early Obama years, when Democrats could still muster 60 votes in the Senate.[50] The support of former Republican secretaries of state George Shultz and Henry Kissinger gave credence to the argument at that time.[51] But those days are unlikely to return soon. It is possible that the impressive endurance of plutonium pits in existing American nuclear weapons and other factors would produce a change of sentiment in the future. Since a second failed ratification could prove counterproductive in sustaining China's restraint and upholding the international norm against testing more broadly, the effort should be made only if 65 or more votes appear within reach from the outset of the effort.

STRATEGIC COMPETITION IN SPACE

One of the greatest dangers to long-term stability in U.S.-China relations is the growing threat of conflict involving space. Each side is increasingly dependent on space-based assets, both as part of its national security strategy and for economic activities. Yet the very high value of these military capabilities, coupled with their inherent vulnerabilities and fragilities, makes them tempting military targets at the outset of a conflict. This fact has led both sides to explore the development of antisatellite capabilities, which create risks of preemptive escalation in a crisis. In addition, there is growing interest in the development of space-based assets for offensive operations, which could pose a substantial danger of a destabilizing arms race. For this reason, the need to develop an approach to mitigate these dangers needs to be near the top of the U.S.-China strategic agenda.[52]

America's new 2010 space policy suggests a greater openness to possible space arms control efforts in the future.[53] But what could they usefully comprise, especially at a time when the United States also rightly expects that space will be a "contested environment?"[54] Certainly Chinese analysts expect the same. As Chinese military journal writers Hong Bing and Liang Xiaoqiu put it recently, "The party with inferior military space forces will be unable to organize a comprehensive and effective defense. It should therefore concentrate its limited military space forces on the offensive." Other authors follow a similar line of reasoning to advocate that China develop further its own space weapons.[55] So discussion of strategic stability in space needs to proceed from a realistic awareness that the United States and China will compete in space and plan to use space for a range of military missions, from surveillance and communications to offense-related military activities including support for command and control and targeting, and possibly even for direct attack.

Given this range of uses, a comprehensive prohibition on "militarizing" space is not realistic. In recent years space has played a central role in American tactical war fighting—as China well understands. This situation constitutes a marked contrast with the early years of satellite technology during the Cold War, when space systems were used principally for communications and surveillance (such as monitoring the production and deployment of nuclear weapons systems and to some extent conventional military assets) and for early warning of attack. As such, they were arguably stabilizing forces and thus gained at least tacit acceptance from both the United States and the Soviet Union.[56]

China's use of space is growing too. It does not yet have early warning satellites for ballistic-missile launch, for example. But it does have $10 billion in space assets by one estimate (relative to a corresponding U.S. figure of perhaps $60 billion) and is increasingly using satellites for reconnaissance and military communications.[57] It also plans a full GPS-like system by 2020, which is now being deployed and employed, and is

TABLE 7.3. Satellites operated by the United States and China
(as of July 31, 2012)

	U.S.	China
USAGE		
Nonmilitary	319	64
Military	90	29
Mixed use[a]	34	0
Total	443	93
ORBIT TYPE		
Low Earth orbit	231	54
Medium Earth orbit	30	3
Geosynchronous orbit	170	36
Elliptical	12	0
Total	443	93
FUNCTION		
Communications	302	23
Navigation/Global positioning	30	15
Technology development	17	6
Earth science/Meteorology	12	2
Electronic surveillance	10	0
Electronic surveillance/Ocean	10	0
Earth science	8	6
Reconnaissance	8	3
Astrophysics	6	0
Communications/Maritime tracking	6	0
Early warning	5	0
Earth observation	5	6
Surveillance	5	0
Meteorology	4	0
Remote sensing[b]	3	22
Space science	3	0
Scientific research	2	2
Amateur radio	1	0
Earth and space science	1	0
Earth observation	1	0
Earth observation/Research	1	0
Solar physics	1	0
Space physics	1	8
Technology development/Communications	1	0
Total	443	93

Source: Union of Concerned Scientists, "UCS Satellite Database," as of July 31, 2012, http:// www.ucsusa.org/nuclear_weapons_and_global_security/space_weapons/technical _issues/ucs-satellite-database.html.

[a] Satellites used by the military and civil, government or commercial agencies.

[b] China numbers include two satellites classified as "Remote Sensing/Research."

improving its all-weather reconnaissance capabilities over land and sea.[58] It has made major strides in its manned space program, with inherent spillovers to potential military applications.

Satellites and antisatellite weapons could play major roles in a future U.S.-China conflict. If the two countries wound up in a war over Taiwan, for example, satellites would be an attractive target from the very outset. For each country, the other's satellites would be capable of identifying, tracking, and helping target its ships and other key military assets and of sharing information to allow the targeting data to be usefully employed. Given their critical military value, each side would be reluctant to give the opponents' unmanned satellites sanctuary while trying to sink each other's ships and shoot each other's pilots out of the sky. Given the range of capabilities already in both sides' arsenals that could damage or destroy satellites, it is difficult to imagine that either could rely on a pledge by the other not to target satellites once a conflict broke out. And trying to limit or roll back those capabilities will be difficult to negotiate, given the dual-use nature of many of these capabilities, for civilian as well as military uses, and for defense as well as offense.

So space arms control is not a given, and not inherently desirable. Any possible treaties need to be assessed very carefully.

A further barrier to space arms control is the need to consider whether any meaningful formal accords would have to be multilateral. Not only the United States and China but countries such as Russia and India and numerous west European nations are important actors in space. Most visions for space-based arms control to date, as discussed at UN fora over the years, have been multilateral in character. This consideration may not preclude certain informal U.S.-China bilateral understandings, though, to constrain their competition in space and perhaps spur action toward multilateral accords.

Verification is another major challenge. This applies to many possible types of space arms control. For example, it is difficult to be sure that a given country's satellite payloads are not explosives that could be used as antisatellite weapons against other countries' satellites once launched into orbit. To prevent that possibility, some might propose inspecting payloads prior to launch. But that is a step that would be very difficult for the United States (and perhaps China) to accept given the sensitive technologies that make up many space payloads, as well as commercial secrecy concerns. Nor would inspections, even if agreed to, necessarily solve the problem. Since satellites can be given the capability for maneuverability without an explosive payload, it will be difficult to preclude this sort of capability (since a satellite with good maneuverability would be very easily turned into an ASAT). A related verification problem could arise in regard to a possible ban on certain types of development tests. For example, a laser can be tested in ballistic-missile defense mode even if there is a ban on ASAT tests. But since the kinematics of low-Earth orbit satellites are so similar to those of ballistic-missile warheads, testing against the latter is a good way to ensure capability against the former.

Still, some arms control steps might be considered—beyond smart unilateral military steps such as making communications and reconnaissance capabilities resilient and redundant enough to reduce preemptive incentives in a crisis.[59] It may make sense, for example, to ban weapons that would be placed in orbit to attack targets on the ground. Because testing of such systems would likely be required before they could be considered usable and would likely be observable, such an accord might be feasible and verifiable, since no such weapons exist today. It bans a hypothetical capability that neither side has shown any real interest in deploying now—which may make it easier to negotiate, even if of only moderate significance once completed.

Bans on actual ASAT tests against satellites could be considered. Their utility would be limited, since as noted earlier the ASAT systems could still be tested in ballistic-missile defense mode as a proxy for testing against actual satellites (at least for low-Earth orbit ASATs), but benefits would still exist. A ban could also be considered on explosions or collisions directed against any object in space that would create debris. Indeed, such prohibitions could probably be usefully codified in a treaty. Both the United States and China have shot down satellites in recent years, and China has continued work on its capabilities since, so in one sense the genie is out of the bottle technologically.[60] But further ASAT tests could be forgone, under mutual accord. And any further tests of ballistic-missile defense systems like those now operated by the United States could be required to take place below a certain altitude, say 1,000 kilometers, to make this kind of pact meaningful while still permitting testing of missile defense systems. So far, tests of the U.S. midcourse missile defense system have occurred around 200 kilometers altitude, so a 1,000-kilometer ceiling may be workable over an extended period of time. This approach would have the benefit of reducing debris in the part of space used most frequently by low-Earth orbit satellites.[61]

Some confidence-building measures may make sense, too. One such idea is keep-out zones around deployed satellites, whether through treaty or informal accord. The logic here is that there is no reason for a satellite to approach within tens of kilometers of another, so a close approach may be reasonably assumed to be hostile. Creating such zones would have only limited utility, as they could be violated in wartime without great difficulty even if respected in peacetime. But a violation of agreed limits could be treated as an indication of hostile intent and provide a justification for taking action—including preemptive measures—to counter the dangers posed by the violation of the commitment.

Another confidence-building measure could be advance notice of space launches. This would make it easier for countries to track each other's satellites and activities in space, increasing confidence that antisatellite weapons were not being tested, for example.

A final useful category of space arms control could be reciprocal unilateral pledges not to develop dedicated ASAT systems. This would not of course preclude continued development of missile defense systems that would have capability against low-Earth orbit satellites in particular, so again, the scope of the accord would be of modest military significance. But it would nonetheless constitute a form of restraint and contribute to a paradigm of U.S.-China strategic reassurance.

It might seem desirable to propose an agreement that, even in the event of limited war, the United States and China not attack each other's key communications satellites to avoid risks of confusion and inadvertent escalation.[62] It is not clear that those assets can realistically be accorded reliable sanctuary, given their roles in conventional war fighting and targeting. But there may be limited benefit to the idea nonetheless—raising the threshold for decision makers contemplating such an action in a crisis—and therefore improving crisis stability at least on the margin.

Beyond the military domain, greater international cooperation in space could foster positive interactions among key actors including the United States, China, and China's neighbors.[63] These could extend to joint manned space exploration, for example. At whatever level of technology and sophistication it might occur, such joint missions would follow in the spirit of U.S.-Russia collaboration on the space station and can contribute to broader sense of shared interests.

CYBER SECURITY

Like space, the cyber domain has become an increasing source of strategic mistrust and competition in the U.S.-China relationship. The two areas share much in common. They are increasingly vital to both civilian and military activities, and the combination of dependence and vulnerability makes them tempting targets for military planners. But unlike the situation with space, the ability to target cyber assets is not limited to highly capable national governments—and the ability to identify the source of cyber attacks is far more challenging. For this reason, the cyber realm poses serious challenges to building U.S.-China strategic reassurance. It also offers real opportunities, since securing cyberspace can serve the interests of both countries. The challenge is to build a framework that enhances cooperation on common threats—against cyber crime and against nonstate actors—while constraining the danger that anxieties about each other's cyber capabilities will lead to arms racing of a new type or strong preemptive incentives during a crisis.[64]

Both countries have identified cyber security as a critical national challenge. The Chinese Ministry of Public Security reports that China is the world's largest victim of cyber attacks by raw numbers.[65] This is partly due to China's excessive use of pirated software, which is more vulnerable to attack. The United States has power grids, chemical plants, and other critical yet potentially vulnerable national infrastructure connected to the Internet in ways that leave them potentially quite vulnerable. The stakes here are enormous. Estimates of possible damage to U.S. systems from all-out cyber attacks exceed $1 trillion, with the potential for hundreds of billions in damage to electric power, oil and gas, water, banking, telecommunications, chemical, transportation, and health care industries. A recent National Academy of Sciences study underscores the severe vulnerability of the electricity grid from cyber threats (as well as traditional terrorist strikes and weather).[66] The number of lives affected—and lives lost—could be very large. And while certain military networks are relatively secure, many are not.[67]

At the core of the problem is each side's growing capacity for offensive cyber operations, along with evidence that each side is prepared to use these capabilities as an element of national security strategy, both for collecting intelligence and for offensive operations. China has recognized the modern American military's unprecedented use of information in its precision warfare techniques and drawn conclusions about the desirability of disrupting computers and computer networks given their roles in collecting, analyzing, and disseminating that information.[68] In response, U.S. officials increasingly worry about the possibility of a "cyber Pearl Harbor." While officials carefully avoid naming potential perpetrators of such an attack, they make clear that only a few states, including China, have the sophistication to conduct devastating operations. As the U.S. Director of National Intelligence put it in 2012, "Among state actors, China and Russia are of particular concern . . . entities within these countries are responsible for extensive illicit intrusions into U.S. computer networks and theft of U.S. intellectual property."[69] The Chinese government also devotes very substantial resources to cyber intelligence efforts and numerous organizations within its armed forces have offensive cyber capabilities and missions as well.[70] To date, China's offensive cyber operations have been probably less noteworthy than America's.[71] But the PRC's strategic intelligence activities are robust and, as the above quote from the Director of National Intelligence suggests, its industrial espionage and intellectual theft activities have few if any parallels.[72]

Although some commentators have questioned the plausibility of a devastating cyber first strike, the competition between the United States and China is unquestionably worrisome for a number of reasons. First, the United States is convinced that China is expanding its offensive cyber operations against American civilian and military targets, fueling suspicions about China's motives. China in turn believes that the United States uses its capabilities to undermine the PRC regime through support of dissident voices as well as other means, a concern fueled by the recent revelations by Edward Snowden concerning alleged NSA operations against China.[73] Second, each side's growing dependence on information technology as part of its military operations means that cyber attacks are increasingly integrated into war-fighting plans, particularly at the early stages of conflict. In some respects, the concern about cyber operations bears similarities to the Cold War fear that the United States or Russia might resort to high-altitude nuclear explosions to generate electromagnetic pulses to blind the adversary prior to initiating kinetic strikes.

U.S. planners are particularly concerned because they appreciate Beijing's general inclination to "asymmetric" military strategies (often characterized as the "assassin's mace," a phrase depicting weapons or tactics with targeted and lethal effects) to counter American technological superiority.[74] In effect, the idea is to turn a U.S. strength into a vulnerability. But this very fear on the U.S. side that China might use cyber preemptively (or at the very early stages of a conflict) leads American planners to consider how to neutralize China's offensive capabilities before they can be deployed against the United States—thus triggering the same crisis instability dynamic as in the space realm.

Because of the challenge of attributing the source of cyber attacks, the dangers may be even greater than in the strategic nuclear or space realm. The ability to attribute attacks is crucial for deterrence. If a potential victim is unable to credibly identify the source of attack (either because of inherent difficulties in cyber attribution or the ability of the attacker to mask and/or deceive), the credibility of a retaliatory response is weakened and the pressures for rapid escalation grow. Yet uncertainty about attribution may lead one side to take risks assuming the other will be deterred from response by the ambiguity of the source of attack—an assumption that may or may not hold in actuality.

The mistrust is further fueled by the scale of industrial espionage and intellectual property theft that the U.S. government and U.S. firms attribute to Chinese hackers, operating with the tacit or even explicit support of the Chinese government. While some of the targets are related to the U.S. military, many appear to be private firms, reflecting attempts by China to pilfer intellectual property in order to achieve a competitive economic advantage. While this form of cyber operations does not directly implicate the strategic competition between the two countries, it certainly undermines mutual confidence. Indeed, it has recently led to a proposal by the Blair-Huntsman commission that U.S. companies might be granted the right to retaliate directly against the perpetrators of such cyber crime and cyber intrusions inflicted upon their information systems. This is a worrying prospect that could deepen the danger of conflict between the two countries triggered by actions of private parties, and it indicates the depth of growing concern on the matter.[75]

Even efforts labeled as "defensive" in the cyber realm pose risks for stability between the United States and China. American officials have begun to discuss an operational concept of "active defense" that could in principle include disabling the source of the attack outside the United States.[76] To be effective, these active defenses might need to be implemented virtually instantaneously through automatic, preprogrammed protocols, without a "man in the loop." These "defensive" operations thus have the potential of triggering a response in kind, triggering an escalatory spiral with little or no opportunity for cooler heads to prevail. Some of the fears of cyber conflict between the United States and China seem overblown. Even if either side was capable of a massive disabling operation, it is hard to imagine the circumstances of a cyber "bolt out of the blue." Our mutual economic dependence means that a powerful strike against the other's cyber infrastructure would boomerang—harming the perpetrator as well the victim. And although attribution is difficult (and techniques for masking continue to be developed), improvements in cyber forensics mean that each side would run a substantial risk that the other would have enough confidence in attributing the source of any attack to justify severe retaliation (even as the risk of mistaken attribution remains considerable).[77]

Of course, these latter considerations are hardly reason for complacency. If nothing else, the mutual sense that one side is developing (and in some cases deploying) cyber capabilities against the other spawns mutual resentment and hostility—not just in government but among wider publics. And while a massive "strategic surprise" cyber attack by either China or the United States seems implausible, the use of cyber in connection with a crisis is highly plausible and will be very tempting, leading to the dangers of escalation and crisis management that are a growing concern across many dimensions of U.S. and Chinese strategy. For this reason, both sides have powerful incentives to try to mitigate, if not eliminate, the dangers.

Many of the requisite tools to address the problem can be developed unilaterally. Resilience is especially critical to strategic reassurance by reducing the hypothetical damage the other side can inflict—thus reducing the incentive for destabilizing "cyber arms races" or operational retaliatory doctrines that would exacerbate crisis instability. Tools that increase resilience include protecting infrastructure against attack by separating some control systems from the Internet, among other steps, while also enhancing redundancy so that single points of computer failure do not lead to the loss of a large capability. Reducing vulnerability lowers the attractiveness of cyber targets and the temptation to launch preemptive or early strikes. Reduced vulnerability also provides greater time for diplomacy and nonescalatory responses to an initial attack (as well as greater time to confirm the accuracy of attribution, thus avoiding the danger of false attribution as well as the temptation of third parties to conduct "false flag" operations that might then lure China and the United States into a conflict that somehow served the interest of said third party). Improved forensics also can help enhance deterrence.

But there are also steps the two sides can pursue together. Developing such a strategy could draw on other areas of U.S.-China cooperation to address common threats, such as in counterterrorism, nonproliferation, and human trafficking. To begin, confidence could be enhanced by directly tackling the problem of cyber theft. Both sides claim to oppose such activities. By developing cooperative strategies to tackle them, they could demonstrate the credibility of the commitment.

Concrete steps could include China acceding to the Budapest cyber crime convention, with its focus on harmonizing national laws to ensure protections against such things as hacking, cyber theft, and xenophobic or racist or pornographic activities, and to allow authorities to monitor certain sites once proper authorities are granted.[78] China could also establish credible domestic mechanisms for investigation of and prosecution of cyber theft. Confidence in the dependability of these efforts would be further buttressed by enhanced information sharing on cyber theft allegations and the creation of joint law enforcement mechanisms for investigation. Although the record remains imperfect, the improved cooperation between the United States and China in addressing U.S. concerns about proliferation-related activities by Chinese nationals (in regard to technologies relevant to weapons of mass destruction) shows that much can be accomplished if the two sides truly share the same goal.[79]

And the converse is also true. If China remains unwilling to cooperate with the United States (and others) to investigate allegations of hacking and theft, Americans are entitled to assume that the activities have at least the acquiescence, if not the support, of the Chinese government. They would then be justified in taking appropriate countermeasures. As the recent Blair-Huntsman commission outlined, these could include more seizures or trade restrictions on goods containing stolen intellectual property, limits on access to American banks for companies repeatedly or blatantly engaged in such theft, prohibitions on such companies being allowed to buy American companies (enforced by the Committee on Foreign Investment in the United States), and modification of the Economic Espionage Act to allow private firms to sue in federal court those stealing their secrets.[80]

Put another way, from the American vantage point, the willingness of China to address effectively and cooperatively U.S. concerns about cyber theft can be an important element of strategic reassurance, and failure to do so would solidify concerns about China's strategic intentions and justify appropriate adjustments in U.S. policy based on those concerns.

Of course, dealing with cyber crime is only a small part of the equation. The core of mistrust derives from each side's concerns about the use of cyber as a direct element of the other's national security strategy. A number of steps have been proposed to address the use of cyber in military operations, including China's advocacy of a multilateral, UN negotiation for a cyber treaty. Proposed elements include a ban on use of offensive cyber tools against civilian targets. The ban could focus on certain kinds of potential targets in particular—electricity grids and large-scale infrastructure more generally, as well as chemical plants and financial institutions. Given the nature of these cyber capabilities, each side would continue to question whether such an agreement would hold in wartime, but as with other destabilizing capabilities (such as chemical weapons or, as we suggest earlier, attacks on space assets) such a norm would raise the threshold for use, thus dampening the dangers of an uncontrolled escalatory spiral.

The issues surrounding verification and enforcement tools that would give high confidence in compliance are substantial. Cyber security, in this regard, is even more daunting than efforts to control the development, stockpiling, and use of biological weapons.[81] But the best need not be the enemy of the good. Most of the discussions about limitations on cyber operations in war or conflict involve whether and how to apply humanitarian law (limiting attacks on civilians) and the law of war (justifying retaliation as a self-defense measure) to cyber operations. Like the laws of war, the development of cyber norms to which both China and the United States subscribe could operate as a constraint on military planning and operations. It could even lead to post-facto enforcement mechanisms like the International Criminal Court. Washington has broadly accepted the applicability of the law of war to cyber; the Chinese position is less clear. The recent U.S. international cyber strategy and Department of Defense cyber strategy both demonstrate increasing openness to the elaboration of norms for cyber activities, and sustained engagement (both bilaterally and multilaterally) by the United States and China on this issue can itself be a confidence-building measure. The inclusion of cyber as a core element of the U.S.-China Strategic Security Dialogue, as well as the recently launched U.S.-China cyber security working group under the Security and Economic Dialogue (SED), provides several promising fora for making progress.[82] This could include increased information on third-party cyber threats, cooperation on enhanced resiliency, discussion of cyber doctrine in military and intelligence channels, establishment of a hotline between top cyber authorities, as well as notification of certain cyber activities at a center like that recently established between the United States and Russia.[83] All of these efforts supplement unilateral efforts to secure networks and make them more redundant.

Additional measures like these could also be considered:[84]

- transparency and confidence-building efforts to ensure that military communications systems, hotlines, and crucial command and control mechanisms for regulating nuclear forces are not targeted by each other, particularly early in any crisis or prospective conflict
- discussion of steps that might amount to a reinvention of how the Internet works, to require in effect a form of electronic self-identification by any user for sensitive domains on the Internet to help further with the attribution challenge
- understanding by Beijing that America will have to continue to limit the investments of Chinese companies like Huawei in U.S. telecommunications for the foreseeable future out of legitimate national security concerns but that it will try to apply such strictures carefully and very selectively and transparently
- modest steps toward preparing for cyber cooperation in future military missions that might involve both countries, for example, future counterpiracy operations and possible future peace operations[85]

Finally, as noted earlier, resilience is critical to limiting the strategic impact of cyber attacks: the more resilient U.S. and Chinese systems become, the less important cyber figures as a source of strategic mistrust. (It is important for U.S. friends and allies in the region that could theoretically be vulnerable to intimidation or attack to do the same, for similar reasons.) Put another way, if each side feels confident it can protect key assets, there will be less need to take measures that deepen strategic competition in cyberspace. This is what the U.S. International Strategy for Cyberspace terms "dissuasion."[86] As one set of potentially useful measures, each side could simply remove some key infrastructure, such as the national electric grid, from the global Internet. Despite their imperfect track record, air gaps can be built into such systems as one added element of resilience, and perhaps also for certain other key infrastructure (such as toxic chemical plants, high-speed rail lines, air traffic control stations, and nuclear power plant control stations). Such defensive measures can be justified not only in the U.S.-China context but as prudent measures against terrorists or others with potentially hostile intent.[87]

CONCLUSION

In strategic military domains, the United States and China do and will continue to compete. But their competition is already somewhat tempered, which should provide reassurance to each. For example, nothing resembling an arms race exists in the nuclear realm, and no all-out competition to develop antisatellite capabilities is under way, even if electronic and cyber domains do witness competition and some destabilizing interactions.

More can be done to dampen the competition and deepen the strategic reassurance without requiring either country to forgo capabilities it considers crucial for its security or desist from types of military competition that it finds legitimate and advantageous. The measures proposed in this chapter draw on the core concepts of transparency and resilience to allow for mutual reassurance without resort to cumbersome formal agreements, yet provide substantial protection against breakout in key areas of nuclear weapons, strategic defense, space, and cyber. In a limited number of cases, it may also be possible to enter into formal accords. The kinds of measures we propose here are vital to prevent deepening strategic mistrust and, if pursued, could provide an important source of mutual reassurance reinforcing the commitment to develop a cooperative rather than confrontational relationship.

8

---◆◇◆---

Bases, Deployments, and Operations

Just as important as the high-level issues of military spending, war plans, and nuclear weapons policies are the more routine matters of how the armed forces of China and the United States routinely interact, primarily in the international zones of the Western Pacific Ocean region. Such seemingly mundane matters can have major implications if each country's military deployments foster distrust and suspicion in the eyes of the other or if accidents or misunderstandings lead to escalating crises.

Chinese and American forces are increasingly in close proximity to one another. The change may not seem so dramatic when one views a static map; after all, U.S. forces have been close to China and in Japan and Korea (and in earlier times in the Philippines and Vietnam) for decades. But China's military is becoming modern and is outwardly orienting into maritime domains for the first time in centuries. In addition, U.S. forces in the region are increasingly focused on China. The interaction between these twin developments poses important risks to managing the bilateral relationship.

U.S. BASING AND DEPLOYMENTS

Since the end of World War II, as the United States took on a global role in connection with the Cold War, it has maintained a robust system of permanent overseas bases and sustained military deployments.[1] These assets and activities have served a variety of roles: reassurance to allies of needed political and military support, sustaining the freedom of navigation, operational flexibility to meet emerging contingencies, and a platform for developing cooperation and interoperability with foreign forces.

U.S. bases in East Asia and the Western Pacific were crucial elements of the containment strategy against the Soviet Union. They also served to solidify the security commitments to Japan and South Korea (and thus contributed to their decisions to forgo nuclear weapons and, in the case of Japan, to refrain from developing a robust offensive military capability) and provided major logistical support for U.S. engagement in Southeast Asia. Basing arrangements have been complemented by less permanent forms of presence, including access rights to foreign ports and, crucially, military exercises.

While some argued that the end of the Cold War should provide a rationale for withdrawing American forces back to the United States from both Europe and the Pacific, in fact the U.S. footprint has not changed dramatically, especially in East Asia, for a number of reasons. The growing threat from North Korea and continued uncertainty around Taiwan (including the informal security relationship implicit in the U.S. policy for a peaceful resolution of Taiwan's status) have provided a strong rationale for continued deployment. Less explicit has been the concern that a U.S. withdrawal would lead both Japan and South Korea to dramatically increase their own military capacity (including possibly developing nuclear weapons), creating new tensions in the region.[2]

The United States has around two hundred thousand military personnel abroad at present. It seeks to possess enough capability in strategically important parts of the world to make a difference in normal day-to-day regional balances of power and to train vigorously with allies on a routine basis. By maintaining presence continuously, it seeks to keep real-time tabs on regional developments and to keep others accustomed to its presence so that it need not take actions seen as escalatory in a crisis (as might be the case if it sent substantial assets into given theater only in times of tension). Not only does the United States have a great deal of firepower stationed abroad, it has the infrastructure, the working relationships, and the transportation and logistics assets needed to reinforce its capacities quickly as needed in crises. No other major power has more than twenty thousand to thirty thousand forces abroad globally, with Britain and France leading the way after the United States. Like China, powers such as Russia and India typically deploy forces totaling only in the thousands in total worldwide, as do several countries that participate frequently in peacekeeping missions.[3]

TABLE 8.1. U.S. troops based in foreign countries
(as of December 31, 2012)

Country or region	Number of troops
Europe	
Belgium	1,165
Germany	45,596
Italy	10,916
Portugal	713
Spain	1,600
Turkey	1,491
United Kingdom	9,310
Afloat	n/a
Other	1,407
Subtotal	72,198
Former Soviet Union	187
East Asia, and Pacific	
Japan	52,692
Korea (now "undistributed")	n/a
Afloat	n/a
Other	1,333
Subtotal	54,025
North Africa, Near East, and South Asia	
Bahrain	2,902
Qatar	800
Afloat	n/a
Other	1,103
Subtotal	4,805
Sub-Saharan Africa	489
Western Hemisphere	
Cuba (Guantanamo)	988
Other	1,117
Subtotal	2,105
Subtotal: All foreign countries, not including war deployments	133,809
Undistributed: Includes classified and unknown locations	39,157
War deployments: Afghanistan	68,000
Total currently abroad	240,966

Sources: Department of Defense, "Active Duty Military Personnel Strengths by Regional Area and by Country," http://siadapp.dmdc.osd.mil/personnel/MILITARY/miltop.htm.

Note: Only countries with at least 500 troops are listed individually. Figures for Afghanistan are now substantially less.

As the PLA has improved, the U.S. deployments have been seen through the lens of America's China strategy—for some, as an implicit but clear element of containment; for others, a framework for encouraging the PRC to focus on peaceful development and to reassure countries of the region that they can develop constructive political and economic relations with China without fear of domination by Beijing. The deployments also support U.S. intelligence activities in the Pacific (including maritime and aerial surveillance of China) and provide a real-time U.S. presence in and around contentious territorial flash points, like the South and East China seas.

Indeed, the Obama administration has identified sustained U.S. presence in the Western Pacific as a centerpiece of its global strategy, not as a counter to China per se but as way of providing public goods that benefit all the countries of the region, including China. As President Obama stated in a speech to the Australian parliament in November 2011:

> Here, we see the future. As the world's fastest-growing region—and home to more than half the global economy—the Asia Pacific is critical to achieving my highest priority, and that's creating jobs and opportunity for the American people. With most of the world's nuclear power and some half of humanity, Asia will largely define whether the century ahead will be marked by conflict or cooperation, needless suffering or human progress.
>
> As President, I have, therefore, made a deliberate and strategic decision—as a Pacific nation, the United States will play a larger and long-term role in shaping this region and its future, by upholding core principles and in close partnership with our allies and friends.
>
> Now, I know that some in this region have wondered about America's commitment to upholding these principles. So let me address this directly. As the United States puts our fiscal house in order, we are reducing our spending. And, yes, after a decade of extraordinary growth in our military budgets—and as we definitively end the war in Iraq, and begin to wind down the war in Afghanistan—we will make some reductions in defense spending.
>
> As we consider the future of our armed forces, we've begun a review that will identify our most important strategic interests and guide our defense priorities and spending over the coming decade. So here is what this region must know. As we end today's wars, I

have directed my national security team to make our presence and mission in the Asia Pacific a top priority. As a result, reductions in U.S. defense spending will not—I repeat, will not—come at the expense of the Asia Pacific.[4]

The president went on to argue that this new policy was not aimed at China, and much of his message was clearly motivated by concern that a decade of wars in the Middle East juxtaposed with pending defense budget cuts had created a false impression of American retrenchment from the region that required correction. This fits with a broader American goal: just as Washington wants to underscore that it remains committed and capable in the Western Pacific, it wants to avoid creating perceptions of trying to contain China or overmilitarizing its foreign policy. Yet Chinese critics of American forward presence often portray the U.S. presence as focusing excessively on reconnaissance or espionage, on sustaining alliances that they see as anachronistic, and on setting up a system of capabilities that they often equate with a containment strategy.[5]

It is clearly difficult to get the overseas basing and deployment balance right, particularly in a time of change. Much of America's increased capacity in the Western Pacific in recent years is modest, yet U.S. officials point to these enhancements as tangible proof that the United States has in fact "rebalanced" toward Asia. This creates an inherent tension as U.S. officials seek to both emphasize and downplay the military significance of the rebalance, risking, on the one hand, stoking China's anxieties and, at the same, undercutting the message of resolve the United States seeks to convey to its allies and partners. For those inclined to interpret America's intent as hostile, the addition of up to 2,500 Marines in Australia and a few more attack submarines on Guam prove their suspicions. For others, the modest scale of these new U.S. activities, as well as the planned periodic rotational deployment of four small warships to Singapore, underscores the limited means employed by America to give credibility to its rebalancing effort. As deeper defense budget cuts loom than even those foreseen by President Obama when giving his 2011 speech in Australia, the difficulty of backing up the rebalancing with real military muscle only grows.

Today America's military has three main concentrations of overseas power. The three regions are roughly comparable in the total numbers of U.S. military personnel they host, though the mix of relevant military capabilities varies considerably from one to another. Each currently features 50,000–100,000 uniformed American personnel. One key area is still Europe, centered on Germany but also with substantial numbers of forces in the United Kingdom and Italy and a more modest presence in a few additional countries like Spain. The second main area of focus is of course in the broader "Central Command" region. GIs in Iraq have now come home, but the United States retains substantial capabilities and bases throughout the Persian Gulf region, on land and at sea. Through at least 2014, the United States will have considerable numbers of troops engaged in combat operations and stabilization activities in Afghanistan. The third major capability is in the dynamic East Asia region, with large standing American forces (air and land) in both Korea and Japan and large numbers of ships routinely on station in the Western Pacific.[6]

In northeast Asia and the broader Western Pacific, the largest U.S. presence is in Japan with up to some 50,000 American uniformed personnel. U.S. capabilities in Korea with almost 30,000 GIs are not far behind. Forces at sea often number 10,000–20,000 military personnel. Hawaii, Alaska, and Guam are of course highly relevant to the Asia-Pacific region, too—and they have about 40,000, 20,000, and 3,000 U.S. uniformed personnel on their territories, respectively. Some 7,000 Marines may soon shift from Okinawa to Guam, though this will essentially be an intratheater reallocation. Modest additional numbers of attack submarines and aircraft may also be added in Guam; for example, a fourth attack submarine may soon be based there.[7]

In playing its worldwide military role, the United States has more than sixty formal allies or other close security partners with whom it teams in one way or another (more than two dozen in Europe, a half dozen in the Asia-Pacific region, nearly a dozen in the broader Middle East, and many in Latin America). Its national security strategy for decades has viewed virtually the entirety of Eurasia's coastal regions as important American national security interests. South Asia and Southeast Asia have sometimes been within this perimeter, sometimes not. But Europe, the Middle East/Persian Gulf region, and East Asia have consistently factored critically into the U.S. national security equation.

The U.S. calculus about these deployments proceeds from a certain reading of history. In this narrative, sometimes oversimplified, after

World War I, U.S. forces went home, and ultimately World War II resulted. After World War II, while some occupation forces remained abroad, most capabilities were demobilized, and then North Korea attacked South Korea. Advocates for U.S. presence and engagement abroad, who, as we discussed in chapter 4, have dominated the American national security debate in modern times, have concluded that sustained peacetime overseas engagement, even if costly and burdensome, is far preferable to the greater risk of war that can result from retrenchment or isolationism.

Even after reductions that followed the Cold War, the U.S. military retains approximately five hundred overseas sites with a combined value of more than $100 billion.[8] The budgetary costs of planned relocations of U.S. forces in Korea and Japan alone could range up to $50 billion. Much of that would be associated with moving seven thousand Marines from Okinawa to Guam while also repositioning remaining Marine assets within Okinawa—costs that would be likely borne in large part by Tokyo, if it can sort out the Japanese domestic politics of getting the basic idea approved in the first place. Opposition on Okinawa to one aspect of the plan that would entail building a new airfield on a different part of the island may or may not sink the whole concept.[9]

In some cases, however, foreign bases in the right place can actually save substantial sums of money, especially once the forces are already established abroad and construction costs paid. This is important to understand for those who would impute aggressiveness to America's forward basing strategy; in fact, it is designed to enhance deterrence and to save money through efficiencies. For example, being able to base U.S. tactical airpower at Kadena Air Base on Okinawa, Japan, arguably saves the United States tens of billions of dollars a year. If the United States had to sustain a comparable airpower capability continuously in that region through other means, the alternative to Kadena might well be a larger Navy aircraft carrier fleet expanded by four or five carrier battle groups with an annual price tag of $25 billion or more.[10]

Concerns over costs are also important to keep in mind when examining current U.S. Navy initiatives. Again, what can appear provocative in some eyes could simply be the triumph of the comptroller, as more efficient ways are found to maintain presence in the region.

Overall, the U.S. Navy is maintaining a robust global presence with only about 286 major warships. That is still a formidable force of generally high-technology and large vessels, including 11 large-deck aircraft carriers, 11 large amphibious ships with aerial capability themselves, and more than 50 state-of-the-art nuclear-powered attack submarines.[11] But it is a fleet only half the size of its peak under Ronald Reagan. Yet it is maintaining 15 percent more overseas deployment time per year than it did just before 9/11. The Navy finds this an uncomfortably high tempo and yet its earlier hopes to expand the fleet by about 10 percent, to 313 ships, are unlikely to prove affordable.[12] The Navy's idea to deploy, on a rotational basis, four midsized Littoral Combat Ships in Singapore in the future is partly a result of this situation. From the perspective of U.S. military leaders, this is not the vanguard of a new containment strategy to China's south but rather a way to maintain American presence in a crucial part of the world on a tight budget.

There are also prepositioned supplies in key overseas theaters that facilitate rapid reinforcement of additional combat capabilities if needed. They include huge ships stocked with enough weaponry and ammunition for roughly two ground combat brigades, based at Guam. These capabilities are not new, but they are being refurbished with the gradual end of the wars in the Middle East. They, too, represent a way to gain meaningful (if hardly huge) military capability in a time of budgetary constraints, and indeed creating more prepositioning stocks might prove useful in the years ahead.

If and when the Navy pursues further port access or similar arrangements for ships abroad, some will be tempted to view such actions as provocative. More accurately, they will probably best reflect an effort to make operations more efficient given the likely downward trajectory of future American defense budgets. Nonetheless, the ambiguity about U.S. intentions that these deployments can engender creates the need to provide reassurance, as will be discussed further.

Yet another way to get more out of a smaller fleet is to homeport more ships near the theaters where they operate. That helps reduce time wasted in transit. Indeed, about a decade ago, the Navy started down the homeporting path in another important way, basing up to six attack submarines on Guam.[13] There is room for the Navy to add several more there in the future and it may well do so. Again, such moves driven by the need to cope with declining budgets and force structure add complexity to managing U.S.-China relations.

These U.S. military enhancements not only are modest in themselves but must also be seen through the prism of the PLA's growing capacities to project power in the region. Nonetheless, there are steps that can be taken to reinforce the limited, stabilizing nature of these measures, as we discuss in detail later in this chapter.

CHINESE BASING AND DEPLOYMENTS

In contrast with the United States, China historically has avoided foreign basing. Indeed, one needs to go back to the fifteenth century to find a Chinese government that had been truly expeditionary beyond its borders. In the Ming era, Admiral Zheng He commanded an impressive fleet of ships, but in 1433 his expeditions were stopped and the fleet was soon destroyed by internal government decision.[14] From that point onward, China focused on its own territorial cohesion and defense. This historical habit has begun to change in the modern era, as deepened global economic engagement means a growing stake for China in maritime security and freedom of navigation, as well as access to resources in areas well beyond the Western Pacific. Chinese great-power ambitions are clearly growing, too. And, of course, PLA naval forces are virtually all located in parts of the world of great interest to the United States and its allies, even when near home waters.

Over the past twenty years, as one indication of growing capability, China has expanded its fleet of major surface combatants from 56 to 77, according to the International Institute for Strategic Studies. Its submarine fleet has declined in size, from 94 to 65 ships, but only because obsolescent vessels have now been retired. China's more modern submarine types have increased in number from 8 to roughly 20.[15] All of these vessels are essentially deployed in important international waters within a very short time after leaving dock. And the more modern vessels tend, naturally, to be optimized for longer-endurance operations than those they have been replacing.

As for actual deployments beyond the international commons of the Western Pacific region, China's activities are growing but still quite modest. A tabulation by the International Institute for Strategic Studies in 2012 estimated that China has about 2,000 personnel in various UN missions around the world and three ships involved in the multilateral Gulf of Aden counterpiracy effort. These kinds of steps have been generally welcomed by the United States.[16] They translate into a total of about 3,000 PLA military personnel worldwide beyond Chinese borders, plus whatever number of Chinese ships are in international waters at any given moment closer to China's own territory. By contrast, as noted, the United States currently bases 50,000–100,000 troops abroad in each of three regions: Europe, the Western Pacific, and the broader Middle East including Afghanistan.[17]

China's role is surely growing, however, as noted. In the period from the mid-1980s through 2000 China averaged less than one foreign port call a year but its Navy then averaged at least two annually over the last decade and the number continues to increase.[18] (Still, to again give perspective on even these increased activities, while 2 PLA ships visited Singapore in 2010, there were 150 American naval visits and 30 Japanese visits there that same year.)[19] Similarly, China's fleet average for sustained submarine patrols has been growing, but again gradually, from a twenty-five-year average of about 2.4 a year to 3.4 annually in recent times.[20] (Depending on precisely how one counts, the commensurate U.S. figure is in the many dozens per year.) This Chinese figure is still modest, but it is growing. And India's military apparently believes it detected Chinese submarines in the Indian Ocean twenty-two times in 2012, a much increased rate.[21]

In 2011, China evacuated 36,000 of its nationals in Libya, but mostly using leased civilian assets from neighboring countries.[22] That same year, for the second time in history, a Chinese officer took command of a UN mission abroad. In the fall of 2011, a Chinese Navy medical ship made a goodwill mission through the Caribbean.[23] In recent years, China has conducted about a dozen military exercises annually with other countries, up substantially from past levels, including two notable two-weeklong exercises in 2012 (with Indonesia and Thailand).[24]

In 2011, senior Chinese military leaders visited about thirty-five countries, nearly double the typical number of just half a decade before, and hosted military officials from thirty-two countries.[25] Chinese military students undertaking foreign study at any time grew from about 200 in 2000 to about 1,000 a decade later; the number of foreign military personnel studying in China at any time grew from around 1,000 to at least 4,000 over roughly that same period.[26]

Chinese are beginning to debate whether they should develop access to overseas military facilities. China has apparently been trying to develop greater expertise in long-range logistics during its participation in the Gulf of Aden counterpiracy operation, as well as other recent missions.[27] State-owned companies have helped build up ports in places such as Gwadar, Pakistan, and Hambantota, Sri Lanka, as well as locations in Burma and Bangladesh, and China's military has used these places as well as facilities in Salalah, Oman, and Aden, Yemen, for refueling and related activities.[28] This informal network is sometimes described as China's "string of pearls." China will also likely continue to use nonmilitary assets, such as Coast Guard capabilities and commercial ships, to expand presence and reconnaissance.

Such increased Chinese activity and access are significant, to be sure, and worthy of continued attention from American policymakers. But the likelihood of these arrangements being upgraded into permanent overseas military bases would seem modest for the foreseeable future at least. Such a development would contradict China's own longstanding complaint about American extraterritorial bases and operations. That might be reason enough to prevent the idea from being pursued. More probable is a continued Chinese penchant to increase contingency access for maintenance, refueling, and the like in a number of places—what the U.S. military habitually referred to as developing "places, not bases" when that lexicon was popular a few years ago—since such facilities serve current PLA interests and needs adequately.[29] Nonetheless, the expanding scope of Chinese basing and operations beyond its home waters has triggered concerns about China's intentions, and for this reason, too, it is imperative for China to provide the United States and regional neighbors clearer reassurance about the purpose and scope of China's activities.

Strategic Reassurance and Resolve in Basing, Operations, and Deployment

This discussion suggests several steps that the United States and China can take to enhance confidence and reduce uncertainty about their intentions behind decisions on basing and operations in the Western Pacific region. These are measures that can be adopted consistent with sustaining the military presence central to demonstrating American resolve in protecting the vital interests of the United States and its allies, a presence that also benefits China because it contributes to regional stability.

Although China from time to time objects to current U.S. basing arrangements as a relic of the Cold War and inconsistent with the "new major power relationship" its leaders advocate, the current situation is not a major source of friction. But future developments could pose a greater risk of stoking strategic mistrust and potentially even conflict. This danger is most evident in considering the question of the role of U.S. military forces in a unified Korean peninsula. As we discuss in chapter 6, the prospect of U.S. forces on China's border following Korean unification would be deeply unsettling to China's leaders. At the same time, it is conceivable that a unified Korea will want to maintain a security tie, backed up with at least a limited U.S. presence, as a counterweight to its large neighbors. As we discussed, this tension could have a significant impact not only on long term diplomacy but, equally important, for the handling of an unexpected crisis. For this reason, it would be desirable now for the United States and China to begin to discuss future arrangements. The United States and the Republic of Korea could make clear that they would be willing to limit voluntarily the scale and location of U.S. forces following unification to provide reassurance of their intentions toward China. China, in turn, should accept the basic proposition that the choice of future security arrangements (including arrangements for hosting foreign forces on a permanent or rotational basis) is the right of a sovereign, unified Korea. These cannot be fully binding commitments, as the precise circumstances in which such future basing might take place cannot yet be specified. Drawing on the experience of German unification, and in the absence of a Chinese threat to the ROK, the United States and the ROK could indicate to Chinese interlocutors that any future postunification U.S. presence (if Seoul ultimately wanted it at all) would be confined south of the 38th parallel and be smaller in size than current U.S. forces in Korea. Indeed it might be focused on capabilities such as infantry training for multilateral stabilization or peace operations that could even sometimes involve PLA forces in joint exercises and operations.

This kind of contingent dialogue would be challenging in advance of unification, particularly in public or formal channels. Each side would have reasons to avoid commitments until absolutely necessary. But leaving the discussion until the problem actually arises incurs costs and risks as well. Quieter dialogues—Track 2 discussions among academics and former officials, as well as so-called Track 1.5 dialogues that also involve some current officials but acting in their "individual capacities"— could lay the groundwork for more official government to government understandings.

There is also value in agreeing on limits on future new basing arrangements, as mutually reinforcing unilateral measures. It is not inconceivable that someday the United States might consider homeporting an aircraft carrier in Hawaii or Guam as a cost-saving measure, for example. But the United States could make clear it does not intend to base a carrier in a new overseas country, as long as China itself takes steps to reassure the United States and its neighbors, for example, through agreeing to a Code of Conduct for maritime operations in the South China Sea and limiting its more assertive military deployments in contested waters. This restraint would be particularly important in connection with sensitive potential basing opportunities, such as Cam Ranh Bay in Vietnam. At a military operational level, each side might be tempted to pursue such bases, but the practical military benefits are probably not worth the strategic cost given the tensions that could result.

Still, the United States should exercise caution in agreeing to limit future basing and related operations, given the need to reassure allies through a demonstration of sustained U.S. resolve, as well as to achieve needed efficiencies. Consider, for example, the U.S. Navy's interest in doing more "crew swaps" abroad, flying in one ship crew to relieve another. As a means of improving the efficiency and economy of America's naval fleet, it may be a wise option for the future in light of budget constraints, and so Washington would need to explain that while it was willing to forgo more forward homeports if China does the same, it might seek to pursue greater use of the sea-swap option and otherwise make modest changes in existing operational practices.

On balance, the situation with regard to major bases in the Western Pacific region should not be unsettling. American bases are not growing greatly in capability or the hypothetical threat they might pose to China. Nor are American allies clamoring for substantially more permanent American basing. That is unlikely to change unless China is seen as highly threatening by regional states in the future. And China has yet to embark on establishing permanent foreign bases, even if Beijing does pursue new access opportunities in places like Burma, Bangladesh, Pakistan, Oman, Yemen, and Sri Lanka. Should China fail to take the kinds of measures of reassurance we suggest in this book to preserve this relatively benign current dynamic, decisions by the United States and its allies to alter the status quo would be justified not as hostility toward China but rather as an appropriate response to China's own ambiguity about its intentions.

But the situation is different with regard to day-to-day employments of forces. Here, the situation is more problematic and more in need of action by both sides to address what is increasingly a source of friction between the two countries.

The United States, despite military downsizing and economic challenges at home, remains active in the region, in order to demonstrate its determination to meet alliance obligations and its more general commitment to the principle of free transit in major global waterways. China, largely as a natural outgrowth of a strengthening economy and military, is becoming more active in those waterways, and further afield, it is participating in the international counterpiracy mission in the Gulf of Aden, carrying out a dozen military exercises a year with others of late, and becoming much more assertive in regard to disputed islands in the South and East China seas.

As a result, the interactions between the militaries of the United States and China have become increasingly precarious in recent years. The issues of concern range from American armed and unarmed reconnaissance patrols just off China's coasts (including in waters China considers "sensitive," such as the Yellow Sea) to China's increasingly assertive use of military power over disputed islands in the South and East China seas and surrounding waterways to the trailing and tracking of each other's military assets.

American withdrawal from the areas which China considers "sensitive" or territorial is not a viable solution to avoiding this growing friction. America has important alliances in these areas. It has rights under international norms of maritime access (even if the United States has not ratified the Law of the Sea Treaty itself, which weakens its legitimacy in seeking to justify U.S. actions). The United States also sees a value, and virtue, in maintaining its presence in a continuous way through the use of visible military assets (rather than employing less visible means). Its allies generally concur with this approach, as do many neutral states.

Much of U.S. operational activity in northeast Asia is associated with the ongoing security threat posed by North Korea. This includes regular joint U.S.-ROK exercises, like Ulchi Freedom Guardian, and ad hoc exercises and deployments during crisis, for example, after the North Korean shelling of Yeonpyeong Island in 2010. Although these exercises are not directed at China, they cause considerable concern in Beijing, both because they lead to enhanced U.S. military capabilities in the region and because they often take place in areas, like the Yellow Sea, which are sensitive to China given the region's geographic proximity to Beijing and its history as an invasion route for past enemies.[30] From Washington's perspective, asserting its prerogatives to sail in international waters in the Yellow Sea was a less destabilizing response to demonstrate U.S. resolve toward North Korea compared with more escalatory alternative responses to North Korean provocations of 2010. To enhance strategic reassurance, the United States should provide advance notification to Beijing of U.S. intentions and operations of this type of "show of force" near Chinese borders.[31] Notification not only can help dispel uncertainties but could contribute to the intended goal of sending a clear message to North Korea of U.S. and allied resolve.

Routine armed and unarmed U.S. patrols near Chinese coasts are another source of political friction because they reinforce Chinese skeptics' view of U.S. intentions and they run a risk of accidental confrontation. These missions are frequent, as can be inferred by the number of dedicated reconnaissance aircraft deployed to Okinawa and other key locations for such purposes (typically a dozen or more at any time).[32] In assessing whether there are steps that could be taken to provide reassurance, it is important to keep in mind the long-term consequences of these operations as well as their near-term tactical benefits. For example, the PLA Navy and Air Force could mimic them—if not necessarily near American shores, then increasingly near Japan and other U.S. allies.[33] As Zbigniew Brzezinski notes, aerial reconnaissance missions pose serious risks of unintentional collisions, since the Chinese often respond by deploying their own fighter planes for up-close inspections or harassment.[34]

Chinese interlocutors increasingly cite concerns about the American presence near the PRC in official interactions (such as the recently established Strategic Security Dialogue) in light of the Chinese perception that it has increased over the last two decades. First the end of the Cold War freed up a higher percentage of American naval assets for monitoring the seas near China (even as the total number of U.S. assets declined); then the Pentagon moved more of its submarine fleet to the Asia-Pacific region; then Secretary of Defense Panetta announced in his 2012 Shangri-La speech that 60 percent of American naval power in general would be based in Pacific waters. As noted, the cumulative effect of these changes may not be great, but there have been a number of them.

Beyond these broad changes, specific interactions between the two sides have produced dangers in the past as well. In 2001, a U.S. Navy EP-3 aircraft was intercepted by a Chinese fighter aircraft, an encounter that led to the accidental death of the Chinese pilot. In 2009, Chinese military assets challenged the U.S. Navy's *Impeccable* and *Victorious* vessels. In 2013, a Chinese vessel maneuvered dangerously close to the U.S.S. *Cowpens*, which was observing China's new carrier in international waters.[35]

The U.S.-China tensions that arise from these dynamics are unlikely to be resolved by an American decision to reduce substantially its regional military activities. Although some scholars and members of Congress have urged the United States to alter its strategy and reduce its military footprint by adopting an approach of "offshore balancing," leading voices in both parties advocate a sustained American presence for reasons that make good strategic sense.[36] Similarly, China's growing naval and air capabilities, along with expanding economic interests, suggest that China is unlikely to dramatically reverse course and reduce its operational activities in these areas.

But despite these inherent tensions, there are steps that both sides can take consistent with current strategies and operational concepts that can reduce the risk of accidental confrontation and increase trust about the underlying purposes of these activities. One potential area for confidence building involves U.S. reconnaissance in and around Chinese territory.

The Open Skies Treaty may provide a useful model. Signed in 1992 and entered into force in 2002, it involves thirty-four members or former members of the Warsaw Pact and NATO. Aircraft involved in the operations are unarmed but equipped with visual, infrared, and radar sensors. Typically the United States hosts six to eight flights a year by Russia while conducting fourteen to sixteen flights a year over Russia. In total, the

United States and Russia are required to accept up to forty-two overflights of their territory annually if requested. Although signed after the Cold War and implemented a full decade after that, the treaty is still notable for the transparency and openness it codifies and facilitates. Russia and the United States still have complex relations on matters such as nuclear security, missile defense, and at times even crisis management (as with Georgia in 2008), so their willingness to allow such overflights over their respective territories is significant. As such it could be a useful model for the U.S.-China relationship in the future.[37] Certainly given the degree of openness of American society—as well as the extent of existing Chinese intelligence activities on American soil through other means—this should not be an unreasonable idea for Washington to consider. For the United States, it could reduce somewhat the need for the airborne reconnaissance missions near Chinese territory that presently tend to lead to the Chinese scrambling of escort aircraft.

That said, open skies arrangements cannot satisfy all U.S. reconnaissance needs. Traditional methods will surely continue to be required as well, since open skies observations are predictable in time and limited in number. American ships and aircraft conducting reconnaissance near China's coasts need to keep up that mission to an extent. If satellites can do more of the work, that might be preferable, but some forward missions will still be needed.

Other steps the United States can consider to reduce frictions include conducting reconnaissance with unarmed or lightly armed systems. It could also limit mock penetrations of Chinese airspace (flying right up to PRC territorial airspace before having planes change course). Certain unmanned aerial vehicles and, in the future, unmanned underwater vehicles could be configured to operate entirely without armaments.

This kind of understanding probably cannot be formalized because it cannot be easily verified given the sensitivity of some American operational practices. It could instead be done informally, in a manner similar to George H. W. Bush's decision back in the early 1990s to announce that the United States would cease deploying tactical nuclear weapons on ships as a routine matter. Bush's announcement was intended in part to elicit Soviet reciprocity and was successful in that regard. In this case, China does not routinely operate armed platforms near American coasts, so the main benefit would be to lower tensions in the Western Pacific while also reducing the scope of any future Chinese temptation to mirror America's deployment patterns with armed patrols near America's West Coast.

But even if these ideas are adopted, American and Chinese ships and planes will sometimes come into proximity with each other. So it is important to consider how their close encounters, involving not just military vessels but possibly others as well, might be conducted in the least risky way possible.

By analogy with the U.S.-Soviet Incidents at Sea (INCSEA) agreement in 1972, the United States and China could agree to set guidelines to avoid threatening or otherwise dangerous approaches between the naval forces of the two sides. INCSEA reaffirms the 1958 Geneva Convention on the High Seas, as well as the International Code of Signals, applicable to all states. It acknowledges that forces will conduct reconnaissance of each other but expects them to do so from a safe distance. It prohibits the mock firing of weapons at each other or the use of high-power beams to disrupt each other's navigation. It requires notification of submarine operations when they are exercising in proximity to other ships. It requires general notification of dangerous activities like weapons tests. It further requires prudence in aircraft carrier operations, including expecting ships not to obstruct or interfere with the operations of the other nation's aircraft carriers.[38] It made a real difference for the better in reducing dangerous encounters at sea.[39] The advantages of this type of agreement to reducing distrust and avoiding unintended confrontation between the United States and China are apparent.

Any understanding would have to take into account the specific character of U.S.-China maritime frictions. Chinese ships that can be sources of conflict are often not naval vessels but those of private fishermen, merchantmen, or other government agencies, so consideration needs to be given to how to include their activities, building on Sino-American cooperation in enforcing fishing laws and conducting search-and-rescue exercises together. (The Chinese might agree not to arm such vessels with anything more than light weaponry needed for their standard and traditional missions, moreover, as part of such an accord or separately.) These cooperative activities have included the U.S. Coast Guard, the China Fishery Law Enforcement Command, and the Chinese Maritime Safety Administration among other entities.[40]

Some may argue that the multilateral International Regulations for Preventing Collisions at Sea already provides the necessary ground rules for avoiding dangerous encounters. But that accord does not relate to vessels that have incentives to shadow or otherwise trail or even provoke each other. Codifying rules of restraint for such vessels could in fact be useful.[41]

Agreements for mutual observation of military exercises are another important avenue for enhancing trust. Here, too, the NATO-Warsaw Pact Cold War experience provides a precedent, this time through the activities of the Organization for Security and Cooperation in Europe (OSCE)—which even today continues to organize more than one hundred annual inspections by the parties to the organization, on each other's territories for confidence building purposes.[42] Already today, the two countries occasionally observe each other's exercises. During his September 2012 visit to China, Secretary Panetta invited a Chinese warship to join a U.S.-led multilateral exercise off the coast of Hawaii known as RIMPAC in 2014. The two countries have exchanged port calls, though these have declined to an average of less than one a year and should be increased. China and the United States participate together in the Gulf of Aden counterpiracy mission. And in 2012, China and the United States conducted a joint command and control exercise simulating a response to a humanitarian disaster.

These kinds of efforts can be broadened and deepened. Other joint activities could be expanded, including joint participation in humanitarian operations and support for UN missions, which would allow for routine U.S.-China interactions on types of operations that would not compromise high-technology secrets on either side but could build working relationships and even some trust. It would also allow their largest respective military services, their armies, to develop working relationships in ways that might be easier than for their navies or air forces.

What about stronger naval cooperation? Some see the Gulf of Aden counterpiracy mission as a useful precedent that could lead to further collaborative steps in light of the two sides' complementary interests in ensuring that sea-lanes are safe for trade.

The Gulf of Aden counterpiracy mission is indeed going well. But it is against a localized threat and a very low-tech one. Each participating navy can basically take a zone of responsibility without having to coordinate air and missile defense, targeting data, most satellite communications, or antisubmarine warfare efforts. Similar forms of naval cooperation elsewhere might be useful, even in the South China Sea and other contentious areas so long as there is a clear understanding that zones of responsibility do not represent an acknowledgment of right to exclusive control. But it will be difficult to cooperate with China on higher-end operations. Doing so would require linking or at least deconflicting air defense, missile defense, and antisubmarine defense operations. The United States would have to worry about protecting sensitive information, and the PLA would be unlikely to wish to reveal its own current capabilities (or in some cases its enduring weaknesses) for such operations.

Still, this fact need not preclude concerted efforts to pursue areas of cooperation in simpler missions. Beyond counterpiracy efforts, there may be opportunities in coordinating coverage of various geographic zones for maritime search and rescue of fishermen or seafarers, in counternarcotics and counterterrorism missions. A U.S. Navy officer and former Brookings fellow, Lt. Cdr. Audry Oxley, has proposed that the United States invite China to join the annual twenty-nation PANAMEX exercise that posits a threat to the Panama Canal.[43] The OSCE model of notification and observation of exercises could be extended to maritime activities in cases where actual participation was not desired. As with our suggestion about advance notice of weapons tests, this type of consultation would of course only contribute to reassurance if it increased transparency rather than becoming a forum for pitched debate about which kinds of tests and exercises were acceptable and appropriate.

CONCLUSION

The day-to-day operations and basing arrangements of the U.S. military and PLA in the Western Pacific are increasing sources of tension between the two sides. Each views the other's activities as a manifestation of hostile intent, while viewing its own efforts as central to its national security (and in the case of the United States, to sustaining alliance commitments). Some friction is inevitable, since neither is prepared to accede fully to the optimal objectives of the other. The United States needs an active, robust presence to reassure its allies and to sustain its ability to operate effectively if a crisis should develop, actions that inevitably pose at least the appearance of potential threat to China. China's increasing capabilities and expanding economic political interests will inevitably lead to greater activity and presence beyond China's adjacent waters—and even beyond the Western Pacific. Though these tensions are inevitable, this chapter suggests that there are modest measures each side can take—including limits on any new bases, creative approaches to reconnaissance, and clearer rules of the road on forward operations—to provide strategic reassurance and reduce the risk of inadvertent conflict without undercutting vital national interests.

9

Conclusion

There is a growing recognition by both policymakers and analysts that the U.S.-China relationship is at a crossroads. The largely amicable relations that characterized strategic interactions between the two during the first forty years after Nixon's historic visit lie in the past—and there is a growing apprehension on both sides of the Pacific that the best days may be behind. These fears are well grounded. Indeed, unless the United States and China recognize the dangers created by their inherently competitive and dynamic relationship and develop a deliberate strategy and associated policies to address those risks, these apprehensions may well become reality for the reasons we discuss at length in this book.

Strategic reassurance is a necessary, but not sufficient, element of a comprehensive strategy. Each side must be prepared to do what it can to reassure the other of its cooperative intentions—but at the same time, each will need to demonstrate that it has the necessary will and capacity to defend its vital interests if necessary. Put another way, *strategic resolve* is the necessary complement to *strategic reassurance*.

While each side must do its part to make this strategy succeed, in our view China, as the rising power, has a special responsibility to demonstrate to its neighbors, the United States, and the wider international community that its pursuit of national security will not come at the expense of others. After all, the United States has shown through its policies and action over the past forty years its willingness to support China's emergence as an economic and political power. China now needs to act in ways that reinforce the continued wisdom of the U.S. approach. For the United States, as the more powerful nation, the challenge is not to alter its course prematurely in the absence of concrete reasons to do so, simply because

China is becoming stronger, and to draw on its longer experience in crisis management and arms control to light the path forward.

Pursuing strategic reassurance comprises several key elements. First, the two sides must endeavor to understand each other's self-images and national security narratives; many high-level policymakers have done so effectively in the years since the famous opening of the 1970s, but a different generation in both countries is gradually taking over and this generation needs to develop the same awareness. Second, each country must look for ways to limit its rivalrous behavior under normal peacetime conditions, even as it also seeks to project strategic resolve and champion its own country's interests. Should major disagreements erupt between the two countries, they must adopt strategies that keep the door open to peaceful resolution and deescalation, avoiding brinkmanship behavior that evokes Schelling's famous phrase of the "threat that leaves something to chance."

The preceding chapters have laid out a number of concrete steps that the United States and China can take in the coming years to reduce the risk of arms racing and conflict. They are summarized in appendix A. Taken individually, many of these actions may seem modest in contrast with the stakes involved. But they should be seen as illustrative of a broader approach, and, taken together, they serve three complementary purposes. First, to provide reassurance that each side does not seek to achieve security at the other's expense. Second, to provide ample time to allow either side to adjust its strategy if the other's intentions prove to be less benign—without requiring premature hedging that would induce self-fulfilling responses predicated on fears of hostile intent. Third, by avoiding premature hedging, to create an opportunity for both sides to work on the positive side of the ledger—deepening cooperation on a broad range of issues of common interest—that, over time, will raise the barrier to conflict by demonstrating the concrete benefits of collaboration. None of these steps requires either to side to rely on benign assumptions about the other's intentions, either short or long term. Nor do they require conceding vital interests, including in the case of the United States, commitments to allies' security. Thus as we have stressed, strategic reassurance is a way of dispelling misperceptions and clarifying what is and is not in real dispute between the two sides.

Throughout this book, we have seen that strategic reassurance can emerge from the creative use of four core elements: restraint, reinforcement, transparency, and resilience. The judicious exercise of *restraint*—forgoing actions that may be misinterpreted as threatening—is a powerful tool for signaling intentions. For this reason we have suggested a number of areas where each side should exercise restraint in both weapons development (such as nuclear weapons, missile defense, and antisatellite capabilities) and operations (basing and exercises). We recognize, however, that restraint runs the risk of being misperceived as a sign of weakness (not only by the other country but by domestic audiences as well). Therefore, *reinforcement* is a vital adjunct: by undertaking reciprocal steps in response to the other's restraint, a virtuous cycle can be initiated that will build confidence, as can be seen in proposals to link actions by each side in areas such as strategic systems and doctrine. *Transparency* not only is a way of dispelling uncertainties about capabilities but also can help give the other side adequate warning of changing intentions (from open skies to observations of exercises), thus reducing the risk of breakout and lowering the potential dangers from unilateral restraint. *Resilience*, too, lowers the risk of exercising restraint and, most important, reduces the need to resort to preemptive or escalatory measures, thus increasing crisis stability and avoidance of conflict through inadvertence (cyber is a particularly powerful domain that exemplifies the stability-enhancing value of enhanced resilience). Strategic *resolve* is important too—each side must clearly identify and communicate its fundamental interests so that deterrence failure does not result from a lack of clarity about them.

This discussion has also shown the limits of confidence building. These steps will prove highly valuable if—but only if—each side is convinced that it cannot achieve its goals unilaterally. In other words, both sides must be convinced that their relationship resembles what game theorists call the prisoners' dilemma. If they cooperate, both sides will achieve their best outcome, but if one unilaterally seeks to improve its position at the other's expense, the second will take steps in response that ultimately will make both sides worse off.

There are powerful reasons to believe that this model accurately characterizes the U.S.-China relationship. China's economic success and growing nationalism mean that China likely will possess both the means and the will to resist U.S. unilateral steps to sustain its primacy in its past form and to hold China vulnerable. Conversely, the United States possesses enormous military capability. Its capacity for technological innovation and the support of key actors in the region suggest that Washington will not accept any Chinese attempts to establish a sort of East Asian Monroe Doctrine that would drive the United States out of the region. If both sides share this perception of a possible negative and dangerous interactive dynamic, they will have a powerful incentive to avoid moving down this slippery slope. The policies we suggest—in their broad philosophies and in their specifics—can help them achieve that.

If, by contrast, either or both misjudge the other's capacity or intentions, the tragedy of the prisoners' dilemma could become a reality. This could come about as a result of an exaggerated sense by each side of its own future capabilities—or an underestimation of the will or capacity of the other. For example, should Chinese strategists become persuaded that the United States is in decline or embracing more isolationist policies, they may be tempted to believe that they could prevail in a head-to-head competition. Similarly, should the United States become convinced that flaws in China's political system or adverse demographics will limit China's ability to keep pace with determined U.S. military modernization, American planners might try to apply what might be called the "Reagan" narrative concerning the end of the Cold War—that the U.S.-Soviet arms race bankrupted the USSR and brought about an era of unipolarity.

A similar result would prevail if either or both sides underweighted the value of cooperation. In game theory terms, if the payoff for cooperation is seen as low (in comparison to the benefits of dominance), the temptation to achieve unilateral security (even if it jeopardized cooperation) would be higher. This might happen if either or both sides became convinced that the prospects for cooperation on nonsecurity issues (economic growth, climate change, etc.) were low or even zero sum in nature. It might also happen if the compromises needed to sustain cooperation were unattractive (e.g., for China, indefinite postponement of unification with Taiwan; for the United States, acceptance of limitations on U.S. military deployments in a unified Korea or continually growing Chinese military presence in the Western Pacific) or if the "payoff" for unilateral hegemony seemed very high in comparison to the benefits of cooperation.

In making these judgments it will be important to consider not only the absolute value to each side of the result achieved either from cooperation or competition but also the probability that each side attaches to being able to achieve that result. Again, to take some examples, each side might judge that the value of cooperation is high but the probability of achieving it (owing to, for example, domestic politics) is low, so the "expected value" is unattractive compared to other alternatives.

The challenge is further complicated because there may be multiple compromises that are ultimately acceptable to both sides but are more or less desirable for each. Put another way, the "pie" may be larger as a result of cooperation (in economists' jargon, cooperation is "Pareto superior"), but how the larger pie should be divided might still be a matter of contention. And though rational actors would generally prefer those pie-splitting outcomes to conflict, the real world suggests that relative gains and losses may color the ability to achieve the necessary compromises, particularly when filtered through the lens of domestic politics. To take an example from recent U.S.-China interactions, the agreement that led to China's accession to the WTO benefits both countries, but many in China believe that the last-minute concessions demanded by Washington undercut the value of the deal, while constituencies in the United States feel the terms were too lenient. The recent effort to avoid a conflict between the Philippines and China is another example; a dangerous conflict was defused, but some in the United States argued that it came in the form of "too high a price" by pressuring the Philippines to withdraw from Scarborough Shoal.

Taking all of this together, the measures we suggest can work if (1) both sides can envision an end state that is (in the best case) an outcome that both sides highly value but (at a minimum) that each "can live with"; (2) they understand the adverse consequences associated with failure to achieve that end state and see such an outcome as worse than the compromises needed to achieve cooperation; and (3) they are in a position to implement the necessary decisions to bring it about. This discussion points to another overarching factor that is familiar to students of game theory: the necessity of deep and candid dialogue. The prisoners' dilemma is only a dilemma when the two prisoners are not allowed to communicate and coordinate their positions; where communication is possible, the optimal outcome is much easier to achieve.

This dialogue must be both strategic and tactical. On the strategic level, both Beijing and Washington must be able to articulate a vision of the future that takes into account each side's vital security interests, in a way that is at least potentially acceptable to its partner. But it must also communicate a firm intention, backed up by capability, to resist the other's attempt to achieve security at its partner's expense. This cannot be simply a matter of abstractions. To date, Chinese professions of a peaceful rise and the parallel American support for a strong and prosperous China have done little to dispel mutual suspicions. That is why the dialogue must address each of the potential elements of conflict, to give credibility to the prospect of an end state—or at least a constructive and reasonably stable ongoing process, likely to last decades as the two world giants establish a new modus vivendi for the twenty-first century—that meets both sides' fundamental concerns. The Strategic Security Dialogue, inaugurated in 2011, is an important framework for these discussions but over time must be able to deliver concrete results as well as candid discussion.

To say that such an optimistic outcome can be achieved is not a guarantee that it will. But it is an important antidote to structural pessimism and, we hope, a spur to policymakers in both countries to redouble their efforts to bring it about. The sheer magnitude of the rise of China, in the face of America's continued power and global network of alliances, is indeed unprecedented in the history of nations. But so too could be the accomplishment of these giants of the twenty-first century in showing that an established superpower and a rising superpower need not allow their relationship to produce hegemonic rivalry or major war.

Appendix A:
Summary of Specific Recommendations

DEFENSE BUDGETS, WEAPONS MODERNIZATION, AND MILITARY DOCTRINE
- For China, level off military budget growth as military budget approaches 50 percent of the U.S. level.
- For the United States, adapt Air-Sea Battle to Air-Sea Operations, and for China, limit development and deployment of antiship ballistic missiles and similar prompt attack capabilities to reduce the risk of preemption and quick escalation in crisis.
- For the United States, restrain modernization and deployment of long-range strike systems, especially precision conventional strike (missiles, bombers, and emerging technologies).
- Mutually show restraint regarding Taiwan: scaling back PRC missile deployments and other military capacities directed at Taiwan to be followed by appropriate adjustments in U.S. arms sales to Taiwan reflecting the reduced threat.
- For the United States, declare that national missile defense systems will not be sized or configured to threaten China's nuclear deterrent.
- Mutually provide advance notification of major tests of advanced weapons.

CONTINGENCIES
- Dialogue and conduct notional contingency planning for upheaval and instability in North Korea, to include measures for security of North Korea's nuclear systems and infrastructure.
- For the United States and ROK, in post Korea-unification scenarios, underscore willingness to forgo U.S. forces stationed north of 38th parallel in return for China's commitment to abide by Seoul's decisions on hosting foreign forces and security alliances.

- For the United States, develop operational strategies to contain escalation in a Taiwan contingency (no early attacks on PRC homeland or ports, possible pressure on Chinese sea lines of communication if PRC blockades Taiwan), while retaining capacity to support Taiwan in resisting coercion.
- For China, commit to exclusively peaceful means toward Taiwan in response to U.S. commitment not to support unilateral Taiwanese declaration of independence
- For the United States, for South China Sea and East China Sea scenarios, develop asymmetrical responses to possible Chinese aggression (including restrictions on Chinese shipping, economic measures, new bases, and enhanced security support to allies).
- For China, join ASEAN Code of Conduct, including a commitment not to use or threaten force to resolve territorial disputes; restrict operations of armed combatants in disputed waters.
- For the United States and China, provide advance notice of military exercises and deployments in the South China Sea and East China Sea.

Nuclear/Space/Cyber
- For China, agree to cap deployment of nuclear warheads in conjunction with next U.S.-Russia agreement for roughly 50 percent warhead cuts.
- For the United States, as noted, offer greater transparency on missile defenses and a commitment not to develop a national missile defense capable of neutralizing the Chinese deterrent.
- For the United States, cap development and deployments of long-range precision-strike capabilities (missiles, bombers, and new technologies) capable of targeting China's nuclear and C^3 capabilities.
- For both, ratify CTBT and agree not to develop new warheads (allowing safety and reliability modification of existing warheads).
- On space, agree to ban collisions/explosions that cause debris above minimal altitudes, ban dedicated antisatellite weapons and tests, ban orbiting weapons for use against Earth, and adopt satellite keep-out zones as well as advance launch notices.

- On cyber, agree to joint investigation of cyber attacks on civilian targets apparently emanating from each other's territory. For China, adhere to Budapest cyber crime convention. Agree not to target civilian infrastructure.
- Create a cyber risk reduction center, a nuclear risk reduction center, hotlines, and improved resilience measures.

COMMUNICATIONS/RECONNAISSANCE

- Develop open skies arrangement and mutual observation of exercises.
- Use unarmed assets for routine surveillance, agree on limits for close approach to other side's surveillance aircraft and vessels.
- Create dedicated military-to-military hotline and Incidents at Sea accord (for all vessels).
- Expand joint peace and humanitarian operations.

Appendix B:
Naval Vessels of the United States and China

TABLE B.1. Major naval ships of China and the United States

China	Number	U.S.	Number
SUBMARINES		SUBMARINES	
Strategic	4	Strategic	14
Tactical	61	Tactical	58
Total:	65	Total:	72
PRINCIPAL SURFACE COMBATANTS		PRINCIPAL SURFACE COMBATANTS	
Aircraft carriers	1	Aircraft carriers	11
		Cruisers	22
Destroyers	14	Destroyers	62
Frigates	62	Frigates	13
		LCS	3
Total:	77	Total	110
MINE WARFARE		MINE WARFARE	
Placement vessels	1	Placement/	
Countermeasure	46	Countermeasure	13
Total:	47	Total:	13
AMPHIBIOUS SHIPS		AMPHIBIOUS SHIPS	
Principal vessels	2	Principal vessels	30
Landing ships	85	(Amphibious craft)	269+
(Landing craft)	151		
Total:	87	Total:	30
LOGISTICS AND SUPPORT		FLEET SUPPORT	
Total:	205	Total:	19

(continued)

TABLE B.1. *(continued)*

China	Number	U.S.	Number
		COMBAT LOGISTICS	
		Total:	34
		NAVAL RESERVE	
		Total:	5

Source: International Institute for Strategic Studies, *The Military Balance 2013* (New York: Routledge, 2013), 74–75, 289–90; Naval Vessel Register, "Ship Battle Forces," http://www .nvr.navy.mil/nvrships/sbf/fleet.htm.

Note: Coastal combatants are not included as part of the U.S. Navy, therefore we have not listed them for China above. However, a conflict with China would possibly involve PLA coastal boats. These are mainly smaller ships, and include 76+ fast guided missile boats, 26 guided missile craft, 75 antiship missile boats, and 34+ patrol boats. We have also listed amphibious craft for each country, but they are not included in U.S. major ship counts. A number of Military Sealift Command (MSC) ships are included above, they are logistics and special operations related. About 140 other ships are part of MSC, and can be activated within a few days to a month. Strategic Sealift and Ready Reserve are included in that count.

U.S. amhibious vessels range from 16,000 to 40,000 tons each, carrying between 750 and 2,000 troops and/or equipment. By comparison, the principal vessels of the PLA Navy are roughly 20,000 tons each, with landing ships mostly between 1,000 and 5,000 tons.

Roughly 60 percent of the U.S. Navy is to be based in the Pacific Ocean.

Notes

CHAPTER 1: INTRODUCTION

1. Remarks of Secretary of State Hillary Rodham Clinton at the U.S. Institute of Peace China Conference, Washington, D.C., March 7, 2012, http://www.state.gov/secretary/rm/2012/03/185402.htm.

2. See, for example, the opening comments by President Obama, "Remarks by President Obama and President Xi Jinping of the People's Republic of China before Bilateral Meeting," Sunnylands Retreat, Palm Springs, California, June 7, 2013, http://www.whitehouse.gov/the-press-office/2013/06/07/remarks-president -obama-and-president-xi-jinping-peoples-republic-china.

3. One formulation of this was expressed at the Sunnylands, California, summit in June 2013, where Chinese President Xi Jinping stated, "We need to think creatively and act energetically so that working together we can build a new model of major country relationship." See "Remarks by President Obama and President Xi Jinping of the People's Republic of China before Bilateral Meeting." For a slightly different "new great power relationship" formulation, see Christian Amanpour, "A Rare Look over the Great Wall: Interview with PRC Ambassador to the United States Cui Tiankai," *cnn.com*, July 8, 2013, http://amanpour.blogs.cnn .com/2013/07/08/a-rare-look-over-the-great-wall.

4. Department of State, "Remarks with Chinese Foreign Minister Yang Jiechi and Secretary of State Hillary Rodham Clinton," Beijing, China, September 5, 2012, http://www.state.gov/secretary/rm/2012/09/197343.htm.

5. See, for example, John J. Mearsheimer, *The Tragedy of Great Power Politics* (New York: W. W. Norton, 2001); and, somewhat less deterministically, Robert Gilpin, *War and Change in World Politics* (Cambridge: Cambridge University Press, 1981).

6. Thucydides, *History of the Peloponnesian War* (New York: Viking Press, 1986), 49 (corresponding to book 1, passage 23 in the original).

7. China's leaders, too, are conscious of this historic legacy. In a speech at the Brookings Institution on September 20, 2013, Chinese Foreign Minister Wang Yi observed: "According to some study of history, there have been about 15 cases of rise of emerging powers. In 11 cases, confrontation and war broke out between the

emerging and established powers." Wang Yi, *Toward a New Model of Major Country Relations between China and the United States*, September 20, 2013, China.org.cn.

8. The White House, "National Security Strategy of the United States," September 2002, p. 30, http://www.state.gov/documents/organization/63562.pdf.

9. See, for example, Justin Vaisse, *Neoconservatism: The Biography of a Movement* (Cambridge, MA: Harvard University Press, 2010), 224–25; Robert Kagan, *The World America Made* (New York: Alfred A. Knopf, 2012); and Aaron L. Friedberg, *A Contest for Supremacy: China, America, and the Struggle for Mastery in Asia* (New York: W. W. Norton, 2011), 266.

10. For example, Rear Admiral Zhang Zhaozhong has stated that the United States would "run like a rabbit" if China went to war with Japan over the Diaoyu Islands and otherwise counseled a more confrontational approach toward the United States. See David Lague, "Special Report: China's Military Hawks Take the Offensive," *Reuters.com*, January 17, 2013, http://www.reuters.com/article/2013/01/17/us-china-hawks-idUSBRE90G00C20130117.

11. See, for example, Robert Axelrod, *The Evolution of Cooperation* (New York: Basic Books, 1984), 7–10, 17–19, 92–113.

12. Robert Jervis, *Perception and Misperception in International Politics* (Princeton: Princeton University Press, 1976), 62–67. Jervis draws on Herbert Butterfield's *History and Human Relations* (London: Collins, 1951) for the term. Jervis calls it the spiral model. "When states seek the ability to defend themselves, they get too much and too little—too much because they gain the ability to carry out aggression; too little because others, being menaced, will increase their own arms and so reduce the first state's security." Jervis explicitly makes the connection to the "prisoner's dilemma."

13. See, for example, Robert O. Keohane, *After Hegemony: Cooperation and Discord in the World Political Economy* (Princeton: Princeton University Press, 1984); G. John Ikenberry, *Liberal Leviathan: The Origins, Crisis, and Transformation of the American World Order* (Princeton: Princeton University Press, 2011); Bernard Brodie, *The Absolute Weapon: Atomic Power and World Order* (New York: Harcourt, 1946); and McGeorge Bundy, *Danger and Survival: Choices about the Bomb in the First Fifty Years* (New York: Random House, 1988). This view has been put forth by Chinese officials as well. In arguing that the past record of conflict between rising and established powers does not apply to U.S.-China relations, Foreign Minister Wang Yi observed, in his September 2013 Brookings speech: " we now live in a different world. China and the United States . . . are part of a community of shared interests. Countries are increasingly interconnected. Neither of us will benefit from confrontation" (*Toward a New Model*).

14. See Aaron L. Friedberg, "The Future of US-China Relations: Is Conflict Inevitable?" *International Security* 30, no. 2 (Autumn 2005): 7–45. Friedberg offers a comprehensive review of how the various schools of international theory view the likely trajectory of U.S.-China relations. He observes that there are two dominant

views with adherents both in the United States and in China: "realist pessimists," who view conflict likely because of China's rising power or the operation of the security dilemma, and "liberal optimists," who expect enhanced U.S.-China cooperation as a result of economic interdependence, the process of democratization in China, and the influence of international institutions. But he also sees other permutations: "realist optimists," who focus on the barriers China faces in sustaining economic growth and military modernization or who argue that the coming U.S.-China bipolarity can be as stable as the mature U.S.-Soviet relationship; and "liberal pessimists," who believe that a more democratic China may become more assertively nationalistic. The latter draws on the work of Edward Mansfield and Jack Snyder, "Democratization and the Danger of War," *International Security* 20, no. 1 (Summer 1995): 5–38. Friedberg also considers "constructivist optimists," who believe that China's international engagement will shape its strategic culture and prevailing norms in ways that favor cooperation. On the latter, see, for example, Alastair Ian Johnston and Paul Evans, "China's Engagement with Multilateral Security Institutions," in Johnston and Robert S. Ross, eds., *Engaging China: The Management of an Emerging Power* (New York: Routledge, 1999), 265. Finally, Friedberg identifies "constructivist pessimists," who focus on the clashing strategic cultures of each side and their deep-seated suspicions of the other's norms and behavior on the international stage. See also Thomas J. Christensen, "The Advantages of an Assertive China: Responding to Beijing's Abrasive Diplomacy," *Foreign Affairs* 90, no. 2 (March/April 2011); and Charles L. Glaser, *Rational Theory of International Politics* (Princeton: Princeton University Press, 2010).

15. For a similar argument about the importance of contingency in assessing the future of China's policy, see Jeffrey W. Legro, "What China Will Want: The Future Intentions of a Rising Power," *Perspectives on Politics* (September 2007): 515–34, http://www.apsanet.org/imgtest/popsept07legro.pdf. Goldstein also emphasizes contingency "shaped by the interdependent choices that leaders in Beijing and elsewhere, especially Washington, make during the coming decades." See Avery Goldstein, *Rising to the Challenge: China's Grand Strategy and International Security* (Stanford: Stanford University Press, 2005), 214.

16. See U.S.-China Joint Statement, "The Two Sides Agreed to Work Further to Nurture and Deepen Bilateral Strategic Trust to Enhance Their Relations," January 19, 2011, http://www.whitehouse.gov/the-press-office/2011/01/19/us-china-joint-statement; Jeffrey Bader, *Obama and China's Rise* (Washington, DC: Brookings, 2012).

17. On Kissinger and Nixon, see Henry Kissinger, *White House Years* (Boston: Little, Brown, 1979), 689–784, 1055–87; and the declassified memcons from Kissinger talks with Zhou, reproduced in William Barr, ed., "The Beijing-Washington Backchannel and Henry Kissinger's Secret Trip to China," National Security Archive Electronic Briefing Book No. 66, February 27, 2002, http://www2.gwu.edu/~nsarchiv/NSAEBB/NSAEBB66/.

18. The maxim, attributed to Deng Xiaoping, in Chinese "tao guang yang hui," has been subject to a variety of translations and equally many interpretations. For example, according to Huang Youyi, "observe calmly, secure our position, cope with affairs calmly, hide our capacities and bide our time, be good at maintaining a low profile, and never claim leadership." Huang argues that the phrase should be interpreted as "be self effacing" and asserts "it could never be translated as 'to hide one's ability and pretend to be weak.'" Yet he also acknowledges that "in a classical context, the phrase is used to indicate a strategic ruse." See Huang Youyi, in *Global Times*, June 15, 2011, http://www.globaltimes.cn/DesktopModules /DnnForge%20-%20NewsArticles/Print.aspx?tabid=99&tabmoduleid=94& articleId=661734&moduleId=405&PortalID=0. See also Dai Bingguo, "Stick to the Path of Peaceful Development," *China Daily*, December 13, 2010, http://www .chinadaily.com.cn/opinion/2010–12/13/content_11690133.htm. The former state councillor argued, "Some people misinterpret the Chinese idiom 'keep a low profile and make due contributions.' They take China's announcement of a peaceful development path as a smokescreen for its real intention before it gets strong enough. This is groundless suspicion. That Chinese idiom was quoted from Comrade Deng Xiaoping's remarks from late 1980s to early 1990s, saying that China should keep modest and prudent, not serve as others' leader or a standard bearer and not seek expansion or hegemony."

19. Jervis, *Perception and Misperception*; Thomas C. Schelling, *The Strategy of Conflict*, rev. ed. (Cambridge, MA: Harvard University Press, 1980); Thomas C. Schelling and Morton H. Halperin, *Strategy and Arms Control* (New York: Pergamon-Brassey's, 1975); Thomas C. Schelling, *Arms and Influence* (New Haven: Yale University Press, 1967).

20. For an interesting discussion of the idea of U.S. retrenchment, see Denny Roy's review of Hugh White's recent book, *The China Choice: Why America Should Share Power* (Collingwood, Australia: Black Inc., 2012). Denny Roy, "The Problem with Appeasement," *Survival* 55, no. 3 (June–July 2013): 183–202.

21. Axelrod, *The Evolution of Cooperation*, 20–30, 75–77.

22. See, for example, George W. Breslauer and Philip E. Tetlock, *Learning in U.S. and Soviet Foreign Policy* (Boulder, CO: Westview, 1991). On repeated interactions and learning more generally, see Robert M. Axelrod, *The Evolution of Cooperation* (New York: Basic Books, 2006).

23. There are structural reasons why negotiating agreements may be difficult where parity is absent. From the perspective of the stronger party, any achievable bargain risks looking like a unilateral concession, while for the weaker party, it may appear to lock in an inferior position.

24. On this point, see Schelling and Halperin, *Strategy and Arms Control*, 77–90.

25. Richard C. Bush, *At Cross Purposes: U.S.-Taiwan Relations since 1942* (Armonk, NY: M. E. Sharpe, 2004), 227–32.

26. Recent archival research casts doubts on whether Acheson's speech affected the decision to invade South Korea. See, for example, James Matray, "Dean

Acheson's Press Club Speech Reexamined," *Journal of Conflict Studies* 22, no. 1 (Spring 2002).

27. For a classic discussion of stability, see Schelling, *Arms and Influence*, 234–59; and Thomas C. Schelling, *The Strategy of Conflict* (Cambridge, MA: Harvard University Press, 1960), 230–54.

28. See "U.S.–China Joint Statement," November 17, 2009, http://www.whitehouse.gov/the-press-office/us-china-joint-statement.

29. For related arguments, see, for example, Patrick M. Cronin, "Flashpoints: The Way Forward in the East and South China Seas," Center for a New American Security, March 2013, cnas.org/files/documents/publications/CNAS_Bulletin_Cronin_TheWayForward.pdf; and David Gompert and Phillip Saunders, *The Paradox of Power: Sino-American Restraint in an Age of Vulnerability* (Washington, DC: National Defense University, 2011).

CHAPTER 2: THE SOURCES OF CONFLICT

1. Thucydides, *History of the Peloponnesian War*, 402 (book 5, passage 89).

2. See, for example, Andrew J. Nathan and Andrew Scobell, "Globalization as a Security Strategy: Power and Vulnerability in the 'China Model,'" *Political Science Quarterly* 128, no. 3 (Fall 2013): 427–253.

3. Jae Ho Chung, *Between Ally and Partner: Korea-China Relations and the United States* (New York: Columbia University Press, 2007), 1–2, 119; Liu Qun and Wu Shan, "The Way Ahead: The Next Decade of PRC-ROK Relations," *Issue Brief No. 47*, Asian Institute for Policy Studies, Seoul, Republic of Korea, March 12, 2013.

4. Department of Defence, Government of Australia, *Defence White Paper 2013* (Canberra, Australia, 2013), 9–11, http://defence.gov.au/whitepaper2013/docs/WP_2013_web.pdf.

5. See "Opening Address at the First Plenary Session of the Chinese People's Political Consultative Conference," September 21, 1949, http://www.marxists.org/reference/archive/mao/selected-works/volume-5/mswv5_01.htm.

6. Xinhua English, "Chinese Dream Awakened by Xi's Speech," December 6, 2012, http://english.sina.com/china/2012/1206/534928.html.

7. Ashton B. Carter and William J. Perry, *Preventive Defense: A New Security Strategy for America* (Washington, DC: Brookings, 1999), 92–122.

8. This perception of benign intent lies at the heart of the security dilemma. Butterfield observed, "[Y]ou know that you yourself mean no harm, and that you want nothing from [the other party] save guarantees for your own safety; and it is never possible for you to realize or remember properly that since he cannot see the inside of your mind, he can never have the same assurance of your intentions that you have." *History and Human Relations*, 19–20; see Jervis, *Perception and Misperception*, 67–78. See also, Nigel Inkster, "Conflict Foretold: America and China," *Survival* 55, no. 5 (October–November 2013), 7–28.

9. For a good discussion of how this concept plays today, see Wu Zhong, "Hu Warns Successors over 'Peaceful Evolution,'" *Asia Times Online*, January 11, 2012, http://www.atimes.com/atimes/China/NA11Ad02.html.

10. Pew Research Center, "America's Global Image Remains More Positive than China's," Washington, D.C., July 18, 2013, p. 2, http://www.pewglobal.org/2013/07/18/americas-global-image-remains-more-positive-than-chinas.

11. Dina Smeltz et al., "Foreign Policy in the New Millennium," Chicago Council on Global Affairs, 2012, p. 35, http://www.thechicagocouncil.org/UserFiles/File/Task%20Force%20Reports/2012_CCS_Report.pdf; P. W. Singer, "D.C.'s New Guard: What Does the Next Generation of American Leaders Think?" Brookings *UpFront* Blog, Brookings Institutions, Washington, D.C., February 2011, http://www.brookings.edu/research/reports/2011/02/young-leaders-singer.

Chapter 3: The Determinants of Chinese Strategy

1. Goldstein suggests that the danger of deliberate misrepresentation is especially great in the case of rising powers, which have particular incentives to conceal intentions to alter the status quo. Goldstein, *Rising to the Challenge*, 39.

2. See Information Office of the State Council, "Defense White Paper 2013: The Diversified Employment of China's Armed Forces," Beijing, April 2013, http://news.xinhuanet.com/english/china/2013–04/16/c_132312681_2.htm.

3. Zheng Bijan, "China's Peaceful Rise to Great Power Status," *Foreign Affairs* 84, no. 5 (September/October 2005), http://www.foreignaffairs.com/articles/61015/zheng-bijian/chinas-peaceful-rise-to-great-power-status; for the evolution of this concept, see Zheng Bijan, *China's Road to Peaceful Rise: Observations on Its Cause, Basis, Connotation, and Prospect* (New York: Routledge, 2011).

4. See Zheng Bijan, " 'Peaceful Rise' and 'Peaceful Development' Are the Same Thing," in Bijan, *China's Road*, ch. 30.

5. A number of these more hawkish voices are active-duty flag officers, including among others General Zhang Zhaozhong, Rear Admiral Yang Yi, Major General Han Xudong, and Major General Luo Yuan. See Willy Lam, "China's Hawks in Command," *Wall Street Journal*, July 1, 2012, http://online.wsj.com/article/SB10001424052702304211804577500521756902802.html. See also David Lai, "The Coming of Chinese Hawks," Strategic Studies Institute, Army War College, Carlisle, Pennsylvania, October 2010, http://www.strategicstudiesinstitute.army.mil/Pubs/display.cfm?pubid=1028.

6. Dai Bingguo, "Adhere to the Path of 'Peaceful Development,'" Xinhua News Agency, December 6, 2010, http://china.usc.edu/ShowArticle.aspx?articleID=2325.

7. It is noteworthy that one of the earlier contemporary references to the "China Dream" came in a speech by the most prominent exponent of the "peaceful rise" approach. See Zheng Bijan, "China's Rise Is a Peaceful Rise," in Bijan, *China's Road*, ch. 39.

8. Consider, for example, this passage from the first chapter of China's 2013 defense white paper, outlining national security priorities:

The diversified employment of China's armed forces adheres to fundamental policies and principles as follows:

Safeguarding national sovereignty, security and territorial integrity, and supporting the country's peaceful development. This is the goal of China's efforts in strengthening its national defense and the sacred mission of its armed forces, as stipulated in the Constitution of the People's Republic of China and other relevant laws. China's armed forces unswervingly implement the military strategy of active defense, guard against and resist aggression, contain separatist forces, safeguard border, coastal and territorial air security, and protect national maritime rights and interests and national security interests in outer space and cyber space. "We will not attack unless we are attacked; but we will surely counterattack if attacked." Following this principle, China will resolutely take all necessary measures to safeguard its national sovereignty and territorial integrity.

9. See, for example, the Joint Statement of Presidents Obama and Hu, Washington, D.C., January 19, 2011: "The two Presidents . . . reaffirmed their commitment to building a positive, cooperative and comprehensive US-China relationship for the 21st century. . . . [They] committed to work together to build a cooperative partnership based on mutual respect and mutual benefit in order to promote the common interests of both countries." See http://www.whitehouse .gov/the-press-office/2011/01/19/us-china-joint-statement.

10. Donald Gross, *The China Fallacy: How the U.S. Can Benefit from China's Rise and Avoid Another Cold War* (New York: Bloomsbury, 2013).

11. Goldstein, *Rising to the Challenge*, 38.

12. Friedberg, *A Contest for Supremacy*, 1–10.

13. For a (skeptical) review of this interpretation of recent Chinese policy, see Alastair Iain Johnston, "How New and Assertive Is China's New Assertiveness?" *International Security* 37, no. 4 (Spring 2013): 7–48; and Michael Swaine, "Perceptions of an Assertive China," *China Leadership Monitor*, no. 32, Hoover Institute, Washington, D.C., May 2010, http://media.hoover.org/sites/default/files /documents/CLM32MS.pdf.

14. See the Chinese sources discussed in Johnston, "How New and Assertive," 43–45.

15. More completely, the statement reads, "Hide our capacities and bide our time; be good at maintaining a low profile and never claim leadership." Or, in Chinese: "Tao gang yang hui."

16. See, for example, Johnston, "How New and Assertive"; Richard H. Solomon, *Chinese Negotiating Behavior: Pursuing Interests through "Old Friends"* (Santa

Monica, CA: RAND, 1995); Bijan, "China's Peaceful Rise to Great Power Status"; and Information Office of the State Council, "Defense White Paper 2013: The Diversified Employment of China's Armed Forces."

17. While the Chinese portray this as a period of imperial benevolence, some of its neighbors have a very different narrative (for Korea, it was obliged to play the role of a tributary state; for Vietnam, its territory was affected by the Ming annexation of the early 1400s).

18. See speech by Wen Jiabao to the United Nations, September 2010, cited in Johnston, "How New and Assertive," 19.

19. For a discussion of the ambiguity of the territorial scope of China's core national interests, see Chris Buckley, "China Affirms Policy on Islands," *New York Times*, January 29, 2013; for a history of the Chinese usage of "core national interests," see Michael Swaine, "China's Assertive Behavior: Part One—Core Interests," *China Leadership Monitor*, no. 34, Hoover Institute, Washington, D.C., February 2011, http://media.hoover.org/sites/default/files/documents/CLM34MS.pdf.

20. Swaine indicates that as a matter of official policy, the scope of "core interests" as applied to territory has been limited. A close examination of the historical record, along with personal conversations with knowledgeable senior U.S. officials, confirms that at least through the time of Swaine's writing, the Chinese government has officially, and repeatedly, identified only three closely related issues as specific core interests: the defense of China's sovereignty claims regarding Taiwan, Tibet, and Xinjiang. See Swaine, "China's Assertive Behavior." See also Dingding Chen and Jianwei Wang, "Lying Low No More?: China's New Thinking on the Tao Guang Yang Hui Strategy," *China: An International Journal* 9, no. 2 (September 2011), http://muse.jhu.edu/login?auth=0&type=summary&url=/journals/china/v009/9.2.chen.html; Andrew Scobell, *China and Strategic Culture* (Carlisle, PA: Strategic Studies Institute, 2002), 11; Kenneth D. Johnson, *China's Strategic Culture: A Perspective for the United States* (Carlisle, PA: Strategic Studies Institute, 2009), 10; and Thomas J. Christensen, "Chinese Realpolitik," *Foreign Affairs* 75, no. 5 (September/October 1996), http://www.foreignaffairs.com/articles/52434/thomas-j-christensen/chinese-realpolitik-reading-beijings-world-view.

21. For an excellent history, see Richard C. Bush, *Untying the Knot: Making Peace in the Taiwan Strait* (Washington, DC: Brookings, 2005).

22. The more or less explicit agreement grew out of conversations involving Prime Ministers Tenaka and Zhou Enlai in 1972 and later between Tenaka and Deng Xiaoping. Deng said, "Our nations face many issues. For example, we call the disputed islands Diaoyu Islands but Japan calls it the Senkaku Islands. This issue is too complicated to discuss at this time. We may not be able to find resolution to this issue due to lack of ideas, but our next generation may be smarter and find a resolution." See Akira Ikegami, "The Reasons Why the Senkaku Islands Are Japanese Territory," reprinted in *Japan Security Watch*, September 14, 2012, http://jsw.newpacificinstitute.org/?p=10500.

23. Martin Fackler, "China and Japan in Deal over Contested Gas Fields," *New York Times*, June 19, 2008, http://www.nytimes.com/2008/06/19/world/asia/19 sea.html.

24. For the debate over the applicability of "core interest" to China's claims in the South China Sea, see Swaine, "China's Assertive Behavior, 8–13. Swaine explains that there is considerable Chinese debate on the subject.

25. See Johnston, "How New and Assertive," 17–20; Bader, *Obama and China's Rise*, 77.

26. See Bonnie Glaser, "Trouble in the South China Sea," *ForeignPolicy.com*, September 17, 2012, http://www.foreignpolicy.com/articles/2012/09/17/trouble _in_the_south_china_sea?page=0,2.

27. See the statement of Chinese Foreign Ministry spokesperson Hua Chunying: "The Diaoyu Islands are about sovereignty and territorial integrity. Of course it's China's core interest." www.nytimes.com/2013/05/12/opinion/sunday/chinas -evolving-core-interests.html; and Michael D. Swaine, "Chinese Views Regarding the Senkaku/Diaoyu Islands Dispute," *China Leadership Monitor*, no. 41 (June 2013).

28. See Li Jinming and Li Dexia, "The Dotted Line on the Chinese Map of the South China Sea: A Note," School of Southeast Asian Studies, Xiamen University, reprinted in *Ocean Development and International Law* 34, issue 3–4 (2003): 287–95, http://cat.middlebury.edu/~scs/docs/Li%20and%20Li-The%20Dotted%20 Line%20on%20the%20Map.pdf.

29. For the Chinese argument, see, for example, Han-yi Shaw, "The Inconvenient Truth behind the Diaoyu/Senkaku Islands," *New York Times*, September 19, 2012, http://kristof.blogs.nytimes.com/2012/09/19/the-inconvenient-truth-behind -the–diaoyusenkaku islands/.

30. Keith Bradsher, "Okinawa Piques Chinese Papers," *New York Times*, May 8, 2013, www.nytimes.com/2013/05/09/world/asia/okinawa-piques-chinese -papers. See also statements by Deputy Chief of the PLA General Staff Lt. Gen. Qi Jianguo at Shangri-La Forum in June 2013, "Shangri-La Dialogue: China Not Disputing Japan Sovereignty over Okinawa," *Straits Times*, June 2, 2013, http://www.straitstimes.com/breaking-news/asia/story/shangri-la-dialogue -china-not-disputing-japan-sovereignty-over-okinawa-2013.

31. Roy Kamphausen and Andrew Scobell, eds., *Right Sizing the People's Liberation Army: Exploring the Contours of China's Military* (Carlisle, PA: Strategic Studies Institute, 2007), 31.

32. Tanvi Madan, "Premier Li Keqiang of China Goes to India," Brookings *Up Front* Blog, Brookings Institution, Washington, D.C., May 18, 2013, http://www .brookings.edu/blogs/up-front/posts/2013/05/18-li-keqiang-china-india -madan.

33. In his last speech as Communist Party secretary on November 8, 2012, Hu Jintao stated, "We should enhance our capacity for exploiting marine resources, resolutely safeguard China's maritime rights and interests, and build

China into a maritime power." http://www.reuters.com/article/2012/11/08/china-congress-hu-idUSL5E8M77P620121108.

34. See Nan Li, "Evolution of Strategy from 'Near Coasts' to 'Far Seas,'" in Phillip Saunders, Christopher Yung, Michael Swaine, and Andrew Nien-Dzu Yang, eds., *The Chinese Navy: Expanding Capabilities, Evolving Roles* (Washington, DC: National Defense University Press, 2011), 129.

35. Erica S. Downs, "China-Middle East Energy Relations," testimony before the U.S.-China Economic and Security Review Commission, Washington, D.C., June 6, 2013, http://www.brookings.edu/research/testimony/2013/06/06-china-middle-east-energy-downs.

36. Bates Gill, *Rising Star: China's New Security Diplomacy*, rev. ed. (Washington, DC: Brookings, 2010), 74–103; Michael D. Swaine, *America's Challenge: Engaging a Rising China in the Twenty-First Century* (Washington, DC: Carnegie, 2011), 251–52.

37. See, for example, the joint statement following the 2013 U.S.-China Strategic and Economic Dialogue, outlining areas of cooperation between the United States and China on nontraditional threats. Department of State, "US-China Strategic and Economic Dialogue: Outcomes of the Strategic Track," July 12, 2013, http://www.state.gov/r/prs/ps/2013/07/211861.htm.

38. The concept of strategic culture arose in connection with studies of U.S. and Soviet approaches to the role of nuclear weapons. Jack Snyder defined strategic culture as "the sum total of ideas, conditioned emotional responses, and patterns of habitual behavior that members of a national strategic community have acquired through instruction or imitation and share with each other with regard to nuclear strategy." Jack L. Snyder, *The Soviet Strategic Culture: Implications for Limited Nuclear Operations* (Santa Monica, CA: RAND, 1977), 8, http://www.rand.org/content/dam/rand/pubs/reports/2005/R2154.pdf. Following Snyder and other early proponents of the concept (such as Colin Grey), a wide-ranging theoretical and empirical literature emerged on both the concept of strategic culture and the various ways it might affect the actual policies pursued by states. For a summary of the evolution of the concept, see Johnston, "How New and Assertive."

39. See John K. Fairbank, introduction to Frank A. Kierman and John King Fairbank, eds. *Chinese Ways in Warfare* (Cambridge, MA: Harvard University Press, 1974), 25–26.

40. Huiyun Feng, *Chinese Strategic Culture and Foreign Policy Decisionmaking* (London: Routledge, 2007), ch. 2. She draws on the work of Nathan Leites and Alexander George for this concept.

41. Ibid., 20.

42. Ibid., 26.

43. Ibid., 27.

44. Geoff Wade, "The Zheng He Voyages: A Reassessment," *Journal of the Malaysian Branch of the Royal Asiatic Society* 77, part 1 (2005): 27–58, cited in Yuan-kang Wang, *Harmony and War: Confucian Culture and Chinese Power Politics* (New York:

Columbia University Press, 2010), 256. Wang disputes the "peaceful" character of Zheng He's voyages. *Harmony and War*, 157–64.

45. Cited in Wang, *Harmony and War*, 2.

46. See, for example, the remarks of Prime Minister Wen Jiabao: "China tomorrow will continue to be a major country that loves peace and has a great deal to look forward. Peace loving has been a time-honored quality of the Chinese nation," Wen Jiabao, "Turning Your Eyes to China," *Harvard Gazette*, December 10, 2003, http://www.news.harvard.edu/gazette/2003/12.11/10-wenspeech.html.

47. Alastair Iain Johnston, "Cultural Realism and Strategy in Maoist China," in Peter J. Katzenstein, ed., *The Culture of National Security: Norms and Identity in World Politics* (New York: Columbia University Press, 1996), 217.

48. Alastair Iain Johnston, *Cultural Realism: Strategic Culture and Grand Strategy in Chinese History* (Princeton: Princeton University Press, 1995), 266.

49. Wang, *Harmony and War*, 178.

50. Other scholars suggest a blend of perspectives, arguing that China is hardly unwilling to use force but there is a certain restraint and long-term purpose in how it tends to do so. Evan Medeiros suggests that perhaps China will continue in this vein as long as it is successful in achieving desirable outcomes. Specifically, he argues that "China has been occasionally assertive but seldom aggressive . . . China's approach . . . is more gravitational than confrontational. It seeks to create an environment in Asia in which states are drawn to, reliant on, and thereby deferential to Beijing, as a way to minimize constraints and maximize its freedom of action." Henry Kissinger focuses on a different aspect of China's approach to the use of force, deriving less from any Confucian spiritual or religious ethos and more from a hardheaded realism. That realism may not make Beijing pacifist, in Kissinger's eyes. But it does tend to incline Chinese leaders to prefer to use only limited amounts of force to shape China's environment and deter its potential enemies—modeled after the Chinese strategy game of wei qi—rather than risk engaging in large-scale and costly war down the road. See Evan S. Medeiros, *China's International Behavior: Activism, Opportunism, and Diversification* (Santa Monica, CA: RAND, 2009), xx; and Henry Kissinger, *On China* (New York: Penguin Press, 2011), 23–25.

51. This was enunciated at the same time that Deng was launching his southern tour in January and February 1992 to revitalize economic reform. Suisheng Zho, "Deng Xiaoping's Southern Tour: Elite Politics in Post-Tiananmen China," *Asian Survey* (August 1993); and Chen and Wang, "Lying Low No More," 197.

52. See Dai Bingguo, "Stick to the Path of Peaceful Development," *China Daily*, December 15, 2010, http://usa.chinadaily.com.cn/2010–12/15/content_11705718 .htm.

53. Tom Christensen has argued that China's leaders' calculus on using force depends in part on the "potential domestic costs of acquiescence and potential political benefits of belligerence to the CCP regime." See Thomas J. Christensen, "The Correlates of Beijing Public Opinion toward the United States," in Alastair

Iain Johnston and Robert S. Ross, eds., *New Directions in the Study of China's Foreign Policy* (Stanford: Stanford University Press, 2006), 53.

54. According to Yong Deng, "both Maoist and contemporary Chinese leaderships have manipulated ideas of foreign threat for popular mobilization in the interests of their domestic agendas and to shore up the regime's legitimacy. In a similar vein, blaming China's security predicament on hostile foreigners helps divert popular attention away from serious problems in the painful domestic transition." Yong Deng, "Reputation and the Security Dilemma: China Reacts to the China Threat Theory," in Alastair Iain Johnston and Robert S. Ross, eds., *New Directions in the Study of China's Foreign Policy* (Stanford: Stanford University Press, 2006), 202n71.

55. See Yufan Hao, "Domestic Chinese Influences on US-China Relations," in David Shambaugh, ed., *Tangled Titans: The United States and China* (Plymouth, UK: Rowman and Littlefield), ch. 6; and Joseph Fewsmith and Stanley Rosen, "The Domestic Context of Chinese Foreign Policy: Does 'Public Opinion' Matter?" in David Lampton, ed., *The Making of Chinese Foreign and Security Policy in the Era of Reform, 1978–2000* (Palo Alto: Stanford University Press, 2001), 151–87.

56. See Christensen, "Correlates," 342.

57. Christensen (ibid., 364–66), for example, argues that the variation in public attitudes among different groups is at least suggestive that party propaganda does not strongly determine public views.

58. See Peter Hays Gries, "Identity and Conflict in Sino-American Relations," in Alastair I. Johnston and Robert S. Ross, eds., *New Directions in the Study of China's Foreign Policy* (Stanford: Stanford University Press, 2006), ch. 11.

59. Zhao Yanrong, "Public Warms to US, as Political Acts Sway Opinion," *China Daily*, January 17, 2011, http://www.chinadaily.com.cn/cndy/2011–01/17/content_11862197.htm.

60. Bruce Drake, "American, Chinese Publics Increasingly Wary of the Other," Pew Research Global Attitudes Project, November 1, 2012, http://www.pewglobal.org/2012/11/01/american-chinese-publics-increasingly-wary-of-the-other.

61. See the Committee of 100, "US-China Public Perceptions Opinion Survey 2012," New York, 2012, http://survey.committee100.org/2012/EN/C100_2012Survey.pdf.

62. Ibid. For the general public, 13 percent thought relations were getting worse in 2007 and 26.3 percent thought so in 2012, compared with 29 percent in 2007 and 23.9 percent in 2012 who thought relations were getting better. For opinion leaders, the trend was more dramatic: in 2012, 22.3 percent thought relations were getting worse compared with 3 percent in 2007. Another poll, by the Carnegie Endowment and Chinese retired general Luo Yuan, found that Chinese view the U.S. more as a competitor than an enemy. See William Wan, "Chinese Don't See United States as an Enemy, Study Finds, but They Distrust Its Government," *Washington Post*, December 11, 2013.

63. Committee of 100, "US-China Public Perceptions Opinion Survey 2012."

64. Ibid.

65. Andrew Jacobs, "China Warns US against Selling F-16s to Taiwan," *New York Times*, February 25, 2010, http://www.nytimes.com/2010/02/26/world/asia/26china.html. Jin Canrong, a professor of international relations at People's University in Beijing, said the United States should pay a price for weapon sales to Taiwan but acknowledged that China's umbrage was largely part of a show aimed at soothing nationalist sentiment, both in the military and among ordinary Chinese. "The domestic political climate is more complicated than before," he said, noting the rise in self-confidence that has accompanied China's economic surge. "The current leadership has to hear all these different voices and to balance all these pressures."

66. Bingguo, "Stick to the Path of Peaceful Development."

67. See Hao, "Domestic Chinese Influences on US-China Relations," 126–29.

68. Lt. Gen. Ren Haiquan, "China's Perspective on Regional Security and Stability in Asia," speech in Melbourne, Australia, November 2012, http://www.lowyinterpreter.org/file.axd?file=2012%2f11%2flt+gen+ren+speech.pdf.

69. See Yan Xuetong, "The Instability of China-US Relations," *World Economy and Politics*, no. 12 (2010).

70. Wu Xinbo, "Chinese Visions of the Future of US-China Relations," in David Shambaugh, ed., *Tangled Titans: The United States and China* (Plymouth, UK: Rowman and Littlefield, 2012), 382.

71. See, for example, Cui Liru, "Decade of Change as Global Power Shifts," *Global Times*, December 23, 2012, http://www.globaltimes.cn/content/751756.shtml.

72. Xinbo, "Chinese Visions of the Future of US-China Relations," 372.

73. Cited in ibid., 371. See also "Beijing's Brand Ambassador: A Conversation with Cui Tiankai," *foreignaffairs.com*, May 27, 2013, http://www.chinausfocus.com/foreign-policy/beijings-brand-ambassador-a-conversation-with-cui-tiankai.

74. At the Singapore meeting, Major General Yao Yunzhu challenged Washington's claims that Obama's "pivot" or "rebalance" to Asia was not aimed against China. "China is not convinced," she said. "How can you assure China? How can you balance the two different objectives—to assure allies, and to build a positive relationship with China?" See http://www.globalresearch.ca/pivot-to-asia-us-military-build-up-in-asia-threatening-china/5337361; see also "China Censures U.S. Asia-Pacific Policy," *Islamic News Daily*, June 4, 2013, http://www.islamicnewsdaily.com/islamic-news/usa/china-censures-asia-pacific-policy.

75. "Overall, statements from authoritative MFA and MND sources have been largely muted and restrained, with abstract, at times even conciliatory, responses given to very specific and sometimes provocative questions about the Pacific Pivot. In addition, most notably, virtually all of these statements have occurred during regular press conferences, in response to media questions." Michael D. Swaine. "Chinese Leadership and Elite Responses to the U.S. Pacific Pivot," *China*

Leadership Monitor, no. 38 (August 2012), http://media.hoover.org/sites/default/files/documents/CLM38MS.pdf.

76. Information Office of the State Council, "Defense White Paper 2013: The Diversified Employment of China's Armed Forces," ch. 1.

77. This is not to suggest that the four factors we discuss are exhaustive. For example, we have not sought to judge whether there are factors specific to the current cast of China's leaders (education, socioeconomic background, prior international experience) that might influence their views.

78. See Legro, "What China Will Want": "When China espouses ideas and action that favor cooperative integration, it makes sense to do as much as possible to ensure that their internal supporters gain positive feedback and 'I told you so' leverage vis-à-vis their domestic critics."

79. Kenneth Lieberthal and Wang Jisi, *Addressing U.S.-China Strategic Distrust* (Washington, DC: Brookings, 2012).

Chapter 4: The Determinants of American Strategy

1. There are, of course, many historical accounts that embrace this historic narrative of America's alleged preference to look inward, as well as those that argue that the United States was more activist. For the latter view, see Robert Kagan, *Dangerous Nation: America's Foreign Policy from Its Earliest Days to the Dawn of the Twentieth Century* (New York: Vintage, 2006).

2. See Barton Gellman, *Contending with Kennan: Toward a Philosophy of American Power* (New York: Praeger, 1984), 38, 121.

3. For a study of the domestic obstacles to Truman's policy and their impact on U.S. policy toward China, see Thomas J. Christensen, *Useful Adversaries: Grand Strategy, Domestic Mobilization, and Sino-American Conflict, 1947–1958* (Princeton: Princeton University Press, 1996).

4. Within this broad concept of "containment" there were many, sometimes conflicting interpretations. See, e.g., John Lewis Gaddis, *Strategies of Containment: A Critical Appraisal of Postwar American National Security Policy* (Oxford: Oxford University Press, 1982). While they differed in many important respects, they all agreed that Soviet expansionism was a threat to U.S. interests that needed to be checked.

5. For the seminal discussion of both concepts, see Jervis, *Perception and Misperception*, 58–83.

6. Raymond L. Garthoff, *A Journey through the Cold War: A Memoir of Containment and Coexistence* (Washington, DC: Brookings, 2001), 1–8.

7. Gaddis, *Strategies of Containment*.

8. A variety of scholars have attempted to characterize "schools" of American strategic thought. See, for example, Walter Russell Mead, *Special Providence: American Foreign Policy and How It Changed the World* (New York: Routledge, 2002).

9. See, for example, Gellman, *Contending with Kennan*, 40.

10. The first accounts of the draft guidance appeared in the *New York Times* on March 8, 1992, in an article by Patrick Tyler, "US Strategy Plan Calls for Assuring No Rivals Develop." Substantial portions of the draft have been declassified and appear at the National Security Archive, "Prevent the Emergence of a New Rival," http://www.gwu.edu/~nsarchiv/nukevault/ebb245/index.htm.

11. "Our forces will be strong enough to dissuade potential adversaries from pursuing a military build-up in hopes of surpassing or equaling the power of the United States." *The National Security Strategy of the United States of America* (2002), http://nssarchive.us/?page_id=32.

12. Derek Chollet and James Goldgeier, *America between the Wars: The Misunderstood Years between the Fall of the Berlin Wall and the Start of the War on Terror* (New York: Public Affairs, 2008), 147–48.

13. Niall Ferguson, *Colossus: The Rise and Fall of the American Empire* (London: Penguin, 2001).

14. For example, Secretary of State James Baker opposed U.S. involvement in the Balkans in 1991 on the grounds that the United States "did not have a dog in the fight." See Tom Gallagher, "Milosevic, Serbia and the West," in Andrew Hammond, ed., *The Balkans and the West* (Farnham, England: Ashgate, 2004), 156–57.

15. See, for example, Richard K. Betts, *American Force: Dangers, Delusions, and Dilemmas in National Security* (New York: Columbia University Press, 2012).

16. See, for example, James Mann, *The Obamians: The Struggle inside the White House to Redefine American Power* (New York: Viking, 2012), 76–99.

17. For example, the "reset" with Russia, support for India's Security Council aspirations, and a new strategic dialogue with Brazil; see also Barack Obama, "Remarks by the President in Address to the Nation on Syria," Washington, D.C., September 10, 2013, http://www.whitehouse.gov/the-press-office/2013/09/10/remarks-president-address-nation-syria.

18. See Chicago Council on Global Affairs "Constrained Internationalism: Adapting to New Realities," 2010, p. 17, http://www.thechicagocouncil.org/UserFiles/File/POS_Topline%20Reports/POS%202010/Global%20Views%202010.pdf.

19. For excellent accounts of the debates surrounding many of these decisions, see Raymond L. Garthoff, *Détente and Confrontation: American-Soviet Relations from Nixon to Reagan*, rev. ed. (Washington, DC: Brookings, 1994); Robert J. Art and Kenneth N. Waltz, *The Use of Force: Military Power and International Politics* (New York: Rowman and Littlefield, 2004); and Vaisse, *Neoconservatism*.

20. For a discussion, see Ivo H. Daalder and Michael E. O'Hanlon, *Winning Ugly: NATO's War to Save Kosovo* (Washington, DC: Brookings, 2000), 212–15.

21. Albright famously challenged Powell over the value of having such a fine military if it would never be used, particularly in regard to Bosnia, whereas Powell considered Albright's views as too casual and incrementalist on the use of force. See, for example, David Halberstam, *War in a Time of Peace: Bush, Clinton, and the Generals* (New York: Scribner, 2001), 378, 385–86, 417.

22. See James B. Steinberg, "A Perfect Polemic: Blind to Reality on Kosovo," *Foreign Affairs 78, no. 6* (November/December 1999).

23. See Condoleezza Rice, "Campaign 2000: Promoting the National Interest," *Foreign Affairs 79*, no. 1 (January/February 2000).

24. See Richard N. Haass, "The U.S. Should Keep out of Libya," *Wall Street Journal*, March 8, 2011; and for a defense of the intervention, Barack H. Obama, "Remarks by the President in Address to the Nation on Libya," National Defense University, Washington, D.C., March 28, 2011, http://www.whitehouse.gov/the -press-office/2011/03/28/remarks-president-address-nation-libya.

25. Donald Rumsfeld typified this view; see Philip H. Gordon and Jeremy Shapiro, *Allies at War: America, Europe, and the Crisis over Iraq* (New York: McGraw-Hill, 2004), 7, 63–64.

26. Chollet and Goldgeier, *America between the Wars*, 91–93.

27. See Richard N. Haass, *The Reluctant Sheriff: The United States after the Cold War* (New York: Council on Foreign Relations, 1997).

28. Robert E. Harkavy, *Bases Abroad: The Global Foreign Military Presence* (Oxford: Oxford University Press, 1989), 2, 26; Stacie L. Pettyjohn, *U.S. Global Defense Posture, 1783–2011* (Santa Monica, CA: RAND, 2012), 25–37.

29. Department of the Navy and United States Coast Guard, "A Cooperative Strategy for 21st Century Seapower," October 2007, http://www.navy.mil/mari time/MaritimeStrategy.pdf.

30. See, for example, Lars Schoultz, *National Security and United States Policy toward Latin America* (Princeton: Princeton University Press, 1987).

31. John Quincy Adams, address to the U.S. House of Representatives, July 4, 1821.

32. For Clinton, see *A National Strategy of Engagement and Enlargement* (White House, 1994), http://nssarchive.us/?page_id=56; for Bush, see *The National Security Strategy of the United States of America* (2002).

33. Speech of George W. Bush to the American Enterprise Institute, February 26, 2003, http://www.guardian.co.uk/world/2003/feb/27/usa.iraq2.

34. Paul Kennedy, *The Rise and Fall of the Great Powers: Economic Change and Military Conflict from 1500 to 2000* (New York: Random House, 1987), 242–49; Kissinger, *On China*, 54.

35. W. Arthur Lewis, *The Evolution of the International Economic Order* (Princeton: Princeton University Press, 1978); G. John Ikenberry, *After Victory: Institutions, Strategic Restraint, and the Rebuilding of Order after Major Wars* (Princeton: Princeton University Press, 2001); and Richard H. Ullman, *Securing Europe* (Princeton: Princeton University Press, 1991).

36. Richard G. Lugar and R. James Woolsey, "The New Petroleum," *Foreign Affairs 78*, no. 1 (January/February 1999), http://www.foreignaffairs.com/articles /54624/richard-g-lugar-and-r-james-woolsey/the-new-petroleum.

37. See, for example, Steven Kull and I. M. Destler, *Misreading the Public: The Myth of a New Isolationism* (Washington, DC: Brookings, 1999), 47.

38. Henry A. Crumpton, *The Art of Intelligence: Lessons from a Life in the CIA's Clandestine Service* (New York: Penguin Press, 2012), 166–67.

39. Kull and Destler, *Misreading the Public*, 23.

40. Pew Research Center Survey and NBC News/*Wall Street Journal* poll, October 2010 and September 2012, respectively, pollingreport.com/priority.htm.

41. Pew Research Center and Council on Foreign Relations, "America's Place in the World 2009," December 2009, p. 12, www.people-press.org/files/legacy-pdf /569.pdf.

42. Chollet and Goldgeier, *America between the Wars*, 328.

43. See Dina Smeltz et al., "Foreign Policy in the New Millennium," Chicago Council on Global Affairs, 2012, p. 16, www.thechicagocouncil.org/UserFiles/File /Task%20Force%20Reports/2012_CCS_Report.pdf; and Gregory Holyk and Dina Smeltz, "Background Brief for Final Presidential Debate: What Kind of Foreign Policy Do Americans Want?" Chicago Council on Global Affairs, October 19, 2012, http://www.thechicagocouncil.org/UserFiles/File/Task%20Force%20Reports /2012_CCS_FPBrief.pdf.

44. Pew Research Center, "America's Global Image Remains More Positive than China's," July 18, 2013, www.media.hoover.org/sites/default/files/documents /CLM41MS.pdf.

45. Luke Johnson, "Afghan War Poll Finds That Two-Thirds Say That It Wasn't Worth the Cost," *Huffington Post*, July 26, 2013, http://www.huffingtonpost.com /2013/07/26/afghan-war-poll_n_3657879.html.

46. See Gaddis, *Strategies of Containment*; Harry Harding, *A Fragile Relationship: The United States and China since 1972* (Washington, DC: Brookings, 1992); and Garthoff, *Détente and Confrontation*, 227–322.

47. See George C. Marshall, "Personal Statement by the Special Representative of the President (General Marshall)," January 7, 1947, http://archive.org/stream /fiftyyearsinchin012639mbp/fiftyyearsinchin012639mbp_djvu.txt.

48. Concerns about the balance of power led some in the Johnson administration to propose preventive strikes against China's emerging nuclear program. See Michael Lumbers, "A Lesson in Restraint: What China Tells Us about Iran," *Washington Post*, October 21, 2012, http://articles.washingtonpost.com/2012–10–21/opinions /35500632_1_nuclear-weapons-nuclear-test-chinese-bomb.

49. Friedberg, *A Contest for Supremacy*, 70.

50. See Robert Ross, *Negotiating Cooperation: The United States and China, 1969–1989* (Stanford: Stanford University Press, 1995), 150. The first concrete step in the security relationship was intelligence sharing and the placement in China of U.S. intelligence-gathering equipment to monitor Soviet compliance with arms control agreements.

51. See, for example, Friedberg, *A Contest for Supremacy*.

52. This is the argument of the Bush 2002 national security strategy.

53. Gross, *The China Fallacy*.

54. Friedberg, *A Contest for Supremacy*, 277.

55. For a related argument, see Nina Hachigian and Mona Sutphen, *The Next American Century: How the U.S. Can Thrive as Other Powers Rise* (New York: Simon and Schuster, 2008).

56. For a clear discussion of the issue, see Friedberg, *A Contest for Supremacy*, 42–45, 188–94.

57. Proponents of this view cite a range of China's actions, including currency manipulation, intellectual property theft, state subsidization, and other nonmarket barriers.

58. Of course, on matters such as this, the debate often has more than two camps; for example, even many proponents of warmer U.S.-China ties have serious reservations about Huawei and about Chinese state-sponsored or state-condoned computer hacking and intellectual property theft.

59. See, for example, Kenneth Lieberthal and Peter W. Singer, *Cybersecurity and U.S.-China Relations* (Washington, DC: Brookings, 2012).

60. What China calls the first island chain essentially covers most of the South China Sea out to the Philippines and the East China Sea out to Okinawa and the main Japanese islands. See Larry M. Wortzel, *The Dragon Extends Its Reach: Chinese Military Power Goes Global* (Washington, DC: Potomac Books, 2013), 49.

61. Richard Bush focuses on the issue of whether the PLA would base military units on Taiwan after possible unification as a key determinant of whether such a scenario would serve U.S. interests. See Richard C. Bush, *Uncharted Strait: The Future of China-Taiwan Relations* (Washington, DC: Brookings, 2013), 223–26.

62. Geopolitics was not the only factor in Bush's decision; the sale also involved the prospect of significant job gains in the U.S. aerospace industry.

63. See U.S.-China Economic and Security Review Commission, http://www.uscc.gov/index.php.

64. Established by Section 1202 of the National Defense Authorization Act for Fiscal Year 2000, Public Law 106–65, it provides that the secretary of defense shall submit a report "on the current and future military strategy of the People's Republic of China. The report shall address the current and probable future course of military-technological development on the People's Liberation Army and the tenets and probable development of Chinese grand strategy, security strategy, and military strategy, and of the military organizations and operational concepts, through the next 20 years."

65. Dina Smeltz et al., "Foreign Policy in the New Millennium," Chicago Council on Global Affairs, 2012, p. 35, http://www.thechicagocouncil.org/User Files/File/Task%20Force%20Reports/2012_CCS_Report.pdf.

66. Ibid., 36.

67. See Committee of 100, "US-China Public Perceptions Opinion Survey 2012."

68. "More than three-quarters of all four samples view China's emergence as a military power as a serious or potential threat. Compared with 2005, the percentage of those who view China's military power as a serious threat rose by 7 percentage points among the general public and 8 percentage points among opinion

leaders." Committee of 100, "2007 C-100 Interactive Report American & Chinese Attitudes toward Each Other," http://survey.committee100.org/2007/2007survey .php?p=2&q=16.

69. Pew Research Center, "America's Global Image Remains More Positive than China's," 24.

CHAPTER 5: MILITARY SPENDING AND MILITARY MODERNIZATION

1. Kagan, *The World America Made*, 87.

2. "Secretary of Defense Donald Rumsfeld's Remarks to the International Institute for Strategic Studies," Singapore, June 4, 2005, Singapore.usembassy. gov/060405.html, as quoted in George J. Gilboy and Eric Heginbotham, *Chinese and Indian Strategic Behavior: Growing Power and Alarm* (New York: Cambridge University Press, 2012), 95.

3. See, for example, Caspar W. Weinberger, *Annual Report to Congress, Fiscal Year 1986* (Washington, DC: GPO, 1985), 17; and Frank C. Carlucci, *Soviet Military Power: An Assessment of the Threat, 1988* (Washington, DC: GPO, 1988), 34, 112, 129, 149.

4. World Bank, "GNI, PPP (current international $)," World Bank table, 2012, http://data.worldbank.org/indicator/NY.GNP.MKTP.PP.CD.

5. Louis Uchitelle, "Subsidies Aid Rebirth in U.S. Manufacturing," *New York Times*, May 10, 2012, www.nytimes.com/2012/05/11/business/subsidies-aid -rebirth-in-us-manufacturing.html.

6. Shipbuilders Association of Japan, "Shipbuilding Statistics," Tokyo, March 2012, sajm.or.j;/pdf/Shipbuilding_Statistics_Mar2012e.pdf.

7. International Organization of Motor Vehicle Manufacturers, "Production Statistics, 2011," Washington, D.C., 2012, oica.net/category/production-statistics.

8. World Steel Association, "World Crude Steel Output Increases by 6.8% in 2011," Washington, D.C., January 23, 2012, www.worldsteel.org/media-centre /press-releases/2012/2011-world-crude-steel-production.html.

9. Marc Humphries, "Rare Earth Elements: The Global Supply Chain," Congressional Research Service, Washington, D.C., June 2012, p. 11, fas.org/sgp/crs /natsec/R41347.pdf.

10. Information Office of the State Council of the People's Republic of China, "China's National Defense in 2010," Beijing, March 31, 2011, p. 18, www.china.org .cn/government/whitepaper/node_7114675.htm.

11. Gilboy and Heginbotham, *Chinese and Indian Strategic Behavior*.

12. World Bank table, 2012, http://data.worldbank.org/indicator/NY.GNP .ATLS.CD.

13. Carnegie Endowment for International Peace, *The World Order in 2050* (Washington, DC: Carnegie, 2010), cited in Zbigniew Brzezinski, *Strategic Vision: America and the Crisis of Global Power* (New York: Basic Books, 2012), 80.

14. Motoko Rich, "U.S. Students Still Lag Globally in Math and Science, Tests Show," *New York Times*, December 11, 2012, http://www.nytimes.com /2012/12/11/education/us-students-still-lag-globally-in-math-and-science -tests-show.html?ref=us.

15. Thom Shanker, "Study Predicts Future for U.S. as Number Two Economy, but Energy Independent," *New York Times*, December 11, 2012, http://www.ny times.com/2012/12/11/world/china-to-be-no-1-economy-before-2030-study -says.html?ref=world.

16. On this debate, see, for example, Dana H. Allin and Erik Jones, *Weary Policeman: American Power in an Age of Austerity* (London: International Institute for Strategic Studies, 2012); Kagan, *The World America Made*; Joseph S. Nye Jr., *The Future of Power* (New York: Public Affairs, 2011); Fareed Zakaria, *The Post-American World* (New York: W. W. Norton, 2008); Brzezinski, *Strategic Vision*; Ikenberry, *Liberal Leviathan*; and Charles A. Kupchan, *No One's World: The West, the Rising Rest, and the Coming Global Turn* (Oxford: Oxford University Press, 2012).

17. On China's economy, see Nicholas R. Lardy, *Sustaining China's Economic Growth after the Global Financial Crisis* (Washington, DC: Peterson Institute for International Economics, 2012), 1.

18. Jianguo Liu and Wu Yang, "Water Sustainability for China and Beyond," *Science* 337 (August 10, 2012): 649, www.sciencemag.org.

19. Michael Beckley, "China's Century?: Why America's Edge Will Endure," *International Security* 36, no. 3 (Winter 2011/2012): 41–78; Daniel Yergin, *The Quest: Energy, Security, and the Remaking of the Modern World* (New York: Penguin, 2011), 704.

20. World Economic Forum, *The Global Competitiveness Report, 2012–2013* (Davos, Switzerland: World Economic Forum, 2012), 15, www3.weforum.org /docs/reports/global-competitiveness-report-2012-2013.

21. See, for example, International Institute for Strategic Studies, *The Military Balance, 1980–1981* (London: International Institute for Strategic Studies, 1980), 96–97.

22. Office of Management and Budget, *Budget of the U.S. Government, Fiscal Year 2013: Historical Tables* (Washington, DC, 2012), 151.

23. Ibid., 149.

24. Alan Simpson, Erskine Bowles, and the National Commission on Fiscal Responsibility and Reform, *The Moment of Truth* (Washington, DC: White House, December 2010), 21.

25. Office of Management and Budget, *Budget of the U.S. Government, Fiscal Year 2013*, 74–75, 102–3, 240.

26. This includes the period 1951–90. See Office of the Under Secretary of Defense (Comptroller), *National Defense Budget Estimates for FY 2012* (2011), 141–46, http://comptroller.defense.gov/defbudget/fy2012/FY12_Green_Book.pdf.

27. International Institute for Strategic Studies, *The Military Balance, 2013* (Abingdon, England: Routledge, 2013), 548–53.

28. Kathleen Ridolfo, "Iraq: Smuggling, Mismanagement Plaguing Oil Industry," Radio Free Europe/Radio Liberty, Washington, D.C., November 13, 2007, http://www.rferl.org/featuresarticle/2007/11/38c235c1-6f71-46ac-9463-4119 f5cb6fea.html.

29. Linda Sieg and Kiyoshi Takenaka, "Japan to Mull Ability to Hit Enemy Bases in Defense Review," Reuters, July 26, 2013, news.yahoo.com/japan-mull -ability-hit-enemy-bases-defense-review-020338380.html; Ministry of Defense, Government of Japan, *Defense of Japan 2013* (Tokyo, 2013), www.mod.go.jp/e/publ /w_paper/2013.html.

30. International Institute for Strategic Studies, *The Military Balance, 2013*, 548– 53; Andrew Davies, "All Comes Down to Priorities," *The Australian*, October 27– 28, 2012, p. SR 1.

31. Information Office of the State Council of the People's Republic of China, "China's National Defense in 2010," 18.

32. Center on International Cooperation, *Annual Review of Global Peace Operations 2012* (Boulder, CO: Lynne Rienner, 2012), 131.

33. See Office of the Under Secretary of Defense (Comptroller), *National Defense Budget Estimates for FY 2012* (2011), 144–46.

34. International Institute for Strategic Studies, *The Military Balance, 2013*, 458–63.

35. International Institute for Strategic Studies, *The Military Balance, 2012* (Oxfordshire: Routledge, 2007), 214–16; Adam P. Liff and Andrew S. Erickson, "Demystifying China's Defence Spending: Less Mysterious in the Aggregate," *China Quarterly* (March 2013): 1–26, journals.cambridge.org/abstract_S0305741013000295; Department of Defense, *Military and Security Developments Involving the People's Republic of China, 2012* (Washington, DC, May 2012), 6, http://www.defense.gov /pubs/pdfs/2012_CMPR_Final.pdf.

36. Andrew S. Erickson and Adam P. Liff, "China's Military Development: Beyond the Numbers," *The Diplomat*, March 12, 2013, www.thediplomat.com /2013/03/12/chinas-military-deevlopment-beyond-the-numbers.

37. Dennis J. Blasko, *The Chinese Army Today: Tradition and Transformation for the 21st Century*, 2nd ed. (New York: Routledge, 2012), 22–30; Chris Buckley, "China Internal Security Spending Jumps Past Army Budget," Reuters, March 5, 2011, http://www.reuters.com/article/2011/03/05/us-china-unrest-idUSTRE7222 RA20110305.

38. David Shambaugh, *China Goes Global: The Partial Power* (Oxford: Oxford University Press, 2013), 275.

39. International Institute for Strategic Studies, *The Military Balance, 2012*, 214– 16; Keith Crane, Roger Cliff, Evan Medeiros, James Mulvenon, and William Overhalt, *Modernizing China's Military: Opportunities and Constraints* (Santa Monica, CA: RAND Corporation, 2005), 101–3.

40. International Institute for Strategic Studies, *The Military Balance, 2013*, 256.

41. Kenneth W. Allen, "Assessing the PLA Air Force's Ten Pillars," *China Brief* 11, issue 3 (February 10, 2011): 6, www.jamestown.org/uploads/media/cb_11_3_03.pdf.

42. International Institute for Strategic Studies, *The Military Balance, 2012*, 215–16.

43. Department of Defense, *Military and Security Developments Involving the People's Republic of China, 2012*.

44. Gilboy and Heginbotham, *Chinese and Indian Strategic Behavior*, 20–129.

45. Ibid., 123.

46. Willard quoted in Thomas G. Mahnken, with Dan Blumental, Thomas Donnelly, Michael Mazza, Gary J. Schmitt, and Andrew Shearer, "Asia in the Balance: Transforming U.S. Military Strategy in Asia," American Enterprise Institute, June 2012, p. 9.

47. Gilboy and Heginbotham, *Chinese and Indian Strategic Behavior*, 100–110.

48. David M. Finkelstein, "Thinking about the PLA's 'Revolution in Doctrinal Affairs,'" in James Mulvenon and David Finkelstein, eds., *China's Revolution in Doctrinal Affairs* (Alexandria, VA: Center for Naval Analyses, 2005), www.defensegroup.com/cira/pdf/doctrinebook.pdf.

49. Kenneth W. Allen, "The Organizational Structure of the PLAAF," in Richard P. Hallion, Roger Cliff, and Phillip C. Saunders, eds., *The Chinese Air Force: Evolving Concepts, Roles, and Capabilities* (Washington, DC: National Defense University Press, 2012), 95; David Shlapak, "Equipping the PLAAF: The Long March to Modernity," in Hallion, Cliff, and Saunders, eds., *The Chinese Air Force*, 191–211.

50. Blasko, *The Chinese Army Today*, 11–13, 18, 59–60.

51. Brzezinski, *Strategic Vision*, 177.

52. In addition, constraining a military competition in a way that is seen as unfair or artificial can simply divert it into different directions. This was the case, for example, with the 1922 Washington Naval Treaty. It failed to limit submarines. Even where it did establish limits on surface vessels, those limits were not widely acceptable to various parties, meaning that it did not survive the strategic challenges of ensuing years.

53. Department of Defense, "Sustaining U.S. Global Leadership: Priorities for 21st Century Defense," Washington, D.C., January 2012, www.defense.gov/news/Defense_Strategic_Guidance.pdf .

54. Office of the Under Secretary of Defense (Comptroller), "Overview of Fiscal Year 2013 Budget Request," Washington, D.C., Department of Defense, February 2012, p. 4–1, www.comptroller.defense.gov/defbudget/fy2013/FY2013_Budget_Request_Overview_Book.pdf.

55. Remarks by Secretary of Defense Leon Panetta at IISS Asia Security Summit, Shangri-La Hotel, Singapore, June 2, 2012, http://www.cfr.org/asia/panettas-speech-shangri-la-security-dialogue-june-2012/p28435.

56. Remarks by Secretary of Defense Chuck Hagel at IISS Asia Security Summit, Shangri-La Hotel, Singapore, June 1, 2013, www.defense.gov/transcripts

/transcript.aspx?transcriptid=5251; Ashton Carter, "The U.S. Strategic Rebalance to Asia: A Defense Perspective," in Aspen Institute Congressional Program Paper Series, *South Asia: Policy Challenges for the U.S.* 28, no. 1 (February 16–24, 2013).

57. Ellis Joffe, "The 'Right Size' for China's Military: To What Ends?" in Roy Kamphausen and Andrew Scobell, eds., *Right-Sizing the People's Liberation Army: Exploring the Contours of China's Military* (Carlisle, PA: Strategic Studies Institute, 2007), 570. A 60–40 split in the submarine force was announced in 2006; see Secretary of Defense Donald Rumsfeld, *Quadrennial Defense Review Report* (February 6, 2006), 47.

58. Michael O'Hanlon, "Rebalancing the U.S. Military in Asia and the Pacific," *Politico*, June 9, 2013, http://www.brookings.edu/research/opinions/2013/06 /09-rebalancing-us-military-asia-pacific-ohanlon.

59. See Michael E. O'Hanlon, *The Science of War* (Princeton: Princeton University Press, 2009), 15.

60. The two military districts covering the western half of the country, as well as all of the nation's land borders with India and Burma about half of those Russia, together hold about 20 percent of major army and air force combat formations. (They are known as the Chengdu and Lanzhou districts.) See International Institute for Strategic Studies, *The Military Balance, 2013*, 292–94.

61. Information Office of the State Council, "Defense White Paper 2013: The Diversified Employment of China's Armed Forces," ch. 1.

62. Vali Nasr, *The Dispensable Nation: American Foreign Policy in Retreat* (New York: Doubleday, 2013).

63. Roger Cliff, Mark Burles, Michael S. Chase, Derek Eaton, and Kevin L. Pollpeter, *Entering the Dragon's Lair: Chinese Antiaccess Strategies and Their Implications for the United States* (Santa Monica, CA: RAND, 2007), 18–23.

64. Roger Cliff, John Fei, Jeff Hagen, Elizabeth Hague, Eric Heginbotham, and John Stillion, *Shaking the Heavens and Splitting the Earth: Chinese Air Force Employment Concepts in the 21st Century* (Santa Monica, CA: RAND, 2011), 187–237.

65. Stephen Biddle, *Military Power* (Princeton: Princeton University Press, 2004).

66. See Governor George W. Bush, "A Period of Consequences," speech at the Citadel, South Carolina, September 23, 1999, www.citadel.edu/pao/addresses /pres_bush.html; Michael E. O'Hanlon, *Defense Policy Choices for the Bush Administration*, 2nd ed. (Washington, DC: Brookings, 2002), 9–10.

67. See Congressional Budget Office, *The Budget and Economic Outlook: Fiscal Years 2012 through 2022* (January 2012), http://www.cbo.gov/publication/42911.

68. See, for example, Michelle Tan, "Deputy SecDef: Major Role for Army in Asia-Pacific Plans," *DefenseNews.com*, October 24, 2012, www.defensenews.com.

69. Andrew Erickson, Lyle Goldstein, and Carnes Lord, "China Sets Sail," *American Interest* (May/June 2010), www.the-american-interest.com/article-bd.cfm ?piece=806.

70. For more on this debate within China, see Andrew S. Erickson and David D. Yang, "Using the Land to Control the Sea?: Chinese Analysts Consider the Antiship Ballistic Missile," *Naval War College Review* 62, no. 4 (Autumn 2009): 53–86.

71. Keith Bradsher, "China Is Said to Be Bolstering Missile Capabilities," *New York Times*, August 24, 2012, www.nytimes.com/2012/08/25/world/asia; Geoffrey Till, *Asia's Naval Expansion: An Arms Race in the Making?* (London: International Institute for Strategic Studies, 2012), 124.

72. National Institute for Defense Studies, *NIDS China Security Report 2011* (Tokyo: National Institute for Defense Studies, 2012), 14–15.

73. Shambaugh, *China Goes Global*, 286–88.

74. Korea Research Institute for Strategy, *The Strategic Balance in Northeast Asia, 2012* (Seoul: Korea Research Institute for Strategy, 2012), 183; Tamir Eshel, "A New Stealth Fighter Unveiled in China," *Defense Update*, September 16, 2012, http://defense-update.com/20120916_new-chinese-fighter-f60-j31.html.

75. Michael D. Swaine, Mike M. Mochizuki, Michael I. Brown, Paul S. Giarra, Douglas H. Paal, Rachel Esplin Odell, Raymond Lu, Oliver Palmer, and Xu Ren, *China's Military and the U.S.-Japan Alliance in 2030* (Washington, DC: Carnegie, 2013), 50.

76. Korea Research Institute for Strategy, *The Strategic Balance in Northeast Asia, 2012*, 178; Jane Perlez, "U.S. General Sees Hope for Chinese Help on Korea," *New York Times*, April 24, 2013, http://www.nytimes.com/2013/04/25/world/asia/us-hopeful-after-talks-with-china. Some references suggest three more carriers may be planned. See Jung Sung-Ki, "S. Korea Envisions Light Aircraft Carrier," *Defense News*, October 28, 2013, 4.

77. Till, *Asia's Naval Expansion*, 88–89, 139; Shambaugh, *China Goes Global*, 290–93.

78. Office of the Under Secretary of Defense (Comptroller), "United States Department of Defense Fiscal Year 2013 Budget Request Overview," February 2012, comptroller.defense.gov/defbudget/fy2013/FY2013_Budget_Request_Overview_Book.pdf, pp. 4–1 through 4–15.

79. See, for example, Mahnken et al., "Asia in the Balance," 16.

80. Department of Defense, *Military and Security Developments Involving the People's Republic of China, 2012*, 7, 21–25, 40.

81. See Andrew F. Krepinevich, *Why Air-Sea Battle?* (Washington, DC: Center for Strategic and Budgetary Assessments, 2010); see also, on a related matter, James M. Acton, *Silver Bullet? Asking the Right Questions about Conventional Prompt Global Strike* (Washington, DC: Carnegie, 2013).

82. From the preface of Air-Sea Battle Office, "Air-Sea Battle: Service Collaboration to Address Anti-Access and Area Denial Strategies," Department of Defense, May 2013, http://navylive.dodlive.mil/files/2013/06/ASB-Concept-Implementation-Summary-May-2013.pdf.

83. On China, see, for example, Friedberg, *A Contest for Supremacy*, 218, 274–77; see also Lieberthal and Jisi, *Addressing U.S.-China Strategic Distrust*, 23–24, 30–31.

84. Bernard Cole, "China's Naval Modernization: Cause for Storm Warnings?" (comments featured at the 2010 Pacific Symposium, National Defense University, June 16, 2010), 4, ndu.edu/inss/docuploaded/PLAN_Cole_Remarks.pdf.

85. See General Norton A. Schwartz and Admiral Jonathan W. Greenert, "Air-Sea Battle Doctrine: A Discussion with the Chief of Staff of the Air Force and Chief of Naval Operations," Brookings Institution, Washington, D.C., May 16, 2012, p. 21, http://www.brookings.edu/~/media/events/2012/5/16%20air%20sea%20 battle/20120516_air_sea_doctrine_corrected_transcript.pdf.

86. See, for example, Mark Gunzinger, *Outside-In: Operating from Range to Defeat Iran's Anti-Access and Area-Denial Threats* (Washington, DC: Center for Strategic and Budgetary Assessments, 2011); and Krepinevich, *Why Air-Sea Battle?*

87. Indeed, another report by the same think tank underscores that while the United States does not see conflict with China as inevitable, China is clearly the most capable potential foe that is now necessitating the new Air-Sea Battle concept. See Jan Van Tol, *Air-Sea Battle: A Point-of-Departure Operational Concept* (Washington, DC: Center for Strategic and Budgetary Assessments, 2010), ix–xvi. See also, Daniel Hartnett, "Air-Sea Battle, China, and the U.S. Rebalance to Asia," Center for National Policy, Washington, D.C., November 2013.

88. For excellent discussions of this notion, see Stephen Peter Rosen, *Winning the Next War: Innovation and the Modern Military* (Ithaca: Cornell University Press, 1991); and Jonathan Shimshoni, "Technology, Military Advantage, and World War I: A Case for Military Entrepreneurship," in Steven E. Miller, Sean M. Lynn-Jones, and Stephen Van Evera, eds., *Military Strategy and the Origins of the First World War*, revised and expanded ed. (Princeton: Princeton University Press, 1991), 134–62. See also Harold Brown with Joyce Winslow, *Star Spangled Security: Applying Lessons Learned over Six Decades Safeguarding America* (Washington, DC: Brookings, 2012), 165.

89. See, for example, Biwu Zhang, *Chinese Perceptions of the U.S.: An Exploration of China's Foreign Policy Motivations* (New York: Lexington Books, 2012), 106–8.

90. See Richard Bush and Michael O'Hanlon, *A War Like No Other: The Truth about China's Challenge to America* (New York: John Wiley and Sons, 2007), 125–30; and Ronald O'Rourke, "PLAN Force Structure: Submarines, Ships, and Aircraft," in Phillip C. Saunders, Christopher Yung, Michael Swaine, and Andrew Nien-Dzu Yang, eds., *The Chinese Navy: Expanding Capabilities, Evolving Roles* (Washington, DC: National Defense University Press, 2011), 158–60. China's forced-entry capabilities, including airborne forces, might roughly equal enough to move one division or a bit more.

91. Mark Cozad, "China's Regional Power Projection: Prospects for Future Missions in the South and East China Seas," in Roy Kamphausen, David Lai, and Andrew Scobell, eds., *Beyond the Strait: PLA Missions Other than Taiwan* (Carlisle, PA: Strategic Studies Institute, 2008), 293.

92. Phillip C. Saunders and Joshua K. Wiseman, "Buy, Build, or Steal: China's Quest for Advanced Military Aviation Technologies," China Strategic Perspectives Paper No. 4, Institute for National Strategic Studies, National Defense University, Washington, D.C., December 2011, p. 2.

93. For a relevant related argument, see Nan Li and Christopher Weuve, "China's Aircraft Carrier Ambitions: An Update," *U.S. Naval War College Review* 63, no. 1 (Winter 2010): 28, www.usnwc.edu.

94. Swaine, *America's Challenge*, 360.

95. Kissinger, *On China*, 384. The six assurances Washington gave to Taipei included the promises that the United States had not set a specific date to end arms sales to Taiwan and that it would not consult with Beijing on those sales or pressure Taipei into negotiations with Beijing.

96. Redeployment of Chinese missiles away from the strait would not achieve the same result since that redeployment could be quickly reversed in a crisis.

97. Some sense of the historical trend line could help inform this process. For example, in the first Bush presidency, the United States notified Congress of $8.2 billion in arms sales to Taiwan from 1990 through 1992. In the two terms of the Clinton presidency, the figures were $3.7 billion and $5.0 billion, respectively; in the George W. Bush administration, they were $5.2 billion and $10.4 billion. In Obama's first three years, the figure was $12.2 billion. See Shirley A. Kan, "Taiwan: Major U.S. Arms Sales since 1990," Congressional Research Service, Washington, D.C., July 23, 2013, pp. 55–58, fas.org/sgp/crs/weapons/RL30957.pdf.

98. U.S. policy speeches tend to focus on the what more than the why of U.S. force deployments in the region. See, for example, Secretary Hagel's Shangri-La speech in June 2013.

99. Other aspects of CFE may have more promising applications to U.S.-China relations. For example, CFE's provision on notification of troop exercises combined with provisions for observing exercises are adaptable to the U.S.-China context.

100. Carter and Perry, *Preventive Defense*, 109.

101. National Institute for Defense Studies, *East Asian Strategic Review 2013* (Tokyo: Japan Times, 2013), p. 135.

CHAPTER 6: MILITARY CONTINGENCIES: ENHANCING CRISIS STABILITY

1. Glaser, *Rational Theory of International Politics*, 276.

2. Michael R. Gordon and Bernard E. Trainor, *Cobra II: The Inside Story of the Invasion and Occupation of Iraq* (New York: Pantheon Books, 2006), 27–35, 457–61; Gregory Fontenot, E. J. Degen, and David Tohn, *On Point: The United States Army in Operation Iraqi Freedom* (Fort Leavenworth, KS: Combat Studies Institute Press, 2004), 46.

3. See Cliff et al., *Shaking the Heavens and Splitting the Earth*; C. Fred Bergsten, Charles Freeman, Nicholas R. Lardy, and Derek J. Mitchell, *China's Rise: Challenges and Opportunities* (Washington, DC: Peterson Institute for International Economics, 2008), 192–97; and Kevin Pollpeter, "Towards an Integrative C4ISR System: Informationization and Joint Operations in the People's Liberation Army," in Roy Kamphausen, David Lai, and Andrew Scobell, eds., *The PLA at Home and Abroad:*

Assessing the Operational Capabilities of China's Military (Carlisle, PA: Strategic Studies Institute, 2010), 193–235.

4. See, for example, "The Dragon's New Teeth," *The Economist*, April 7, 2012, pp. 27–31.

5. Forrest E. Morgan, Karl P. Mueller, Evan S. Medeiros, Kevin L. Pollpeter, and Roger Cliff, *Dangerous Thresholds: Managing Escalation in the 21st Century* (Santa Monica, CA: RAND, 2008), 57, 61.

6. T. X. Hammes, "Offshore Control: A Proposed Strategy for an Unlikely Conflict," Strategic Forum Paper No. 278 (Washington, DC: National Defense University, June 2012), www.ndu.edu/inss.

7. For a related argument, see Paul Bracken, *The Second Nuclear Age: Strategy, Danger, and the New Power Politics* (New York: Henry Holt, 2012), 209–11.

8. The partial exception to this statement is perhaps Taiwan, which China sees as crucial not only for restoring the territorial integrity of the state but also for preventing further secessionism elsewhere. But the United States is sufficiently aware of this Chinese view, and Chinese leaders have to date shown a measure of patience in pursuing reunification, that there are reasons to hope the issue can be managed, as we discuss later in the chapter.

9. See, for example, Barry R. Posen, *Inadvertent Escalation: Conventional War and Nuclear Risks* (Ithaca: Cornell University Press, 1991), 28–67, 159–96.

10. See Michael J. Mazarr, "The Angry Pacific: Why the United States Is Not Ready for Conflict in Asia," *Foreignpolicy.com*, November 2, 2012; and Robert S. Ross, "The Problem with the Pivot: Obama's New Asia Policy Is Unnecessary and Counterproductive," *Foreign Affairs* 91, no. 6 (November/December 2012): 81.

11. "International Law's Unhelpful Role in the Senkaku Islands," *University of Pennsylvania Journal of International Law* 29, issue 4 (2008), https://www .law.upenn.edu/journals/jil/articles/volume29/issue4/RamosMrosovsky29U .Pa.J.Int'lL.903(2008).pdf.

12. Schelling, *The Strategy of Conflict* (1980 ed.), 187–203.

13. For an assessment along these lines, see Thomas J. Christensen, "Posing Problems without Catching Up: China's Rise and Challenges for U.S. Security Policy," *International Security* 25, no. 4 (Spring 2001): 5–40.

14. Center for Strategic and International Studies, "U.S. Force Posture Strategy in the Asia Pacific Region: An Independent Assessment," Washington, D.C., June 2012, p. 5, http://apo.org.au/research/us-force-posture-strategy-asia-pacific -region-independent-assessment.

15. On these concepts, see, for example, Thomas C. Schelling and Morton H. Halperin, *Strategy and Arms Control*, Twentieth Century Fund ed. (New York: Pergamon-Brassey's, 1985).

16. See, for example, Don Oberdorfer, *The Two Koreas* (New York: Perseus Books, 1997).

17. Martin Fackler and Mark McDonald, "South Korea Reassesses Its Defenses after Attack," *New York Times*, November 26, 2010, http://www.nytimes.com/2010/11/26/world/asia/26korea.html.

18. On North Korea's reactor ambitions, see Kelsey Davenport, "North Korea Makes Progress on Reactor," *Arms Control Today* 42, no. 8 (October 2012): 26–27; on the earlier crisis, see Carter and Perry, *Preventive Defense*, 123–42.

19. See, for example, Bruce E. Bechtol Jr., "Maintaining a Rogue Military: North Korea's Military Capabilities and Strategy at the End of the Kim Jong-Il Era," *International Journal of Korean Studies* 16, no. 1 (Spring/Summer 2012): 160–91.

20. For a similar view, see James Dobbins, "War with China," *Survival* 54, no. 4 (August–September 2012): 9.

21. Larry M. Wortzel, "PLA 'Joint' Operational Contingencies in South Asia, Central Asia, and Korea," in Roy Kamphausen, David Lai, and Andrew Scobell, eds., *Beyond the Strait: PLA Missions Other than Taiwan* (Carlisle, PA: Strategic Studies Institute, 2008), 360.

22. See Kissinger, *On China*, 80–82; Brzezinski, *Strategic Vision*, 85; Kagan, *The World America Made*, 126; and Friedberg, *A Contest for Supremacy*, 176.

23. Yong-Sup Han, "The ROK-US Cooperation for Dealing with Political Crises in North Korea," *International Journal of Korean Studies* 16, no. 1 (Spring/Summer 2012): 70–73.

24. Daalder and O'Hanlon, *Winning Ugly*, 176.

25. Comments by Professor Andrew Erickson of the Naval War College, Henry L. Stimson Center, Washington, D.C., July 30, 2012, used with Erickson's permission.

26. Blainey also usefully debunks the type of conventional wisdom that many invoke to argue that such dangers are not serious today—the myths that relatively even balances of power naturally promote peace, that countries busy making money tend not to fight, and that countries with lots of interactions among their leaders and citizens are inoculated against war with each other. Geoffrey Blainey, *The Causes of War* (New York: Free Press, 1973), 245–49.

27. For a related argument, see David C. Gompert, "North Korea: Preparing for the End," *Survival* 55, no. 3 (June/July 2013): 21–45.

28. "Memorandum of Understanding between the United States of America and the Union of Soviet Socialist Republics Regarding the Establishment of a Direct Communication Link," Geneva, Switzerland, June 20, 1963, www.state.gov/t/isn/4785.htm.

29. See, for example, Bader, *Obama and China's Rise*, 71.

30. Gong Li, "The Official Perspective," in Carola McGiffert, ed., *Chinese Images of the United States* (Washington, DC: Center for Strategic and International Studies, 2005), 30; Lieberthal and Jisi, *Addressing U.S.-China Strategic Distrust*, 13.

31. Related to this argument, we believe that, should both sides ever agree to it, peaceful reunification of Taiwan and China would not be a major setback for the United States. Some analysts suggest that China would become far more powerful

if it could project force into the Western Pacific from bases on Taiwan, too. But we consider this hypothesis to be overstated. Forceful conquest of Taiwan by China would represent a disaster, to be sure. But a peaceful reunification scenario would not be. Possessing bases on Taiwan would extend the PLA's starting point for projecting force one hundred to two hundred miles farther east than is the case today. That would complicate regional dynamics, but it would not be a radical shift on geostrategic scales. It might ultimately require U.S. allies to develop backup plans in the unlikely event that China sought to harass or interdict shipping in the South China Sea. But countries like Japan and Korea would still be able to use the oceans for commerce and their own national sustenance.

32. See, for example, Robert L. Suettinger, *Beyond Tiananmen: The Politics of U.S.-China Relations, 1989–2000* (Washington, DC: Brookings, 2003), 200–263.

33. Blasko, *The Chinese Army Today*, 96–104, 186–90.

34. Suettinger, *Beyond Tiananmen*, 383–84.

35. See, for example, Bush and O'Hanlon, *A War Like No Other*; and Swaine, *America's Challenge*, 174–76.

36. David A. Shlapak, David T. Orletsky, Toy I. Reid, Murry Scot Tanner, and Barry Wilson, *A Question of Balance: Political Context and Military Aspects of the China-Taiwan Dispute* (Santa Monica, CA: RAND, 2009), 89.

37. See, for example, ibid., 139; and O'Rourke, "PLAN Force Structure," 144–49.

38. See Capt. Wayne P. Hughes Jr., *Fleet Tactics and Coastal Combat*, 2nd ed. (Annapolis, MD: Naval Institute Press, 2000); and O'Hanlon, *The Science of War*, 85–103.

39. Morgan et al., *Dangerous Thresholds*, 67.

40. For a related argument, see Avery Goldstein, "First Things First: The Pressing Danger of Crisis Instability in U.S.-China Relations," *International Security* 37, no. 4 (Spring 2013): 49–89.

41. Dobbins, "War with China," 23; Andrew F. Krepinevich Jr., "Strategy in a Time of Austerity: Why the Pentagon Should Focus on Assuring Access," *Foreign Affairs* 91, no. 6 (November/December 2012): 65.

42. Hammes, "Offshore Control: A Proposed Strategy for an Unlikely Conflict."

43. U.S. Energy Information Administration, "China Analysis Brief," Washington, D.C., May 2011, www.eia.gov/countries/cab.cfm?fips=CH. In 2010, China obtained 65% of its oil from abroad. Of its imports, 19% came from Saudi Arabia, 16% from Angola, 7% from Oman, 5% from Sudan, 5% from Iraq, 4% from Kuwait, 3% from Libya, and another 3% from Brazil. A further 19% came from various small providers, some of them not connected to China by pipeline. Of those nations with direct land routes to China, 9% of its crude oil imports came from Iran, 6% from Russia, and 4% from Kazakhstan. See Abby Joseph Cohen and Rachel Siu, "Sustainable Growth in China: Spotlight on Energy," Global Markets Institute, Goldman Sachs Global Investment Research, New York, August 13, 2012, p. 14.

44. Michael Pillsbury, "The Sixteen Fears: China's Strategic Psychology," *Survival* 54, no. 5 (October–November 2012), 152.

45. A corollary to this idea is that the United States needs to enhance U.S. resilience by reducing vulnerability to possible Chinese economic reprisal measures such as embargoes on exports, rare Earth metals, semiconductors, or other crucial precursors to its own high-technology industries or any consumer goods that it cannot quickly obtain elsewhere. (Chinese officials seem to appreciate that even in the realm of rare Earth metals, where they used their quasi-monopoly to punish Japan for a dispute over the Senkaku/Diaoyu Islands in 2010, other providers will erode their dominance in this sector in coming years—which will of course be a desirable outcome for the United States.)

46. Some other disputes do not involve China. South Korea and Japan both assert ownership of the Takeshima/Dokdo islets, for example. See Zhang Yunbi, "Bitter Remarks Ramp Up Dispute between Seoul, Tokyo," *China Daily*, August 23, 2012, www.chinadaily.com.cn.

47. Kosuke Takahashi, "China Is Changing Status Quo by Force, Says Japan," *Jane's Defence Weekly*, July 8, 2013, http://www.janes.com/article/24315/japanese-white-paper-accuses-china-of-changing-status-quo-by-force.

48. Tomotaka Shoji, "Vietnam, ASEAN, and the South China Sea: Unity or Diverseness?" *NIDS Journal of Defense and Security*, no. 13 (December 2012): 15.

49. National Institute for Defense Studies, *NIDS China Security Report 2012* (Tokyo, 2012), 18–20; Reuters, "Second Thomas Shoal 'Could Be the Next Flashpoint,'" *Taipei Times*, May 30, 2013, http://www.taipeitimes.com/News/front/archives/2013/05/30/2003563520.

50. Michael A. McDevitt and Catherine K. Lea, "Workshop Overview," in Michael A. McDevitt and Catherine K. Lea, eds., "Workshop One: The Yellow and East China Seas," Conference Report, Center for Naval Analyses, Alexandria, Va., May 2012, p. 10; National Institute for Defense Studies, *NIDS China Security Report 2012*, 18–20.

51. Chris Buckley, "China Denies Directing Radar at Japanese Military," *New York Times*, February 8, 2013, www.nytimes.com/2013/02/09/world/asia.

52. International Crisis Group, "Stirring Up the South China Sea," *Asia Report No. 223* (Brussels, April 2012), 8–28, http://www.crisisgroup.org/en/regions/asia/north-east-asia/china/223-stirring-up-the-south-china-sea-i.aspx; STRATFOR, "China's Maritime Law Enforcement Reorganization," March 12, 2013, https://apps.militaryperiscope.com/SpecialReports/ShowReport.aspx?report=690.

53. Jane Perlez, "Chinese, with Revamped Force, Make Presence Known in East China Sea," *New York Times*, July 27, 2013, http://www.nytimes.com/2013/07/28/world/asia/chinese-with-revamped-force-make-presence-known-in-east-china-sea.html?emc=eta1&_r=0.

54. Jane Perlez, "China Sends Troops to Disputed Islands," *New York Times*, July 23, 2012.

55. "Each Party recognizes that an armed attack against either Party in the territories under the administration of Japan would be dangerous to its own peace and safety and declares that it would act to meet the common danger in accordance with its constitutional provisions and processes. Any such armed attack and all measures taken as a result thereof shall be immediately reported to the Security Council of the United Nations in accordance with the provisions of Article 51 of the Charter. Such measures shall be terminated when the Security Council has taken the measures necessary to restore and maintain international peace and security." http://www.mofa.go.jp/region/n-america/us/q&a/ref/1.html.

56. "Each Party recognizes that an armed attack in the Pacific Area on either of the Parties would be dangerous to its own peace and safety and declares that it would act to meet the common dangers in accordance with its constitutional processes." Mutual Defense Treaty between the United States and the Republic of the Philippines, August 30, 1951, Article IV, http://avalon.law.yale.edu/20th _century/phil001.asp.

57. Bader, *Obama and China's Rise*, 105.

58. On some of these trends, see Bonnie S. Glaser, "Potential Flashpoints in the East China Sea," in Michael A. McDevitt and Catherine K. Lea, eds., "Workshop One: The Yellow and East China Seas," Conference Report, Center for Naval Analyses, Alexandria, Virginia, May 2012, pp. 37–41.

59. Carlos Ramos-Mrosovsky, "International Law's Unhelpful Role in the Senkaku Islands," *University of Pennsylvania Journal of International Law* 29, no. 4 (2008): 903–46.

60. David Rosenberg, "Managing the Resources of the China Seas: China's Bilateral Fisheries Agreements with Japan, South Korea, and Vietnam," *Japan Focus*, June 2005, www.japanfocus.org/-David-Rosenberg/1789?rand=137521202.

61. See John Pike, "South China Sea Oil and Natural Gas," *Globalsecurity.org*, November 7, 2011, http://www.globalsecurity.org/military/world/war/spratly -oil.htm.

62. Guo Rongxing, "Territorial Disputes and Seabed Petroleum Exploitation: Some Options for the East China Sea," Brookings Institution, Washington, D.C., 2008, http://www.brookings.edu/~/media/research/files/papers/2010/9/east%20 china%20sea%20guo/09_east_china_sea_guo; see also David Lai, *The United States and China in Power Transition* (Carlisle, PA: Strategic Studies Institute, 2011), 147.

63. Yomiuri Shimbun, "Japan-Taiwan Deal Strategic Tool to Protect Senkaku Islands," April 14, 2013, reprinted in *The Nation*, http://www.nationmultimedia .com/opinion/Japan-Taiwan-deal-strategic-tool-to-protect-Senkak-30204021 .html.

64. For a good discussion of the earlier part of this period, see Richard C. Bush, *The Perils of Proximity: China-Japan Security Relations* (Washington, DC: Brookings, 2010).

65. The United States and Japan discussed such exercises in 2012 following increased provocations by China around the Senkaku Islands. Zhao Shengnan

and Dong Fangyu, "Military Official's U.S. Visit Linked to Islands," *China Daily*, August 23, 2012, www.chinadaily.com.cn.

66. Wendell Minnick, "Is China Laying Down Stakes at Disputed Scarborough Shoal?" *Defense News*, September 6, 2013, http://www.defensenews.com/article/20130906/DEFREG03/309060013/Is-China-Laying-Down-Stakes-Disputed-Scarborough-Shoal.

67. U.S.-China Policy Foundation, "ASEAN Regional Forum Held in Cambodia," Washington, D.C., July 12, 2012, http://uscpf.org/v3/2012/07/12/asean-regional-forum-held-in-cambodia; Carlyle A. Thayer, "ASEAN's Code of Conduct in the South China Sea: A Litmus Test for Community-Building?," *Asia-Pacific Journal* 10, issue 34, no. 4 (August 20, 2012), http://www.japanfocus.org/-Carlyle_A_-Thayer/3813.

68. China's views on the subject are hardening; see, for example, National Institute for South China Sea Studies, "What One Needs to Know about the South China Sea," Haikou, Hainan Province, 2011.

Chapter 7: The Strategic Domain: Nuclear, Space, and Cyber

1. Gompert and Saunders, *The Paradox of Power*, xiv.

2. Dingli Shen, "Revitalizing the Prague Agenda," *Washington Quarterly* 36, no. 2 (Spring 2013): 124.

3. The 2010 *Nuclear Posture Review Report* talks of working toward a stable, transparent, and nonthreatening strategic relationship with both Russia and China. See Department of Defense, *Nuclear Posture Review Report 2010* (Washington, DC, 2010), 7, 28–29, 46, www.defense.gov/npr.

4. Desmond Ball, "The Development of the SIOP, 1960–1983," in Desmond Ball and Jeffrey Richelson, eds., *Strategic Nuclear Targeting* (Ithaca: Cornell University Press, 1986), 57–83.

5. Friedberg, *A Contest for Supremacy*, 70.

6. Bundy, *Danger and Survival*, 531–32.

7. Michael Mazza and Dan Blumental, "China's Strategic Forces in the 21st Century: The People's Liberation Army's Changing Nuclear Doctrine and Force Posture," in Henry D. Sokolski, ed., *The Next Arms Race* (Carlisle, PA: Strategic Studies Institute, 2012), 95.

8. See, for example, Christopher F. Chyba and Karthika Sasikumar, "A World of Risk: The Current Environment for U.S. Nuclear Weapons Policy," in George Bunn and Christopher F. Chyba, eds., *U.S. Nuclear Weapons Policy: Confronting Today's Threats* (Washington, DC: Brookings, 2006), 15–17.

9. Lawrence Freedman, *The Evolution of Nuclear Strategy* (New York: St. Martin's Press, 1983), 274–82; Bundy, *Danger and Survival*, 525–35; Janne E. Nolan, *Guardians of the Arsenal: The Politics of Nuclear Strategy* (New York: Basic Books, 1989), 70–71, 93–98.

10. Federation of American Scientists, National Security Blog, August 22, 2012, www.fas.org/bloh/ssp/2012/08/china-nukes.php. The article cites STRATCOM Commander General Kehler: "I do not believe that China has hundreds or thousands more nuclear weapons than what the intelligence community has been saying . . . that the Chinese arsenal is in the range of several hundred [nuclear warheads]."

11. Wendell Minnick, "New U.S. Law Seeks Answers on Chinese Nuke Tunnels," *Defense News*, January 7, 2013, p. 1. Shambaugh thinks the Chinese nuclear arsenal could include 400 to 600 warheads; see Shambaugh, *China Goes Global*, 295.

12. Mark B. Schneider, "The Nuclear Forces and Doctrine of the Russian Federation and the People's Republic of China," testimony before the House Armed Services Subcommittee on Strategic Forces, October 14, 2011; Michael S. Chase, "Chinese Nuclear Force Modernization: How Much Is Enough?" *China Brief*, Jamestown Foundation, 12, issue 8 (April 12, 2012); Kathleen E. Masterson, "China Cited by Foes of Nuclear Budget Cuts," *Arms Control Today*, December 2011.

13. See Gompert and Saunders, *The Paradox of Power*; Thomas Fingar, "Worrying about Washington," *Nonproliferation Review* 18, no. 1 (2011): 51–68; Wu Riqiang, "Survivability of China's Sea-Based Nuclear Forces," *Science and Global Security* 19, no. 2 (2011): 91–120; Gregory Kulacki, "Chickens Talking with Ducks: The U.S.-Chinese Nuclear Dialogue," *Arms Control Today* (October 2011); and Hans M. Kristensen, Robert S. Norris, and Matthew G. McKinzie, *Chinese Nuclear Forces and U.S. Nuclear War Planning* (Washington, DC: Federation of American Scientists, 2006), 35–40, www.fas.org/nuke/guide/china/Book2006.pdf.

14. See M. Taylor Fravel and Evan S. Medeiros, "China's Search for Assured Retaliation: The Evolution of Chinese Nuclear Strategy and Force Structure," *International Security* 35, no. 2 (Fall 2010): 48–87; for a recent Chinese view, see Li Bin, "Revisiting No First Use and Minimum Deterrence," in Lora Saalman, ed., *The China-India Nuclear Crossroads* (Washington, DC: Carnegie Endowment for International Peace, 2012), 47–57.

15. Yao Yunzhu, "No First Use of Nuclear Weapons," *China Daily*, April 25, 2013, http://www.chinadaily.com.cn/opinion/2013–04/25/content_16447477_2.htm.

16. Tom Z. Collina, "Pentagon Defends '3+2' Plan for Warheads, *Arms Control Today* 43, no. 7 (September 2013): 35–37.

17. See Department of Defense, *Nuclear Posture Review Report* (April 2010), http://www.defense.gov/npr/docs/2010%20nuclear%20posture%20review%20report.pdf .

18. White House, Nuclear Weapons Fact Sheet, 2013, www.whitehouse.gov/the-press-office/2013/06/19/fact-sheet-nuclear-weapons-employment-strategy-united-states.

19. Carter and Perry, *Preventive Defense*, 107.

20. On these issues, see Teng Jianqun, "Sino-American Nuclear Dialogue: Retrospect and Prospect," China Institute of International Studies, Beijing, August 3, 2011, www.ciis.org.cn/english/2011–08/03/content_4380644.htm.

21. One possible future U.S.-Russia arms accord might continue the gradual downsizing of strategic arsenals while also placing some controls for the first time on tactical and surplus warheads. For example, the United States and Russia might each reduce their deployed strategic nuclear inventories to 1,000 warheads and their additional inventories in the form of nondeployed strategic and nonstrategic nuclear warheads to another 1,000–1,500. That would require roughly a 50 percent cut in existing arsenals, in aggregate. If Moscow and Washington agreed to this, they would retain a clear numerical dominance over the medium nuclear powers. But the disparity in numbers would no longer be quite so great as before. It would keep the traditional nuclear superpowers clearly in a class by themselves but begin to limit their dominance. In the general spirit of reducing reliance on nuclear weapons, the two superpowers might further reduce the alert levels of their nuclear weapons as part of this process if they had not done so already. That could include adopting ways to be sure that intercontinental missiles (ICBMs and SLBMs) could not be promptly launched. See Steven Pifer and Michael O'Hanlon, *The Opportunity: Next Steps in Nuclear Arms Control* (Washington, DC: Brookings, 2012).

22. Remarks by President Obama at the Brandenburg Gate, Berlin, Germany, June 19, 2013, http://www.whitehouse.gov/the-press-office/2013/06/19/remarks-president-obama-brandenburg-gate-berlin-germany.

23. John D. Steinbruner, *Principles of Global Security* (Washington, DC: Brookings, 2000), 227. Herman Kahn's writings are relevant here, too, for understanding Chinese concerns, even if they were originally intended to underscore America's challenges in deterring the Soviet Union across many kinds of scenarios and under many types of circumstances. See Herman Kahn, *On Thermonuclear War* (New Brunswick, NJ: Transaction Publishers, 2007), 557.

24. For more on Chinese views, see Lora Saalman, "China and the U.S. Nuclear Posture Review," Carnegie-Tsinghua Center for Global Policy, Washington, D.C., February 2011, scribd.com/doc/49855154/China-and-the-U-S-Nuclear-Posture-Review.

25. See, for example, "Former STRATCOM Head Calls for Cuts," *Arms Control Today* (June 2012): 27.

26. Gompert and Saunders, *The Paradox of Power*, 76–88.

27. Teng Jianqun, "Sino-U.S. Nuclear Dialogue: Retrospect and Prospect," in Teng Jianqun, ed., *Global Nuclear Posture Review 2011/2012* (Beijing: Center of Arms Control Research, China Institute of International Studies, 2012), 71; and Wu Riqiang, "China's Anxiety about U.S. Missile Defence: A Solution," *Survival* 55, no. 5 (October–November 2013), 29–52.

28. Yao Yunzhu, "Linking Strategic Stability and Ballistic Missile Defense: The View from China," in Lora Saalman, ed., *The China-India Nuclear Crossroads* (Washington, DC: Carnegie Endowment for International Peace, 2012), 73.

29. Personal communication to Michael O'Hanlon by a Chinese official at Beijing University, August 23, 2012.

30. Tom Z. Collina, "Strategic Misdirection: Are the Latest U.S. Moves on Missile Defense Making It Less Safe?" *ForeignPolicy.com*, October 26, 2012, http://www.foreignpolicy.com/articles/2012/10/26/strategic_misdirection.

31. See Bradsher, "China Is Said to Be Bolstering Missile Capabilities"; and Lora Saalman, "China's Evolution on Ballistic Missile Defense," Carnegie Endowment Blog, August 23, 2012, carnegieendowment.org/2012/08/23.

32. Teng Jianqun, "Sino-U.S. Nuclear Dialogue," in Jianqun, ed., *Global Nuclear Posture Review, 2011/2012*, 73.

33. For more discussion of this, see Brad Roberts, "Asia's Major Powers and the Emerging Challenges to Nuclear Stability among Them," IDA Paper P-4423 (Alexandria, VA: Institute for Defense Analyses, 2009), 9–10; and Saalman, "China and the U.S. Nuclear Posture Review," 1–2.

34. Swaine, *America's Challenge*, 180–81.

35. Tom Z. Collina, "Report Critiques U.S. Missile Defense," *Arms Control Today* 42, no. 8 (October 2012): 30–32.

36. Steve Fetter, *Toward a Comprehensive Test Ban* (Cambridge, MA: Ballinger Publishing, 1988), 72–78.

37. R. J. Hemley et al., "Pit Lifetime," JSR-06–335, Massachusetts Institute of Technology, McLean, Virginia, January 2007, http://www.fas.org/irp/agency/dod/jason/pit.pdf; Matthew L. Wald, "U.S. Has No Need to Test Atomic Arsenal, Report Says," *New York Times*, March 31, 2012, http://www.nytimes.com/2012/03/31/science/earth/us-tests-of-atomic-weapons-not-needed-report-says.html?scp=1&sq=nuclear%20test%20ban&st=cse.

38. See National Research Council, *The Comprehensive Nuclear Test Ban Treaty—Technical Issues for the United States* (Washington, DC: National Academy of Sciences, 2012), 16, www.nap.edu/catalog.php?record_id=12849.

39. U.S. Nuclear Weapons Cost Study Project, "Fifty Facts about Nuclear Weapons," Brookings Institution, Washington, D.C., http://www.brookings.edu/projects/archive/nucweapons/50.aspx.

40. See Secretary of Defense Robert Gates, "Gates: Nuclear Weapons and Deterrence in the 21st Century," Carnegie Endowment for International Peace, Washington, D.C., October 28, 2008, www.carnegieendowment.org/files/1028.transcrip_gates_checked.pdf.

41. Stephen M. Younger, *The Bomb: A New History* (New York: Ecco, 2010), 219.

42. National Nuclear Security Administration, "Reliable Replacement Warhead Program," March 2007, www.nnsa.doe.gov/docs/factsheets/2007/NA-07-FS-02.pdf.

43. Damien J. LaVera, "Looking Back: The U.S. Senate Vote on the Comprehensive Test Ban," *Arms Control Today* (October 2004), www.armscontrol.org/act/2004_10/LookingBack_CTBT.

44. Zhang Hui, "Revisiting North Korea's Nuclear Test," *China Security* 3, no. 3 (Summer 2007): 119–30.

45. National Research Council, *The Comprehensive Test Ban Treaty*, 97–100.

46. On China's nuclear forces, see Swaine, *America's Challenge*, 40, 246; Friedberg, *A Contest for Supremacy*, 226–27; and David Shambaugh, "China's Military Modernization: Making Steady and Surprising Progress," in Ashley J. Tellis and Michael Wills, eds., *Military Modernization in an Era of Uncertainty* (Washington, DC: National Bureau of Asian Research, 2005), 97.

47. See Gates, "Gates: Nuclear Weapons and Deterrence in the 21st Century."

48. See Jeff Lindemyer, "Potential U.S. Ratification of the Comprehensive Nuclear Test Ban Treaty (CTBT) Fact Sheet," *Center for Arms Control and Non-Proliferation*, Washington, D.C., April 15, 2008, www.armscontrolcenter.org/policy/nuclearweapons/articles; and Nuclear Age Peace Foundation, "Public Support for a Nuclear Test Ban Treaty Remains High," *NuclearFiles.org*, July 20, 1999, www.nuclearfiles.org/menu/library/opinion-polls/test-ban/test-ban-treaty-support-remains-high.htm.

49. Terry L. Deibel, "The Death of a Treaty," *Foreign Affairs* 81, no. 5 (September/October 2002); Helen Dewar, "Senate Rejects Test Ban Treaty; Nuclear Pact Falls 51 to 48 as GOP Deals Clinton Major Defeat," *Washington Post*, October 14, 1999, p. A1.

50. John Isaacs, "A Strategy for Achieving Senate Approval of the CTBT," *Bulletin of the Atomic Scientists*, April 15, 2009, www.thebulletin.org/print/web-edition/features.

51. George P. Shultz, William J. Perry, Henry A. Kissinger, and Sam Nunn, "A World Free of Nuclear Weapons," *Wall Street Journal*, January 4, 2007, p. A15.

52. For a related view, see Michael P. Pillsbury, "An Assessment of China's Anti-Satellite and Space Warfare Programs, Policies, and Doctrines," report prepared for the U.S.-China Economic and Security Review Commission, Washington, D.C., January 19, 2007, p. 48.

53. James Clay Moltz, *Asia's Space Race: National Motivations, Regional Rivalries, and International Risks* (New York: Columbia University Press, 2012), 205.

54. Deputy Secretary of Defense William J. Lynn III, "Remarks on Space Policy," U.S. Strategic Command Space Symposium, Omaha, November 2010, www.defense.gov/speeches/speech.aspx?speechid=1515, as reprinted in Gompert and Saunders, *The Paradox of Power*, 29.

55. Quoted in Morgan et al., *Dangerous Thresholds*, 74–76.

56. John Lewis Gaddis, *The Long Peace: Inquiries into the History of the Cold War* (New York: Oxford University Press, 1987), 195–206.

57. Gompert and Saunders, *The Paradox of Power*, 58, 96; Department of Defense, *Military and Security Developments Involving the People's Republic of China, 2012*, 8.

58. Information Office of the State Council, "China's Space Activities in 2011," Beijing, December 2011, http://news.xinhuanet.com/english/china/2011–12/29/c_131333479.htm; Michael McDevitt, "The PLA Navy's Antiaccess Role in a Taiwan Contingency," in Phillip C. Saunders, Christopher Yung, Michael Swaine, and Andrew Nien-Dzu Yang, eds., *The Chinese Navy: Expanding*

Capabilities, Evolving Roles (Washington, DC: National Defense University Press, 2011), 206.

59. See, for example, Bruce W. MacDonald, *China, Space Weapons, and U.S. Security*, Council Special Report No. 38 (September 2008), 11, cfr.org/china /china-space-weapons-us-security/p16707.

60. Mark Stokes and Ian Easton, "China and the Emerging Strategic Competition in Aerospace Power," in Henry D. Sokolski, ed., *The Next Arms Race* (Carlisle, PA: Strategic Studies Institute, 2012), 146; Kevin Pollpeter, "The PLAAF and the Integration of Air and Space Power," in Richard P. Hallion, Roger Cliff, and Phillip C. Saunders, eds., *The Chinese Air Force: Evolving Concepts, Roles, and Capabilities* (Washington, DC: National Defense University Press, 2012), 166, 175; Andrea Shalal-Esa, "U.S. Sees China Launch as Test of Anti-Satellite Muscle: Source," *Reuters.com*, May 15, 2013, www.reuters.com/assets/print?aid=USBRE94E07D20130515.

61. See Michael Krepon and Samuel Black, "An International Code of Conduct for Responsible Space-Faring Nations," in Michael Krepon, ed., *A Code of Conduct for Responsible Space-Faring Nations* (Washington, DC: Stimson, 2010), 53–58. China's 2007 successful intercept of a satellite, after three failed attempts, occurred at about 850 kilometers altitude. See Swaine et al., *China's Military and the U.S.-Japan Alliance in 2030*, 58.

62. Barry R. Posen, *Inadvertent Escalation: Conventional War and Nuclear Risks* (Ithaca: Cornell University Press, 1991).

63. James Clay Moltz, *Asia's Space Race: National Motivations, Regional Rivalries, and International Risks* (New York: Columbia University Press, 2012), 193–95.

64. See, for example, Richard A. Clarke, *Cyber War: The Next Threat to National Security and What to Do About It* (New York: HarperCollins, 2010).

65. Lieberthal and Singer, *Cybersecurity and U.S.-China Relations*, 4–5.

66. Matthew L. Wald, "Terrorist Attack on Power Grid Could Cause Broad Hardship, Report Says," *New York Times*, November 15, 2012, p. A23.

67. Gompert and Saunders, *The Paradox of Power*, 119; Clark Kent Ervin, *Open Target: Where America Is Vulnerable to Attack* (New York: Palgrave Macmillan, 2006), 152–53.

68. See, for example, Monika Chansoria, "Defying Borders in Future Conflict in East Asia: Chinese Capabilities in the Realm of Information Warfare and Cyberspace," *Journal of East Asian Affairs* 26, no. 1 (Spring/Summer 2012): 105–27.

69. James R. Clapper, Director of National Intelligence, "Unclassified Statement for the Record on the Worldwide Threat Assessment of the U.S. Intelligence Community for the Senate Committee on Armed Services," February 7, 2012, p. 7, http:// www.armed-services.senate.gov/statemnt/2012/02%20February/Clapper %2002–16–12.pdf.

70. Hearing to Receive Testimony on the Current and Future Worldwide Threats to the National Security of the United States, Senate Committee on Armed Services, Washington, D.C., March 10, 2011, p. 29, armed-services.senate.gov /Transcripts/2011/03March/11–11–3-10–11.pdf; U.S.-China Economic and

Security Review Commission, *2012 Report to Congress* (2012), 147–69, http://www
.globalsecurity.org/military/library/report/2012/2012-china-economic-secur
ity-review.htm.

71. David E. Sanger, *Confront and Conceal: Obama's Secret Wars and Surprising
Use of American Power* (New York: Crown, 2012), 141–240.

72. Lieberthal and Singer, *Cybersecurity and U.S.-China Relations*, 2–4; Loren
Thompson, "Averting Catastrophe in Cyberspace: Core Requirements," Lexing-
ton Institute, Arlington, Virginia, July 2012, p. 3; Soren Olson, "Shadow Boxing:
Cyber Warfare and Strategic Economic Attack," *Joint Forces Quarterly*, issue 66 (3rd
quarter 2012), 19; and Department of Defense, *Military and Security Developments
Involving the People's Republic of China, 2012*, 9.

73. Evan Osnos, "Why China Let Snowden Go," *New Yorker* blog, June 24, 2013,
http://www.newyorker.com/online/blogs/evanosnos/2013/06/why-china
-let-snowden-go.html.

74. See, for example, John Arquilla, "Beijing's 'Bitskrieg,'"*Foreignpolicy.com*,
May 13, 2013, www.foreignpolicy.com/articles/2013/05/13/beijings_bitskrieg?

75. David E. Sanger, "As Chinese Leader's Visit Nears, U.S. Is Urged to Allow
Counterattacks on Hackers," *New York Times*, May 21, 2013, www.nytimes.com
/2013/05/22/world/asia/as-chinese-leaders-visit-nears-us-urged-to-allow
-counterattacks-on-hackers.

76. Ellen Nakashima, "When Is a Cyberattack a Matter of Defense?" *Washington Post*, February 27, 2012, http://www.washingtonpost.com/blogs/checkpoint
-washington/post/active-defense-at-center-of-debate-on-cyberattacks/2012
/02/27/gIQACFoKeR_blog.html.

77. Zachary Fryer-Biggs, "DoD's New Cyber Doctrine: Panetta Defines Deterrence, Preemption Strategy," *Defense News*, October 15, 2012, p. 1.

78. European Union, "Convention on Cybercrime," Budapest, Hungary, November 23, 2001, http://conventions.coe.int/Treaty/en/Treaties/Html/185.htm.

79. See U.S. Department of State, "Adherence to and Compliance with Arms
Control, Nonproliferation, and Disarmament Agreements and Commitments,"
July 2010, p. 61, http://www.state.gov/t/avc/rls/rpt/197085.htm. "In past years,
the United States shared with Chinese Government officials information on
known-to-be-completed transactions of nuclear proliferation concern, and on sus-
pected proliferation activities believed to be planned for the future. The United
States consistently has urged Chinese authorities to share the results of their inves-
tigations, to include information on export control enforcement actions, and to
publicize cases of export control violations. On the basis of U.S.-provided information (on which China routinely seeks more detail) and evidence that it ascer-
tained on its own, China has in some cases prevented or ceased the transfer of
proliferation-sensitive nuclear materials or technology and has punished Chinese
entities."

80. Dennis C. Blair, Jon M. Huntsman Jr., and the Commission on the Theft
of American Intellectual Property, *The IP Commission Report*, National Bureau of

Asian Research, Washington, D.C., May 2013, pp. 4–6, ipcommission.org/report /IP_Commission_Report_052213.pdf.

81. On biological arms, see, for example, John D. Steinbruner, *Principles of Global Security* (Washington, DC: Brookings, 2000), 175–93; and Michael A. Levi and Michael E. O'Hanlon, *The Future of Arms Control* (Washington, D.C.: Brookings, 2005), 74–93.

82. Bill Gertz, "U.S., China Talk Cyber Theft at Strategic Dialogue," *Washington Free Beacon*, July 8, 2013, http://freebeacon.com/us-china-talk-cyber-theft-at -strategic-dialogue.

83. See Ellen Nakashima, "U.S., Russia Agree to Set Up Computer Security Link," *Washington Post*, June 18, 2013, p. A10.

84. Gompert and Saunders, *The Paradox of Power*, 145–49; Lieberthal and Singer, *Cybersecurity and U.S.-China Relations*, 29.

85. Franklin D. Kramer, "Cyberpower and National Security: Policy Recommendations for a Strategic Framework," in Franklin D. Kramer, Stuart H. Starr, and Larry K. Wentz, eds., *Cyberpower and National Security* (Washington, DC: National Defense University, 2009), 21.

86. The White House, "U.S. International Strategy for Cyberspace," Washington, D.C., May 2011, pp. 12–14, http://www.whitehouse.gov/sites/default/files /rss_viewer/international_strategy_for_cyberspace.pdf.

87. Clarke, *Cyber War*.

Chapter 8: Bases, Deployments, and Operations

1. In fact, the United States had some limited presence abroad before the world wars, as in the Philippines and in other parts of the Americas, and to an extent in China as well, but not what might be described as a global network. See Pettyjohn, *U.S. Global Defense Posture*, 34. At least since the time of President Theodore Roosevelt, American naval strategy has accorded an important role to U.S. presence in the Western Pacific.

2. Such arguments carried the day against a possible major downsizing of U.S. forces in South Korea during the Carter administration, when the idea was seriously considered; see Stuart E. Johnson with Joseph A. Yager, *The Military Equation in Northeast Asia* (Washington, DC: Brookings, 1979), 78–80.

3. Center on International Cooperation, *Annual Review of Global Peace Operations, 2011* (London: Lynne Rienner, 2011), 4, 109, 146.

4. "Remarks by President Obama to the Australian Parliament," Canberra, Australia, November 17, 2011, http://www.whitehouse.gov/the-press-office/2011 /11/17/remarks-president-obama-australian-parliament.

5. See Lieberthal and Jisi, *Addressing U.S.-China Strategic Distrust*, 13–14.

6. For an earlier version of some of this material, see Michael O'Hanlon, *The Wounded Giant: America's Armed Forces in an Age of Austerity* (New York: Penguin, 2011).

7. Shirley A. Kan, "Guam: U.S. Defense Deployments," Congressional Research Service, Washington, D.C., September 27, 2013, pp. 1–5, http://www.fas.org/sgp/crs/row/RS22570.pdf.

8. Frances Lussier, *Options for Changing the Army's Overseas Basing* (Washington, DC: Congressional Budget Office, May 2004), 52, 54; Government Accountability Office, *DoD's Overseas Infrastructure Master Plans Continue to Evolve,* GAO-06–913R (August 22, 2006), p. 15.

9. Government Accountability Office, "Defense Management: Comprehensive Cost Information and Analysis of Alternatives Needed to Assess Military Posture in Asia," Washington, D.C., May 2011, www.gao.gov/new.items/d11316.pdf.

10. Michael O'Hanlon, "Restructuring U.S. Forces and Bases in Japan," in Mike Mochizuki, ed., *Toward a True Alliance* (Washington, DC: Brookings, 1997), 161.

11. See Statement of General James F. Amos before the House Armed Services Committee on the 2011 Posture of the United States Marine Corps, March 1, 2011, p. 13, http://armedservices.house.gov/index.cfm/files/serve?File_id=6e6d479e-0bea-41a1-8f3d-44b3147640fe.

12. Statement of Admiral Gary Roughead, Chief of Naval Operations, before the House Armed Services Committee, March 1, 2011, pp. 3–5, navy.mil/navydata/people/cno/Roughead/Testimony/CNO%20Roughead_Testimony_030111.pdf.

13. With the fleet response program, the Navy no longer insists on scrupulously maintaining an absolutely continuous presence in the Mediterranean, Persian Gulf, and Western Pacific regions. Now it is more inclined to make deployments unpredictable, sometimes using more and sometimes fewer assets than before.

14. Kissinger, *On China,* 9–10.

15. International Institute for Strategic Studies, *The Military Balance, 1991–1992* (Oxford: Brassey's, 1991), 152; International Institute for Strategic Studies, *The Military Balance, 2013,* 289.

16. See Hillary Rodham Clinton, "Remarks at the U.S. Institute of Peace China Conference," Washington, D.C., March 7, 2012, www.state.gov/secretary/rm/2012/03/185402.htm.

17. International Institute for Strategic Studies, *The Military Balance, 2012,* 66–68, 241–42.

18. Heidi Holz and Kenneth Allen, "Military Exchanges with Chinese Characteristics: The People's Liberation Army Experience with Military Relations," in Roy Kamphausen, David Lai, and Andrew Scobell, eds., *The PLA at Home and Abroad: Assessing the Operational Capabilities of China's Military* (Carlisle, PA: Strategic Studies Institute, 2010), 446.

19. Ian Storey, "China's Bilateral Defense Diplomacy in Southeast Asia," *Asian Security* 8, no. 3 (2012): 306.

20. Till, *Asia's Naval Expansion,* 104–5.

21. Rahul Singh, "China's Submarines in Indian Ocean Worry Indian Navy," *Hindustan Times,* April 7, 2013, http://www.hindustantimes.com/India-news/

NewDelhi/China-s-submarines-in-Indian-Ocean-worry-Indian-Navy/Article1
-1038689.aspx.

22. David Shambaugh, *China Goes Global: The Partial Power* (Oxford: Oxford University Press, 2013), 270.

23. Department of Defense, *Military and Security Developments Involving the People's Republic of China, 2012.*

24. U.S.-China Economic and Security Review Commission, *2012 Report to Congress* (Washington, DC, 2012), 138, http://www.uscc.gov/.

25. Office of the Secretary of Defense, *Annual Report to Congress*, 33–36.

26. Holz and Allen, "Military Exchanges with Chinese Characteristics," 443.

27. Michael McDevitt, "PLA Naval Exercises with International Partners," in Roy Kamphausen, David Lai, and Travis Tanner, eds., *Learning by Doing: The PLA Trains at Home and Abroad* (Carlisle, PA: Strategic Studies Institute, 2012), 81–126; Abraham M. Denmark, "PLA Logistics in 2004–2011: Lessons Learned in the Field," in Kamphausen, Lai, and Tanner, eds., *Learning by Doing*, 297–336.

28. Daniel J. Kostecka, "Places and Bases: The Chinese Navy's Emerging Support Network in the Indian Ocean," *Naval War College Review* 64, no. 1 (Winter 2011): 59–78; Ashley S. Townshend, "Unraveling China's 'String of Pearls,'" *Yale-GlobalOnline*, September 16, 2011, yaleglobal.yale.edu/print/7305.

29. Michael S. Chase and Andrew S. Erickson, "Changes in Beijing's Approach to Overseas Basing?" *China Brief* 9, issue 19 (September 24, 2009), www.jamestown.org.

30. John Pomfret, "U.S. Carrier Dispatched to Yellow Sea," *Washington Post*, November 25, 2010, p. A1; Elisabeth Bumiller and Edward Wong, "China Warily Eyes U.S.-Korea Drills," *New York Times*, July 20, 2010.

31. Bader, *Obama and China's Rise*, 149–50.

32. See http://www.globalsecurity.org/military/agency/navy/patrecon wing1.htm.

33. Unofficial Chinese comments suggest that China is contemplating just such an action. See "Is China 'Reciprocating' US Maritime Surveillance?" June 1, 2013, http://www.lowyinterpreter.org/post/2013/06/01/Is-China-reciprocating -US-maritime-surveillance.aspx. See also Rory Metcalf, "Maritime Game Change Revealed at Shangri-La Dialogue," *The Diplomat*, June 2, 2013, http://thediplomat .com/flashpoints-blog/2013/06/02/maritime-game-changer-revealed-at-shangri -la-dialogue.

34. Brzezinski, *Strategic Vision*, 176–77.

35. Swaine, *America's Challenge*, 165; Kurt Campbell and Richard Weitz, "The Limits of U.S.-China Military Cooperation: Lessons from 1995–1999," *Washington Quarterly* 29, no. 1 (Winter 2005–6), 169–86; Ian Storey, "China's Bilateral Defense Diplomacy," *Asian Security* 8, no. 3 (September–December 2012): 302–6. See James Steinberg and Michael O'Hanlon, "China's Air Defense Zone: The Shape of Things to Come?" *Reuters.com*, December 16, 2013.

36. On offshore balancing and military deployments abroad, see, for example, Barry Posen, "Pull Back: The Case for a Less Activist Foreign Policy," *Foreign Affairs* 92, no. 1 (January/February 2013): 116–29.

37. Office of the Spokesperson, "Fact Sheet: Open Skies Treaty," Department of State, Washington, D.C., March 23, 2012, www.state.gov/r/pa/prs/ps /2012/03/186738.htm.

38. "Agreement between the Government of the United States of America and the Government of the Union of Soviet Socialist Republics on the Prevention of Incidents on and over the High Seas," signed in Moscow, May 25, 1972, http:// www.fas.org/nuke/control/sea/text/sea1.htm.

39. Sean M. Lynn-Jones, "A Quiet Success for Arms Control: Preventing Incidents at Sea," *International Security* 9, no. 4 (Spring 1985): 154–84.

40. Stephanie Young, "International Partnership Nabs Another Drift Net Violator," *Coast Guard Compass*, August 17, 2012, coastguard.dodlive.mil/2012/08 /international-partnership-nabs-another-drft-net-violator; Zhang Dan, "China, US Conduct Sea Exercises in Hawaii," CCTV News, July 9, 2012, English.cntv.cn /program/newsupdate/20120907/107179.shtml.

41. Pete Pedrozo, "The U.S.-China Incidents at Sea Agreement: A Recipe for Disaster," *Journal of National Security Law and Policy* 6 (August 2012), jnslp.com /wp-content/uploads/2012/08/07_Pedro20_Master.pdf .

42. Organization for Security and Cooperation in Europe, "Confidence- and Security-Building on Agenda at OSCE Implementation and Assessment Meeting in Vienna," 2013, http://www.osce.org/fsc/99961.

43. Lieutenant Commander Audry Oxley, "Dragon Training at Home: Exploring the Possibilities for Collaboration between the U.S. and Chinese Navies in the Western Hemisphere," 21CSI Paper, Brookings Institution, Washington, D.C., July 2012, http://www.brookings.edu/~/media/research/files/papers /2012/7/10%20china%20us%20defense/10%20china%20us%20defense.pdf. The participation of Chinese troops in a humanitarian assistance exercise in November of 2013 was a useful step forward, too.

Index